D1241370

BENEATH THE SURFACE

# A NATURAL HISTORY OF A FISHERMAN'S LAKE

*Bruce M. Carlson*

*Illustrations by Bruce Granquist*

# Beneath *the* Surface

MINNESOTA HISTORICAL SOCIETY PRESS

© 2007 by the Minnesota Historical Society. All rights reserved. No part of this book may be used or reproduced in any manner whatsoever without written permission except in the case of brief quotations embodied in critical articles and reviews. For information, write to the Minnesota Historical Society Press, 345 Kellogg Blvd. W., St. Paul, MN 55102-1906.

www.mhspress.org

The Minnesota Historical Society Press is a member of the Association of American University Presses.

Manufactured in the United States of America

10 9 8 7 6 5 4 3 2 1

♾ The paper used in this publication meets the minimum requirements of the American National Standard for Information Sciences—Permanence for Printed Library Materials, ANSI Z39.48-1984.

International Standard Book Number
    ISBN 13: 978-0-87351-578-8 (cloth)
    ISBN 10: 0-87351-578-1 (cloth)

LIBRARY OF CONGRESS CATALOGING-IN-PUBLICATION DATA
Carlson, Bruce M.
Beneath the surface : a natural history of a fisherman's lake / Bruce M. Carlson ; illustrations by Bruce Granquist.
    p. cm.
Includes bibliographical references and index.
ISBN-13: 978-0-87351-578-8 (cloth : alk. paper)
ISBN-10: 0-87351-578-1 (cloth : alk. paper)
  1. Lake ecology—Minnesota.
  2. Fishing—Minnesota.
  3. Lakes—Minnesota.
  I. Title.

QH105.M55C37 2007
577.63'09776—dc22

                                                          2006039473

*To my mother, Esther Granquist Carlson,*

*who introduced me to the beauty*

*and mysteries of nature*

*Publication of this book was supported, in part, with funds provided by the Joseph and Josephine Ruttgers Descendants Fund of the Minnesota Historical Society and through a grant from the University of Michigan.*

# CONTENTS

## ACKNOWLEDGMENTS

OVER THE YEARS many people have asked me about lakes, fish, and fishing, and although no one single question started my writing, the overall effect of their queries was to plant the seed for this book. To all of those who have, perhaps unwittingly, inspired me, I offer my thanks.

If this book is well received, it will be due as much to the illustrations as the text. The illustrator, Bruce Granquist, is actually a relative of mine—the son of a cousin. I scarcely knew him until December 2004, when my wife and I visited with him after a conference in his adopted island of Bali. In those few hours he taught me more about the meaning of art than I had learned during the first sixty-some years of my life. Knowing that he had already illustrated a number of publications on Southeast Asian and island ecology, I thought he would be the perfect person to illustrate my lake book. Our mutual endeavor turned into a wonderful working partnership in which he took many cues from my text but then turned loose his creative talents on making the text come alive through his illustrations. Simple thanks are not enough. Thanks also goes to Pt. Primascan Citragraphika and Pt. Dian Raykat for their careful work in scanning Bruce's illustrations and to Wijaya Bontoh and Ngurah Yasa for their technical assistance.

As always, thank you to my wife, Jean, who has been very supportive of yet another book-writing project. Her enthusiasm, despite the occasional deposit of fish and aquatic plants on the kitchen counter or in the refrigerator, convinced me that there were people who would actually read such a book.

A number of people read and commented on early drafts of chapters and greatly helped improve the text. These include Jean, Tom and Carol Beech, Wes Daining, Jim and Marlys Hyslop, John Alden, Tom Cox, and Jim Limburg. My thanks to all of them.

Much detail on Ten Mile Lake came from records in the Walker, Minnesota, branch of the Fisheries Division of the Minnesota Department of Natural Resources. I thank Harlan Firestine and the rest of the staff there for permitting me access to all of their records on the lake. I would also like to thank Donna Perleberg and Paul Radomski of the Ecological Services Division of the Minnesota Department of Natural Resources for permission to use unpublished data from the ongoing studies of aquatic vegetation and nongame fish and to Larry Kallemeyn and Paul Hauck from the Biological Resources Division of the U.S. Geological Survey for permission to use their unpublished data on the ages of whitefish sampled from Ten Mile Lake.

Last, I wish to express my delight in working with Ann Regan and the rest of the folks at the Minnesota Historical Society Press, not only for their rapid handling of the manuscript and the efficient production process but for genuinely pleasant interactions. Michael Hanson efficiently guided the overall process of turning the manuscript into an actual book. Will Powers and Cathy Spengler imaginatively married text and artwork into a pleasing format, and the efforts of marketing director Alison Vandenberg were responsible for getting this book into your hands. Every author should have such an experience.

FROM OUR SUMMER CABIN'S STUDY, I look out over a lake whose still, gray waters meet a soft curtain of mist and a forest dripping from an all-day rain. Yet I know that with an advancing cold front this same lake tomorrow will be bright blue, with white-capped waves driven by a brisk northwest wind. As interesting as these visible changes may be, events underwater are even more fascinating. Beneath the surface is a world both separate from and connected to our own. Except for scuba divers and those with expensive aquatic viewing systems, people rarely experience this world directly, yet an abundance of indirect means of sampling—thermometers, sonar devices, nets, dredges, even angling— has allowed me to better understand how a lake works.

As I talk to friends and associates who live on or visit lakes, I realize that what has become purely instinctive to me is completely foreign to many others. Nevertheless, when I explain what is happening in a lake, people seem genuinely interested in learning more. This book attempts to answer, in understandable language, their many questions about how a typical north country lake is put together and how it functions.

For over fifty years I have been vacationing on and studying Ten Mile Lake near Hackensack, Minnesota. Although in many respects it is a classic northern Minnesota lake, Ten Mile possesses some unique characteristics—such as great depth (at 208 feet it is the third-deepest lake in Minnesota) and a huge population of dwarf ciscoes that is estimated to run into the millions—and therefore this lake has caught the interest of aquatic biologists for many decades. They have provided extensive documentation about various aspects of the lake, and such documentation, along with my own experiences and observations, provides a coherent picture of a north country lake's main workings. And in knowing the dynamics of this particular lake, you will better appreciate your own favorite lake.

This book comprises a mix of natural history, biology, and information on fishing. It is not intended to be a textbook, but much of the material is presented in sufficient depth to allow a real understanding of lakes. Nor is it designed to fine-tune fishing techniques for the hard-core angler. I discuss fishing technology in a basic manner intended for novices. Most anglers, however, regardless of their technical skills, are likely to benefit from the vignettes that connect fish biology with how to find fish and how to tempt them to bite. I have always held that the better you understand fish biology, the better success you will have in fishing.

Although I have spent my entire professional career as a medical researcher and as a teacher, in a previous life I worked my way through college as an aquatic biologist for the Minnesota Department of Natural Resources and soon after got a master's degree in ichthyology. I then became fascinated with the phenomenon of regeneration, which has occupied my professional attention for the past forty-five years. I have continued to be a devotee of lakes and fishing and for twenty years have regularly researched and written articles on fishing and lake biology for *In-Fisherman*. With every advance in technology, I have learned more about the lake, but with each advance I have also become aware of how much I still don't know. Nevertheless, I hope this book will provide you with a better sense of what goes on beneath the surface of your favorite lake and perhaps encourage you to find out even more.

*Bruce M. Carlson*
June 2006

*T*ime spent on a north country lake is something special. Hearing the haunting call of a loon, catching a big fish, or just watching a thunderstorm develop across the distant horizon leaves an impression like few other experiences. The experience can vary greatly, however, from person to person, and to a large extent what you take away from a lake depends upon your understanding of how it functions. Someone with little wine knowledge can thoroughly enjoy a glass of fine wine, for example, but a connoisseur could drink the same glass and detect subtleties that would make the experience much different. You can similarly have a wonderful time swimming, water skiing, and fishing without knowing much about lakes, but the experience would be immeasurably deeper if you understood a lake's essential workings.

Like a living being, a lake is born, matures, and eventually dies. And like most animals and plants, a lake hosts a wide variety of life-forms. A lake can also get sick from pollution or other causes, and it can often recover, even from serious insults. Just as a knowledge of anatomy, physiology, and pathology gives us a good understanding of the human body, real knowledge of a lake requires knowing something about its structure, its physical and biological rhythms, and its reactions to disturbing influences.

Putting this all together can be quite complex, but one doesn't have to master all the details to have a good working understanding of what is happening beneath the waves. Physical characteristics of a lake, such as temperature, oxygen levels, and light penetration, impact the plant and animal life within the lake and how the many forms of life inhabiting a lake interact. For the angler, in particular, knowledge of the rhythms and constraints of underwater life can be directly transferable into strategies and techniques that will significantly increase fishing success.

North country lakes come in many shapes and sizes, and instead of trying to cover all the possible variations among lakes, I have decided to use as a model a lake that I have studied intensively for a half century, Ten Mile Lake in Cass County, Minnesota. Although this lake has some unique features, the majority of what is presented here applies to most northern lakes.

## The Life Cycle of a North Country Lake

Like most northern Minnesota lakes, Ten Mile Lake owes its existence to the last glacier that covered the northern part of the state more than 10,000 years ago. As the lobes of the glacier retreated, the melting ice dropped large masses of rock and gravel in the form of miles-long terminal moraines northwest and southeast of the lake. Glacial rivers formed by the melting ice deposited large masses of sand and gravel in other areas. The main body of the lake was probably formed by the action of the glacial ice itself (fig. 1.1). Some geologists consider Ten Mile to be an ice block lake. As the last glacier retreated, a huge block of ice that had gouged a hole in the ground was left behind, forming the main lake basin and filling it as the ice melted. Others have conjectured that the deepest holes in the lake represent sites at the base of massive glacial waterfalls or other swift currents where the rapidly moving water eroded huge cavities in the earth. On a lesser scale similar holes form beneath waterfalls or dam outlets in present-day streams.

Glaciers leave behind many clues about their origin and path. Small hills just west of the lake represent the soil materials (moraines) that were pushed out from the present lake basin by the forward-moving glacier. The presence of these glacial hills suggests that the glacier that formed them flowed from east to west. This is similar to the small mound of sand that forms in front of your foot when you are walking on a sandy beach. Glaciers pick up rocks in their path and carry them along, much like a stream of water carries pieces of wood. I still remember my surprise upon reaching an overlook beside the Tasman glacier near Mt. Cook in New Zealand. My initial reaction was "Where is it?" because the entire glacier was covered with a layer of rock and debris to the point where the ice was invisible from the top. On the beaches of Ten Mile Lake, one can find beautiful agates of the type found along the north shore of Lake Superior. These, plus other types of characteristic rocks, were swept from the Lake Superior region by the advancing Superior lobe of the last glacier and deposited along its path when the glacier melted.

Other likely residues of the glacier are the rocky underwater islands that are favorite sites for both walleyes and anglers to gather at night. Such rock ridges typically represent areas where a small stream coming

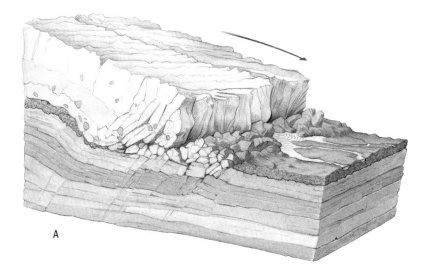

A

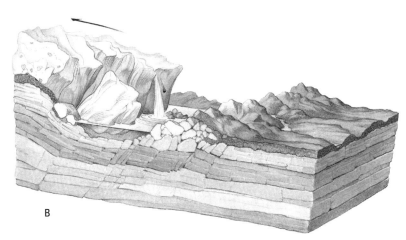

B

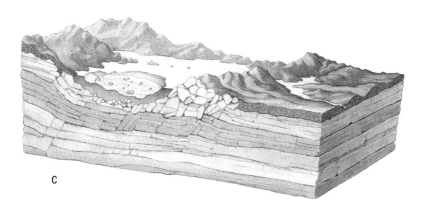

C

**Fig. 1.1.**

. . . . . . . . . . . . . . . . . . .

*Likely scenarios for the origin of a glacial lake.* **A**, *As the weather warmed, the ice at the end of the glacier began to break up and melt, causing water to pool and streams to run away from the glacier.* **B**, *Meltwater from the glaciers formed waterfalls, which may have concentrated rocks carried along by the glacial ice. As the glacier receded, the rocks got caught up in ridges, which may account for the formation of some of the boulder-strewn underwater islands in glacial lakes.* **C**, *In some areas a large block of ice embedded in the earth formed a deep lake basin as it melted.*

from a melting glacier concentrates and deposits rocks. Because these structures have remained underwater since the time of the glacier and have been protected from the elements and erosion, they are very representative of what the overall terrain must have looked like after the glaciers had just melted.

Most of our northern lakes owe their existence to the last glacier that covered most of northern North America until about 12,000 years ago. As the weather warmed, the melting glacier retreated to the north, leaving in its wake immense amounts of meltwater. In a huge area covering most of Manitoba, western Ontario, eastern North Dakota, and northwestern Minnesota, the water left by the glacier formed an enormous lake. Named after Louis Agassiz, a prominent nineteenth-century biologist, Lake Agassiz was, at its maximum extent, over 700 miles long and 200 miles wide and contained much more water than all the Great Lakes do today (fig. 1.2). Lake Agassiz began to form about 12,500 years ago and persisted for about 4,000 years. During this time its shape changed tremendously, as did its drainage channels. At various times its massive drainage channels emptied through the present Minnesota River valley, and also into Lake Duluth (the western part of present Lake Superior), and the region where Hudson's Bay was taking shape. Most of the waters of Lake Agassiz drained out through these large outlets, but wherever the glacier had scooped depressions in the ground, water remained as lakes of various sizes. Some of the huge present-day lakes in this region (Lake Winnipeg, Lake Manitoba, Lake of the Woods, and the Upper and Lower Red Lakes) represent the last big remnants of this former inland sea. Because of their common origin from a single lake, these lakes also contain many common forms of aquatic life.

**Fig. 1.2.**

. . . . . . . . . . . . . . . . . . .

*Maximal extent of glacial Lake Agassiz. This huge glacial lake was situated along the edge of the receding glacier. At no one time was it ever as large as the area indicated on this map.*

Although not a remnant of former Lake Agassiz, Ten Mile Lake likely shares the same postglacial history as that of most other lakes which took their origins from the melting glaciers. Its waters were originally very cold and crystal clear, with little vegetation or animal life. Over the course of the intervening thousands of years, all of these lakes have undergone a gradual evolution, but at different rates. Some lakes, such as those in the rocky areas of Minnesota's Arrowhead region or the Boundary Waters Canoe Area Wilderness, remain in an almost pristine condition with very clear, infertile water, mostly rocky bottoms, little vegetation, and cold-water fish such as lake trout, whitefish, walleyes, and northern pike. Such lakes are called *oligotrophic lakes* (fig. 1.3A).

Ten Mile Lake has passed from the purely oligotrophic condition and is slowly becoming a mesotrophic lake, the next stage in the natural evolution of a lake (fig. 1.3B). Although, like Ten Mile, a mesotrophic lake may still have very clear water, the influx of substances that support plant growth has made the water more fertile, and abundant plant growth fills its shallower waters. Most mesotrophic lakes do not contain trout, because of their higher water temperature, but deep mesotrophic lakes retain a lower layer that if sufficiently oxygenated, can support cold-water fish such as trout and whitefish. Most of the fish in a mesotrophic lake are cool-water fish like walleyes, northern pike, muskies, bass, and panfish.

The next stage in the evolution of a lake is called *eutrophication*, during which the lake bottom fills with silt and organic debris. With this filling-in, the lake becomes shallower. The waters warm and typically become severely oxygen depleted in their lower levels in both the summer and the winter (fig. 1.3C). Water clarity in a eutrophic lake is commonly poor. It is not uncommon to be able to see only a foot or two below the surface. Cool-water fish such as walleyes, northern pike, and smallmouth bass give way to warm-water fish such as largemouth bass, panfish, bullheads, and carp.

The terminal stage in the life history of a lake occurs when the bottom debris fills it in to the point where it becomes a wetland or swamp (fig. 1.3D). This can take place rapidly in a geological time scale. In my lifetime I have seen several small, shallow lakes transition into swamps. For historical perspective it is important to recognize that the northern parts of the United States and much of Canada are still in the process of drying out from the last glacial period over 10,000 years ago. In any given region there is a climatic ebb and flow, with centuries-long cyclical variations in both temperature and rainfall. These cyclical conditions can dramatically affect a lake, although from our personal perspective the past history of a lake is not likely to be apparent without careful observation.

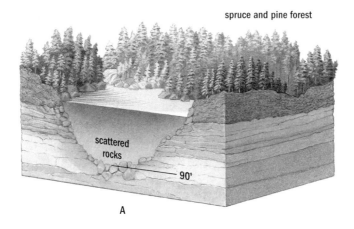

spruce and pine forest

scattered rocks

90'

A

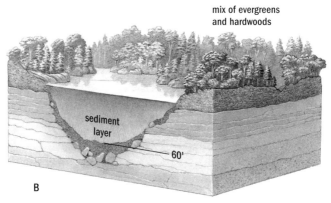

mix of evergreens and hardwoods

sediment layer

60'

B

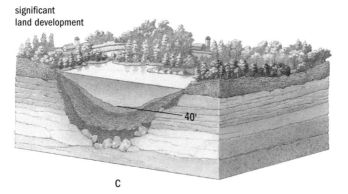

significant land development

40'

C

**Fig. 1.3.**
. . . . . . . . . . . . . . . . . .

*Maturation of a lake from its pristine origins to its becoming a swamp:*
**A**, *oligotrophic lake;*
**B**, *mesotrophic lake;*
**C**, *eutrophic lake;*
**D**, *swamp. Note that the initially rocky lake bottom becomes progressively filled with layers of sediment.*

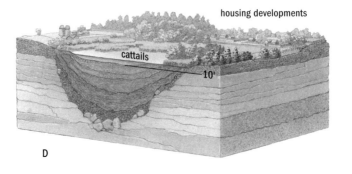

housing developments

cattails

10'

D

While our population is rapidly expanding, the number of natural lakes remains constant. The increasing number of cabins that ring our lakes and the boats that crowd them is a ready reminder that lakes are a shared resource. A recent flight over the western Chicago suburbs on a summer Sunday afternoon impressed upon me how much some lakes are actually used. Many of us have witnessed firsthand how the quality of the water, the fishing, and the surrounding shoreline of some popular lakes has deteriorated within our lifetime. Yet other similar lakes have more successfully maintained their quality. Although some of these differences are due to locally uncontrollable factors, the actions or negligence of immediate users of lakes are also significant. Ignorance or disregard of lake dynamics is one of the surest recipes for hastening deterioration, whereas an enlightened approach based upon knowledge has proven to be the basis for not only maintaining but also improving the quality of a lake and slowing the inevitable cycle of eutrophication.

## Background on Ten Mile Lake

Ten Mile Lake covers roughly 5,000 acres, with a large main basin and several smaller bays extending from it (fig. 1.4). In many respects it is a nearly self-contained system since it has no inlet stream but is fed by springs, swamps, and groundwater seepage from a small and largely undeveloped watershed (10,432 acres) only about twice the area of the lake itself. It has one small outlet stream (the Boy River), with a water flow of about 20 cubic feet per second. The Boy River leads through a chain of smaller lakes—with names like Baby, Girl, and Woman—before entering Leech Lake, one of the largest lakes in Minnesota. Ten Mile is a very deep lake (the third deepest in Minnesota), with a maximum depth of 208 feet and a significant portion of the main basin deeper than 100 feet (fig. 1.5). One island, situated close to the mainland, is connected to the shore by a road.

The water is clear, with Secchi disk readings—a measure of water transparency in open waters—of up to 25 feet in the main basin. In addition to springs, swamp drainage, and groundwater seepage, the other main source of water in the lake is rainfall, averaging 26 inches per year. The contribution by rainfall is roughly equivalent to the amount of evaporation, meaning that the influx of water from springs, swamps, and groundwater approximates the efflux of lake water into the outlet stream. This equilibrium of water coming into and leaving the lake results in quite stable water levels, with variations measured only in inches. A beaver dam in the outlet stream sometimes causes the lake level to rise several inches.

Both the contours and composition of the lake bottom are quite

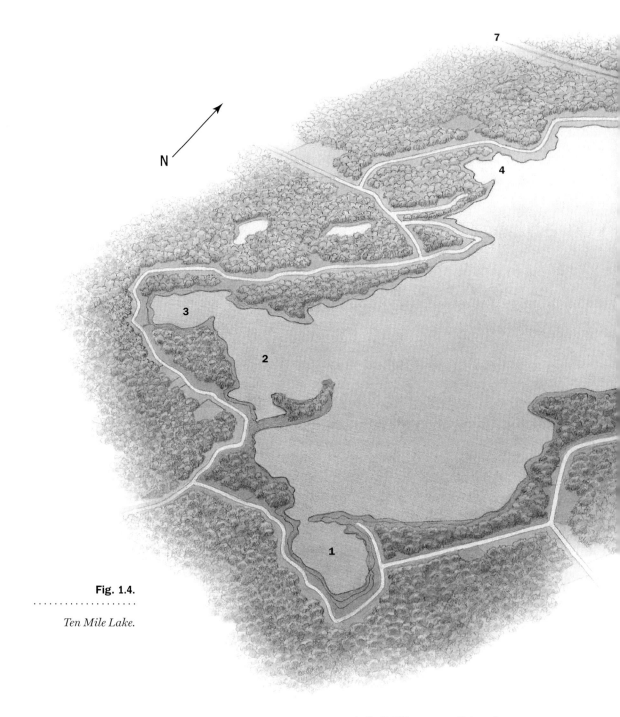

**Fig. 1.4.**

*Ten Mile Lake.*

1. Kenfield Bay     5. Long Bay
2. Robinson's Bay     6. Boy River
3. Lundstrom's Bay     7. Bicycle trail
4. Flowerpot Bay     8. Highway 371

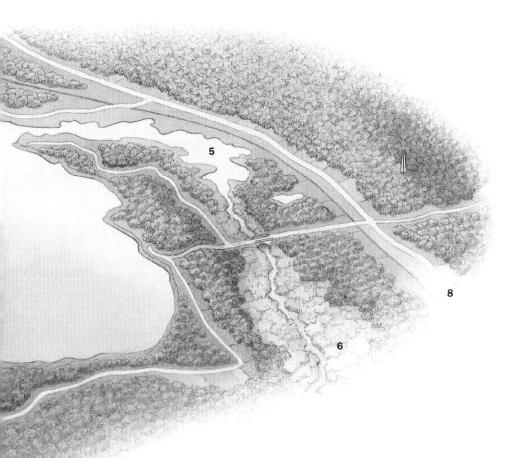

varied, especially in the main lake basin
(fig. 1.5). Overall, the bottom along the shoreline consists of 40 percent sand, 25 percent boulders, 20 percent rubble, 10 percent marl, and 5 percent clay. Large sand beaches in
several locations continue into the lake, some for significant distances. In other more rocky areas, underwater humps rise from depths
as great as 70 feet to within 10 feet of the surface. These tend to be rocky,
with most rocks ranging from 6 inches to 3 feet in diameter. The humps
that rise to within 10 to 15 feet of the surface are covered with varying
amounts of aquatic vegetation, whereas the few humps topping out at
30 feet are devoid of plant life. One such deep underwater ridge consists
of large rocks at one end and sand at the other. The bottom composition
has a significant effect on the distribution of fish—walleyes in particular. Humps in areas near sandy beaches may have sandy or silty tops, but
their steep sides are almost always rocky. Long bars extending from
points on shore are for the most part rocky, but a very long and shallow
bar extending north from the island is mostly sand and gravel. During
the day, in particular, fish are commonly concentrated around structural
irregularities rather than over large expanses of unchanging bottom.

The bays are quite different in character from the main lake basin, and each bay has its own special characteristics (fig. 1.4). Kenfield Bay, located on the south end of the lake, is unique in that much of the springwater that enters the lake flows into this bay from shoreline seepage and underwater sources. Although over 40 feet deep in one spot, the area near the springs is choked with calcium carbonate deposits (marl) and vegetation.

On the west side of the lake, Lundstrom's Bay is very shallow (less than 12 feet deep) and weedy, with abundant marshes along much of its perimeter. The bottom is silty, and the water clarity is considerably less than that of the rest of the lake. Although quite cut off from the main lake by a shallow entrance, this bay is very important because in the spring it serves as a main spawning area for northern pike, bass, and many panfish. In many respects Lundstrom's Bay has the

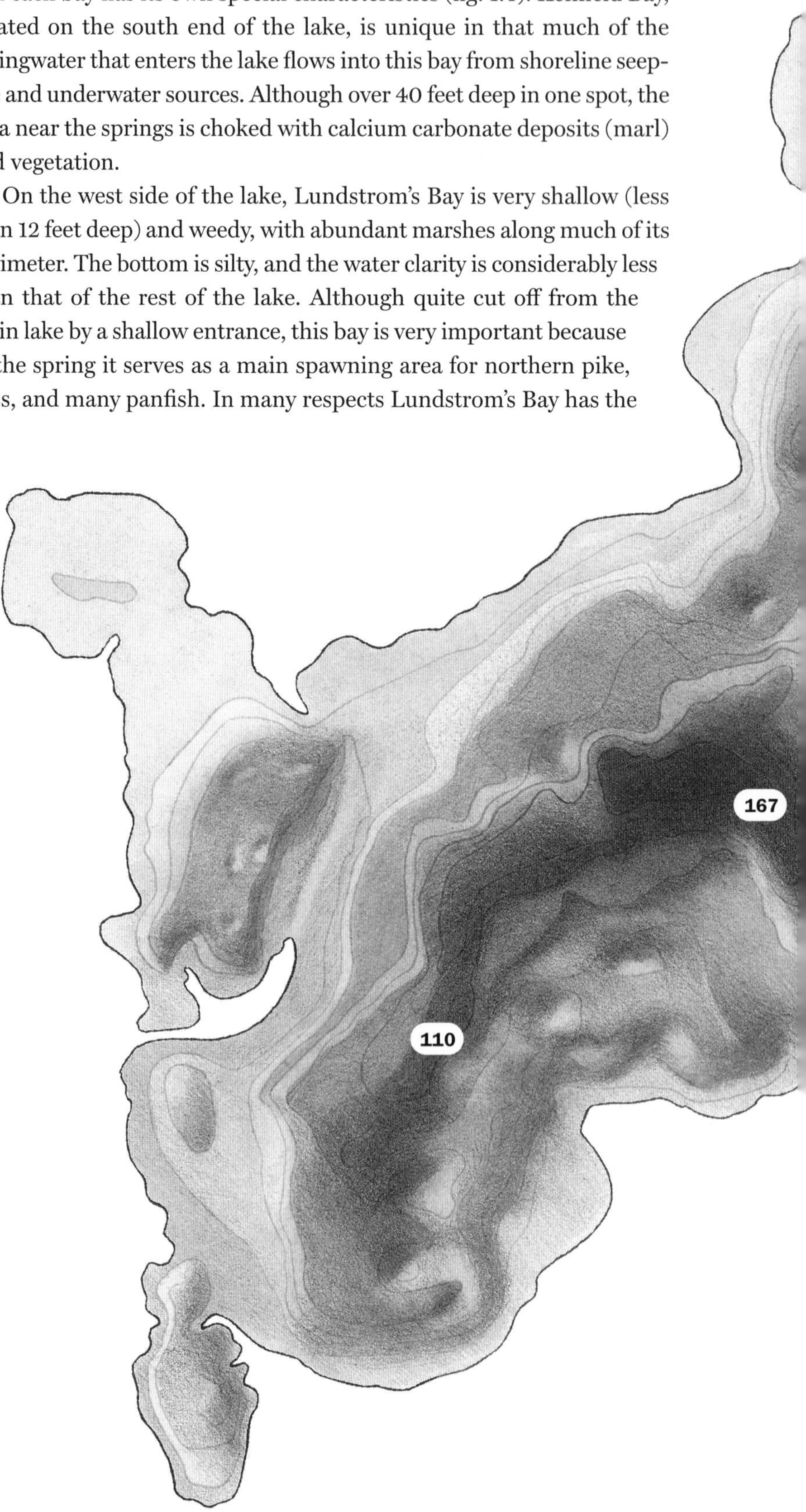

**Fig. 1.5.**
. . . . . . . . . . . . . . . . . . . .
*Topographic map of Ten Mile Lake. Depth measured in feet.*

167

110

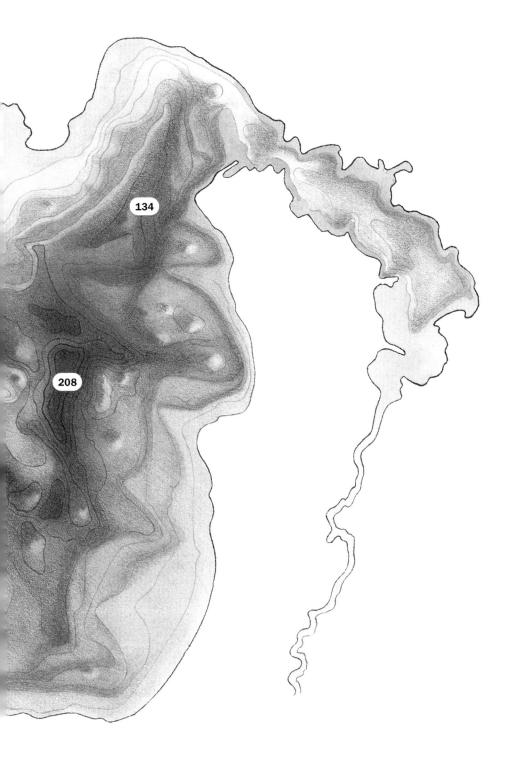

characteristics of many small lakes (10 to 25 acres) in the area and is quite different from the rest of Ten Mile.

On the northwest side Flowerpot Bay, though quite similar in size to Lundstrom's Bay, is totally different in character. Although it has a wide entrance into the main lake, that entrance is completely traversed by a bar that comes within a couple feet of the surface. Despite the fact that it is very shallow (less than 10 feet), its water is considerably clearer than that of Lundstrom's Bay because of its broad connection to the main lake. Much of the bay is occupied by beds of bulrushes.

The last major bay, Long Bay, comes off the north end of the lake, and because of its narrow and shallow entrance, it almost has the character of a separate lake. The Boy River leaves Long Bay from a broad, shallow, and weedy neck area. Because it is much shallower than the main basin of the lake (about 40 feet maximum) and is almost completely separated from it, Long Bay warms up much more quickly after ice-out than does the main lake basin. As a result many fish, especially walleyes, migrate into Long Bay in the early spring.

Although Ten Mile Lake, which has over 22 miles of shoreline, is ringed by about 450 cabins, their direct impact has been considerably less than is the case with many lakes. The shoreline of the main lake basin has historically not been lined with bulrushes or other emergent aquatic vegetation, and even in the more weedy bays, many of the bulrush beds have remained for the most part intact. Interestingly, the principal direct impact of cabins on the main lake has been the presence of numerous docks and boat lifts, which provide additional cover for bass and panfish. A significant indirect impact of human habitation has been leakage from faulty septic systems and runoff from property with chemically fertilized lawns. The vigilance of an active lake association has resulted in a significant improvement in lake water quality over the past few decades.

One of the most noticeable features of the animal life associated with the lake is the large population of loons that congregate on the lake. Throughout the summer it is not uncommon to see aggregations of as many as 30 to 40 loons in the evening. Many of these birds nest in nearby smaller lakes and come to Ten Mile to fish. Ten Mile has a huge population of the unique dwarf fish called *ciscoes*. Present in the lake in the millions, these fish, which measure from only 4 to 6 inches when mature, are the perfect eating size for not only loons, gulls, and terns but also game fish such as walleyes and northern pike. Many significant biological characteristics of the lake are strongly influenced by these little bite-sized creatures. Later chapters will devote significant attention to the role of the dwarf ciscoes in the overall biology of the lake. Fish-eating ducks, such as mergansers, are also plentiful on the lake because of the availability of abundant fish food. The presence of these birds has also attracted top-of-the-line predators such as ospreys and eagles that regularly patrol the lake for fish, young ducks, and loons. Although not so visible, the lake also hosts aquatic mammals—beavers, muskrats, and even otters. At times beavers make regular evening and night patrols along the shoreline. The mammals that have most strongly influenced the lake, however, are humans. To date, the areas of greatest human impact have been water quality, the nature of the fish populations, and the appearance and composition of the shoreline.

What is fascinating about dealing with lakes and oceans is that no matter how much you know there is always much more that you don't. Piecing together a story from largely indirect evidence is both interesting and risky, but when you get a working knowledge of lake dynamics, your appreciation of the beauty and complexity of the workings of a lake makes your time on a lake a much more meaningful experience.

## 2  THE LAKE ON A SUMMER'S DAY

*I*magine your favorite lake on a nice July day. The air temperature is 80 degrees; the sky is bright blue with white, puffy clouds; and a light wind blowing from the west kicks up small waves. Below the waves lies a different world that few people understand or appreciate. What makes this world different? Day or night the underwater world is much darker than ours, and colors do not look the same. Plants can live only to a certain depth because of the lack of light in deeper water. And almost all of the animals are cold-blooded. Their distribution and activity levels are limited by both the water temperature and the availability of oxygen. The physical properties of water—density and sound conductance, for example—strongly affect animal behavior, as well.

### Water Temperature and Oxygen

Knowledge of the temperature profile within a lake is critically important to understanding its overall dynamics because virtually all of the animal life in a lake is cold-blooded, and the distribution of these animals, especially fish, is highly dependent upon water temperature. The importance of temperature will be a recurring theme throughout this book.

In any body of water there is much less daily variation in temperature than there is in the air, creating a relatively stable environment for the creatures that inhabit the lake. Although the temperature of the shallow water at the beach is likely to be in the mid to upper 70s in July, it gradually becomes colder as the water gets deeper (fig. 2.1). At a certain depth (often from 30 to 40 feet below the surface in July), the water temperature drops dramatically—typically from the low 70s to the high 50s—within a range of about 10 feet. Below this level the water temperature continues to decrease gradually until it levels off at the mid-40s. Such a temperature profile is seen in most lakes, although the level at which this rapid decrease in water temperature occurs varies from lake to lake.

Scientists who study lakes (limnologists) have given names to the three main temperature layers of a lake. The middle zone of rapid temperature change is called the *thermocline.* The warm layer above the thermocline is called the *epilimnion,* and the cold layer beneath it is called the *hypolimnion.*

Associated with the temperature profile of a lake is the oxygen content of the water. Like life above the water, aquatic animals require oxygen to survive, but in a lake the oxygen is dissolved in the water. Whereas the oxygen content in air is expressed as a percentage (roughly 21 percent), the oxygen content in water is commonly reported as parts per million (PPM). Cold water has a greater capacity to carry dissolved oxygen than does warm water. In fact, the theoretical oxygen-carrying capacity of the upper water on a July day is only about two-thirds that of the coldest water at the bottom of the lake. The actual quantity of dissolved oxygen at the lower depths differs greatly, however, from this amount because the concentration of oxygen present at any given depth depends primarily upon what supplies oxygen to the water and what removes it. The main sources of oxygen are green plants, which produce oxygen as a by-product of photosynthesis, and diffusion from the air at the surface of the lake. Oxygen is removed from the water mainly by decaying organic matter at the bottom of the lake. By comparison the amount removed by fish and other animals is negligible.

The upper layer of the lake (epilimnion) contains the most oxygen-rich water in the lake—often 8 to 9 PPM near the surface on a wavy day. Like temperature, oxygen content tends to decrease with increasing water depth. Sometimes, however, the oxygen concentration actually increases by 1 or 2 PPM at the level of the thermocline, likely as a result of oxygen production by suspended algae in this layer. The oxygen concentration usually decreases dramatically below the thermocline. In

**Fig. 2.1.**

. . . . . . . . . . . . . . . . . . .

*Cross section of an oligotrophic lake showing,* **left***, the rapid drop of temperature in the thermocline layer and,* **right***, the concentration of dissolved oxygen.*

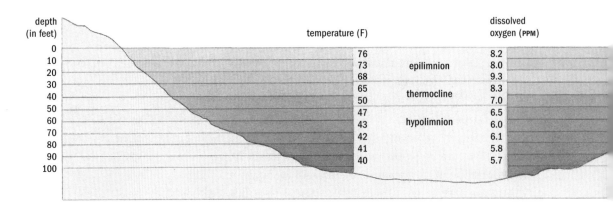

| depth (in feet) | temperature (F) | | dissolved oxygen (PPM) |
|---|---|---|---|
| 0 | | | |
| 10 | 76 | | 8.2 |
| 20 | 73 | epilimnion | 8.0 |
| 30 | 68 | | 9.3 |
| 40 | 65 | thermocline | 8.3 |
| 50 | 50 | | 7.0 |
| 60 | 47 | | 6.5 |
| 70 | 43 | hypolimnion | 6.0 |
| 80 | 42 | | 6.1 |
| 90 | 41 | | 5.8 |
| 100 | 40 | | 5.7 |

many lakes the oxygen levels below the thermocline are too low to sustain most animal life because the oxygen is consumed by the organic detritus at the bottom of the lake and there are no green plants to replenish it. In the summertime the water above and below the thermocline rarely mixes. Most fish require a minimum of 2.5 to 3.5 PPM of dissolved oxygen for survival in the summer. The waters of Ten Mile Lake are well oxygenated, however, and even at its greatest depths the oxygen content is normally sufficient to support fish life (fig. 2.1). Measurements taken in September have shown a dissolved oxygen concentration of 3.2 PPM at 200 feet.

## Light

. . . . . . . . . . . . . . . . . .

Light is a subtle determinant in the life of a lake, and water has an important filtering effect on light. A familiar example of the filtering of light by the air will help in understanding what takes place underwater. During midday, when the sun is at its greatest height, it is so bright that it is very dangerous to look at it directly. As sunset approaches and the sun sinks toward the horizon, its color changes from yellow to a deep red orange because tiny particles in the lower layers of the air filter the light. Similarly, the moon, as it peeks above the eastern horizon, appears a coppery yellow but then gradually turns silver as it rises in the night sky. Light on a bright, sunny noonday is white light with a balanced mix of red, green, and blue wavelengths. The color of light at sunset or moonrise is yellow-orange because of the lack of penetration of the blue components through the atmospheric haze.

Water affects the properties of light even more strongly than does air and often with different effects, depending upon the color of the water. Filtering of light in water occurs in two main ways. First, the total amount of light that penetrates the water decreases with depth; second, specific light wavelengths are filtered out as water depth increases. Both of these filtration phenomena heavily depend upon the nature of the

water, namely its color and clarity (turbidity). In many north country lakes, including Ten Mile, the water is colorless. The water in other lakes is tinted, however, by varying degrees of brown or green. Although metallic ions such as iron often contribute to the brownish color of some lakes, the dark brown color seen in some northern lakes is caused by bog drainage into the lake. Tannins, brownish pigments released by decaying leaves and other organic matter, stain the water and have a profound effect on the light that penetrates the brown lake waters. Similarly, green water, usually caused by algal growth, has a great but somewhat different effect on the amount and type of light that enters the lake.

One of the standard methods of measuring the overall clarity of a lake is to use Secchi disk readings. A Secchi disk is a roughly 8-inch metal disk usually painted black and white in alternate quadrants. The disk is lowered into the water on a string, and the depth at which the disk is no longer visible to the observer in a boat is the Secchi disk reading. Secchi disk readings are convenient indicators of both water clarity and water quality, and monitoring these readings over the years gives a good indication of whether the overall water quality of a lake is becoming better or worse over time. As examples of Secchi disk readings, the reading in Lake Superior, a highly infertile, clear-water lake, is typically up to 65 feet, whereas many small lakes around the Twin Cities that have been ringed by homes for many decades have readings often as low as 2 to 4 feet. In Ten Mile Lake readings in the main basin of the lake have been from 20 to 25 feet, but in shallow, more fertile bays readings of 16 feet are more common. For many north country lakes readings of 7 to 12 feet are typical.

Why spend so much time on Secchi disk readings? In addition to their general value as indicators of overall water quality, they also serve as a guide to the ability of light to penetrate the water. It is sometimes assumed that the Secchi disk reading equals the depth of light penetration. This is not the case. Light actually penetrates a considerable distance below the reading.

Probably the most profound effect of total light penetration is on the vertical distribution of aquatic plants. Almost all plants, whether above or below the water, require light because photosynthesis, the means by which plants derive energy, is light dependent. At depths where the total amount of light falls below a critical level, plants simply cannot produce enough energy to exist, which means that below a certain water depth most plant life is absent. In Ten Mile Lake plants grow well as deep as 30 to 34 feet, whereas in lakes with stained, turbid water, plant growth may cease within 5 feet of the surface. One exception to this rule is the dark-colored, wiry alga, sometimes called *moss* by walleye anglers who encounter it while fishing deep water in the late fall. On the slopes of an underwater island near the deepest part of Ten Mile, lush beds of this alga have been recorded as deep as 55 feet below the surface.

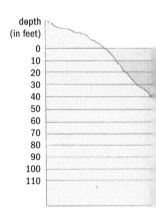

As a convenient reference point, plant life in a lake usually ceases at a depth where the intensity of the light is reduced to about 1 percent of that hitting the surface at midday. Below 1 percent the amount of light is insufficient for the plants to carry out photosynthesis. If we use Ten Mile Lake as an example, this means that 99 percent of the light has been filtered out by the time it has penetrated from 30 to 34 feet—the lower limit of plant growth. The absorption of light, however, is not a linear process. Instead, for every equal unit of depth in the water column (about 5 feet for Ten Mile), the amount of light that passes through it is halved (fig. 2.2).

The location of vegetation, in turn, has profound effects on the distribution and behavior of animal life within the lake, because vegetation attracts both fish and insects, along with the animals that they eat. Regardless of the presence or absence of vegetation, fish, in particular, react to the amount of light that hits them. Although there are certainly exceptions, most fish prefer relatively low light levels because the iris of their eye does not adjust as easily as ours to different intensities of light. This leads fish to head for deeper waters or to seek shade on bright, sunny days. If shade is available, fish can be found in amazingly shallow water, even on the brightest of days. On a clear, calm day you can find bass or rock bass positioned exactly in the thin shadow of a submerged tree branch or an underwater plant. As the sun moves across the sky and shadows correspondingly change position, fish move to remain in these shadows. On very dark overcast days, when the light levels may be over a hundred times less than those on a sunny day, fish are more active and much more likely to be cruising the shallow waters.

Another aspect of light intensity that has a profound effect on ani-

**Fig. 2.2.**

**Left**, *the amount of light penetration (extrapolated from indirect data) at different depths in Ten Mile Lake.* **Right**, *depths at which various colors wash out in a lake with very clear, colorless water.*

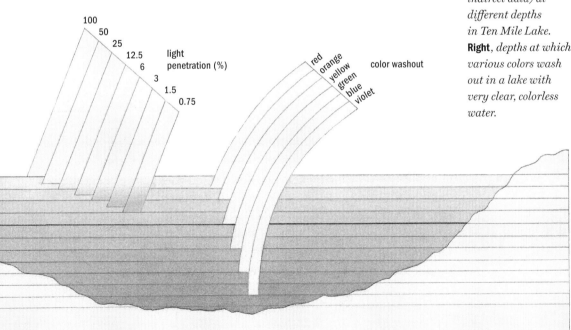

mal behavior is the diurnal change at sunrise and sunset. As the sun approaches or leaves the horizon, the intensity of light above and below the surface of the water changes dramatically (table 2.1). The most noticeable effect of this is seen by anglers, who find that fish bite much better around sunrise or sunset. For some fish, such as perch, this is due to the way their eyes process light. In other cases it is a response to diurnal changes in the behavior of other creatures that inhabit the lake (see chapter 4).

**Table 2.1: Approximate Levels of Light Intensity under Different Conditions**

| Condition | Light intensity |
| --- | --- |
| Noon on a clear summer's day | 100,000 lx |
| Sun at the horizon at dusk | 1,000 lx |
| Dark, overcast day | 100 lx |
| Twilight | 10 lx |
| Full moon | 0.1 lx |
| Clear, starry night | 0.001 lx |
| Overcast night | 0.0001 lx |

*Note: Light intensity is measured in lux, a unit of illuminance.*

The other major effect of water on light is the filtering out of specific wavelengths with increasing depth. This can get very complex because the color of the water has an important influence on which wavelengths are filtered out and at what level this occurs. For simplicity's sake we will cover in detail only what happens in a clear-water lake like Ten Mile.

The light that hits the water's surface contains the entire spectrum of wavelengths, but within a few feet below the surface, the longer wavelengths, mainly the reds, no longer penetrate. (Note that the very short wavelengths of ultraviolet light that are beyond our range of vision have also been assumed to be filtered out by particulate matter within millimeters of the surface, but recent studies on the effects of the southern ozone hole in the atmosphere suggest that the increased uv rays that penetrate into the atmosphere may affect plankton many meters below the surface of the ocean.) As the water gets deeper, other colors get filtered out, and the visual world becomes increasingly somber in hue (fig. 2.2). Generally speaking, as the water depth increases, colors get filtered out according to decreasing wavelength. In colorless water the colors would disappear in the strict sequence of red, orange, yellow, green, blue, and violet, but there is surprising variation from lake to lake. A good rule of thumb is that below 5 to 10 feet what looks like red to us above the water appears black or dark gray, depending on the intensity of the color. Orange and yellow will turn gray at middepths, and in the deepest water the only colors that are likely to be seen as colors are greens, blues, and some violets.

This phenomenon of color washout is of considerable relevance to anglers because many of the exquisitely colored baits that are sold in the tackle store do not look anything like these colors to the fish that see them in the water. In lakes with greenish or brownish water, blue is strongly absorbed by these pigments, so blue as a color would not be visible much below the surface. When fishing at levels below 25 to 30 feet in such lakes, one is in a world of dull gray, brown, and greenish hues. In a clear-water lake like Ten Mile, virtually all colors except reds are likely to be visible at the depths at which most anglers typically place their baits. On a cloudy day when the light intensity is much less, colors in the water wash out at shallower depths than they do on sunny days. In this era when red hooks are being strongly pushed by the tackle industry, it is worthwhile remembering some of the above basic facts about color washout, especially on the red end of the spectrum.

## Sound

One of the major myths propagated in many literary works is that of the silent deep. Water is a dense medium that carries sound very well and very quickly. In fact, sound travels five times faster in water than it does in air. In addition, water is an excellent medium for transmitting vibration, to the extent that much of fish behavior is related to their ability not only to hear but also to pick up low-frequency vibrations with their lateral lines. In our example of a July day on the lake, fish would be subject to the frequent roar of boat motors charging overhead or, in some locales, to industrially generated noise that is sometimes so intense that there is real concern about the potentially harmful effects of underwater noise pollution. Noise pollution is a much greater problem in the oceans, where massive noise from military exercises and other sources has been shown to have a highly detrimental effect on communication among whales and porpoises.

All underwater noise is not man-made, however. Around the time of World War II, sonar operators were having great difficulty in determining which underwater sounds were really important to them. This led to a long series of research studies, mainly supported by navies of various countries, to learn more about the sources and nature of underwater sounds. They discovered that many oceanic animals, ranging from whales to shrimp, regularly produce a wide variety of underwater sounds as different as moans and soft clicks and that the oceans are really very noisy places. Because there are few enemy submarines in freshwater lakes, studies on natural sound production in lakes have

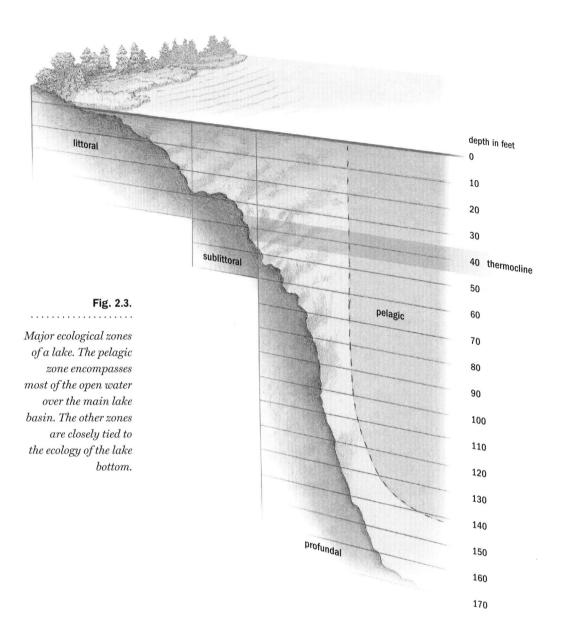

littoral

depth in feet
0

10

20

30

sublittoral

40 thermocline

50

**Fig. 2.3.**
. . . . . . . . . . . . . . . . . . .

pelagic 60

70

*Major ecological zones
of a lake. The pelagic
zone encompasses
most of the open water
over the main lake
basin. The other zones
are closely tied to
the ecology of the lake
bottom.*

80

90

100

110

120

130

140

profundal 150

160

170

lagged far behind those on oceanic sounds. Despite this relative lack of attention, we do know that some freshwater fish, such as carp and drums (sheepshead), emit well-defined sounds. At a much more subtle level even the muscular movements of a fish produce detectable sound. Among the invertebrates, animals with shells or exoskeletons, such as crayfish, produce clicking sounds when they move, which can alert fish to their presence.

Superimposed on all the man-made and animal-made sounds are the sounds made by big waves over the body of the lake and those made by the waves hitting the shore. All of this makes an auditory mélange that is part and parcel of the normal environment of a lake. It is worth noting that sounds in the air above the surface of the water are not very efficiently translated into aquatic noise. Therefore, talking in a boat will have minimal or no effect on fishing success, but dropping a pair of pliers on the bottom of an aluminum boat will produce a noise in the water that will scare the daylights out of most nearby fish.

Now that we have set the stage for our mid-July day on the lake, how do the physical parameters described above relate to life in the lake? By midsummer the steadily warming water temperature has allowed the luxuriant growth of aquatic plants in areas suitable for plant growth, and most of the lake animals have completed their reproductive period. This is a time of feeding and growth. The lake is a beehive of activity, but the actors and the unfolding dramas vary considerably in different regions of the lake.

## Ecological Zones in a Lake

A lake is divided into a number of ecological zones, each of which has unique characteristics and aggregations of plant and animal life (fig. 2.3). By midsummer the zones are well delineated and are quite stable. The band of water from the shoreline to the depth at which plants no longer grow is called the *littoral zone.* By convention this zone is often assumed to be the first 15 feet from the surface, but on Ten Mile Lake plant growth extends down to about 30 feet. This zone, which is comparatively well lit, is teeming with a wide variety of plant and animal life. The next zone, often coinciding with the thermocline, is called the *sublittoral zone.* Here the large plants are no longer present because of the reduced light, but oxygen is very plentiful, often more than at the surface. The region of lake bottom below is called the *profundal zone,* and this dark region consists largely of silt or exposed rocks. The water is cold and of nearly uniform temperature. In many lakes this region is poorly oxygenated by midsummer. The last zone is the region of open water over the main lake basin. Called the *pelagic zone,* it is home to many free-swimming animals, mainly plankton and fish. Blooms of small algae often dominate the pelagic zone in fertile lakes.

### The Littoral Zone

The littoral zone contains several recognizable regions. Around the perimeter of the lake is a very shallow rim where the water is less than a foot or two deep. In most areas this rim is completely or mostly weed free due to the actions of waves and ice. The bottom consists of sand or rubble or, in some of the bays, silt covered by varying degrees of vegetation (fig. 2.4). This is the part of the lake most familiar to folks with small children or to those who frequent the beaches. At first glance it

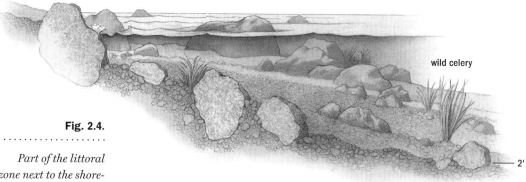

wild celery

2'

**Fig. 2.4.**

. . . . . . . . . . . . . . . . . .

*Part of the littoral
zone next to the shore-
line. In this narrow
band, wave action
reduces the amount
of vegetation.*

may not seem that much is happening in this part of the lake, but in reality it is a vital region of the lake, bustling with activity. Most noticeable to swimmers are the schools of minnows that cruise the shoreline and occasionally nibble their toes. Along with true minnows are the tiny young of many game fish that inhabit the shallowest waters during their first summer of life. These young fish are called *fry.*

Although the shallow water protects these tiny fish from large fish, the eat-or-be-eaten cycle of nature goes on even here. The minnows and fry are often vegetarians, and they eat organic material that collects near the shoreline. In turn, they may become the meal of slightly larger predators, such as 3-inch bass or large insect larvae. A good example of how nature works is the relationship between perch and walleyes. In Ten Mile and most northern Minnesota lakes, walleyes lay their eggs in late April, followed a few weeks later by the spawning time for perch, one of the walleye's main foods. Even in their first summer the predator-prey relationship holds true, because by the time the perch eggs hatch, the several-weeks-older walleyes are already large enough to eat the newly hatched perch. Small fish in the shallows are individually quite vulnerable, and they can even be eaten by large water beetles or dragonfly larvae (fig. 2.5). Most newly hatched fish do not make it past their first summer.

If the shoreline is rocky and wave swept, the shallow waters will also be inhabited by crayfish and tiny relatives of perch and walleyes called *darters.* In addition, many insect larvae live in these waters; these can vary in size from 2-inch-long dragonfly or damselfly larvae (fig. 2.6) to the tiny larvae of caddis flies, which build a tube of sand or organic debris around themselves for protection (see fig. 3.2).

As the water gets deeper, the lakescape is dominated by a succession of different types of vegetation. First is emergent vegetation, such as bulrushes and cattails, which commonly take root in water 2 to 4 feet deep (fig. 2.7). Bulrushes, in particular, provide excellent cover for both small fish and larger predators such as bass and pike. Numerous aquatic

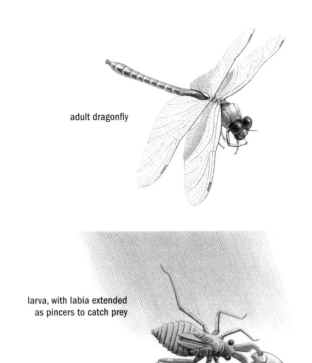

adult dragonfly

larva, with labia extended
as pincers to catch prey

**Fig. 2.5.**

. . . . . . . . . . . . . . . . . . .

*Larval and adult
forms of the
dragonfly. Cast-off
exoskeletons of larvae
(1 to 1½ inches long)
are often seen stuck
to window screens or
cabin porches that
are near river and
lake shores.*

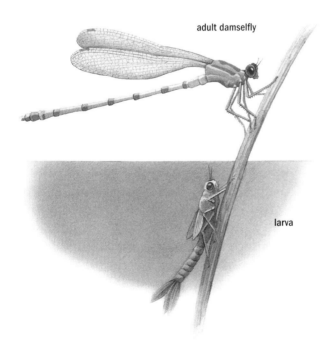

adult damselfly

larva

**Fig. 2.6.**

. . . . . . . . . . . . . . . . . . .

*Larval and adult
forms of the
damselfly. Note the
difference in the way
damselflies and
dragonflies carry
their wings when
at rest.*

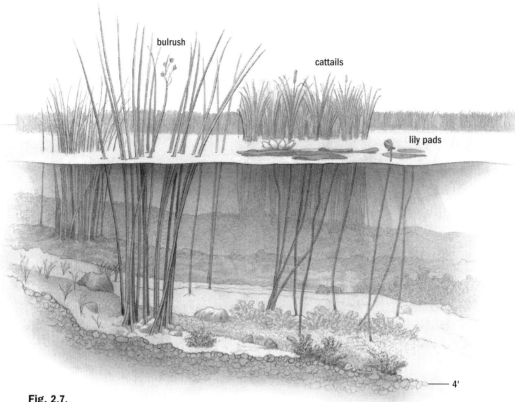

bulrush

cattails

lily pads

4'

**Fig. 2.7.**

*Typical ecological scene in the shallow waters of the littoral zone. These plants would be most likely seen in the shallow bays.*

insects and leeches inhabit bulrush beds, as well. In bays with silt or muck bottoms, water lily beds are important features. The large leaves of the lilies provide both shade and cooling during the hot days of summer. Water lily beds are home to many insects, small fish, and frogs. This attracts larger predators, including largemouth bass. Protected corners of small bays are sometimes covered by masses of tiny floating green plants called *duckweed.* Duckweed plants, whose leaves range from one-eighth to one-quarter inch in length, send down tiny roots that dangle in the water.

Farther from shore, in water up to 6 to 8 feet deep, one finds plants that send their stems up to the surface and often have leaves that spread out over the top of the water (fig. 2.8). Prominent types of plants are the pondweeds *(Potamogeton),* which may have thin leaves along the stem and then a different type of broad shiny leaf lying on the surface of the water. These plants also send their flowers into the air. Another inhabitant of this region is Canadian waterweed, often called *Elodea.* This is the type of plant commonly sold in aquarium stores.

Still deeper is the region containing plants that rise toward the surface but do not reach it. These include other members of the pondweed family, some of which have luxuriant, broad leaves. Broad-leafed pondweeds, known to anglers as *cabbage,* provide prime ambush habitat for the largest of the game fish. In a few bays common northern milfoil may grow in large clumps 2 to 4 feet high. Toward the deep end of the littoral zone, usually at depths from 22 to 26 feet in Ten Mile, are stands of coontail, highly branched plants that rise to about 15 feet below the surface (fig. 2.9). Throughout the littoral zone in Ten Mile and many other clear lakes are dense masses of the spongy alga *Chara*. This plant, which forms a green carpet over much of the bottom, has a characteristically musky odor—hence its common names, *stinkweed* or *muskgrass*—and provides excellent cover for a variety of animal life. Below 25 feet the density of plant life decreases until, by 30 to 34 feet, it is represented mainly by isolated clumps of *Chara*. This marks the last of the vegetation, and it often coincides with the upper limits of the thermocline.

The littoral zone is teeming with animal life, and it is the region where most of the game fish are concentrated in the early summer. The vegetation attracts large numbers of tiny aquatic invertebrates, which constitute the main food source for many minnows and young-of-the-year game fish. These, in turn, become the food of panfish, such as rock bass and crappies, as well as their large cousins, the bass. Small- to medium-sized northern pike, another top-of-the-line predator, use vegetation as camouflage as they lie in wait to ambush their unlucky prey. The bass, panfish, and pike are mostly stay-at-home types that operate within a relatively limited range, but the littoral zone is also a frequent stopping place for more nomadic fish like perch and walleyes.

Each species of fish seems to have a distinct personality when viewed through an underwater camera. Smallmouth bass are very curious and swim around the camera or even follow it for up to 50 feet, whereas largemouth bass often come right up to the lens and seem to try to

**Fig. 2.8.**
. . . . . . . . . . . . . . . . . . .

*The middepths of the littoral zone abound in plant life. The plants seen here are characteristic of this part of many north country lakes.*

emergent pondweed

cabbage

assorted
pondweeds

stand
of *Elodea*

clump
of milfoil

6'

algae-
covered
rocks

8'

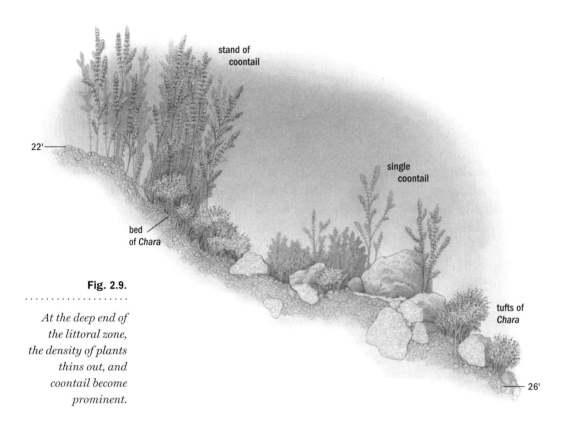

stand of
coontail

single
coontail

22'

bed
of *Chara*

tufts of
*Chara*

26'

**Fig. 2.9.**

*At the deep end of
the littoral zone,
the density of plants
thins out, and
coontail become
prominent.*

stare it down. Understandably, perch are very skittish, acting as if the camera wants to eat them. Walleyes glide past the camera like silent submarines, usually without acknowledging its presence, whereas a pike, lurking near the bottom, often gets frightened by it and darts away amidst a cloud of silt with a quick swoosh of its tail.

Perch form dense schools that often extend from just above the bottom to near the surface, and from sunup to nearly sunset, they move through the weeds and also in open water looking for food. Hovering around the edges of the perch schools are walleyes and northern pike. Typically, these predators patrol the outside lower edges of the school. Most of the time they seem to be merely accompanying the densely massed perch, but periodically, for reasons that are not understood, the walleyes and northerns dive into the school, slashing at the hapless perch. During major feeding frenzies, the school dissolves, and individual perch flee in all directions, trying to make themselves as inconspicuous as possible.

### The Sublittoral Zone

Just past the littoral zone is a transitional zone that in Ten Mile is often seen on the steep down-sloping sides of bars or underwater islands. These steep slopes often consist of large rocks and boulders, and in July it often coincides with the level of rapid temperature change at the top of the thermocline. This is a region where large fish tend to congregate because of favorable light and temperature conditions. Interestingly, in the summertime the oxygen concentration in this zone is higher than it is at the surface of the lake—sometimes as much as 12 PPM.

In many regions of the lake, the bottoms of both the littoral and sublittoral zones are not carpeted with vegetation. For the most part the amount of animal life is correspondingly reduced. With a few exceptions it is rare to see many fish in such areas unless the monotony of the bottom is broken by patches of rocks.

### The Profundal Zone

Below 35 to 40 feet is a cold, dark zone located below the thermocline. The summertime temperature at these great depths is typically in the mid to upper 40s. This region, which constitutes the bulk of the bottom of a deep lake like Ten Mile, has been little explored by anyone and is almost unknown to the average cabin owner or angler. Much of the bottom consists of fine silt, but in areas where there are sharp drop-offs, massive rock formations are often present. The silt comes from both the decaying bodies of plankton and from fecal pellets deposited by invertebrates after eating tiny floating algae. Rooted in the silt at depths in the 50-foot range are rare fragments of plants, like coontails, that have dropped down from the shallower waters and taken hold. These plants are doomed, however, because the dim light isn't adequate to meet their needs for survival.

Although the profundal zone often looks like the surface of the moon, it is not devoid of animal life. Living within the bottom silt are enormous numbers of midge larvae. The presence of some species, like bright red *Chironomus* larvae, indicates a poorly oxygenated region, whereas other species are found in the silt only when the water is well oxygenated. In unpolluted lakes mayfly larvae abound in the bottom silt in the profundal zone. When pollution and low oxygen take over a lake, the disappearance of mayflies is one of the first indicators of trouble. When the mayflies go, their niche becomes occupied by pollution-tolerant chironomid and tubifex larvae.

Bottom depths just below the thermocline, where the water temperature is in the mid-50s, are the haunts of the whitefish. These fish, usually weighing 2 to 4 pounds in Ten Mile, frequent the slopes or bottom edges of drop-offs and commonly cruise around in schools of several dozen, looking for 1- to 2-inch perch, darters, and insect larvae. Another unexpected denizen of the depths is the common sucker. Contrary to a popular conception, the adult sucker is not a warm-water fish and in the summer spends a great deal of time in densely packed schools lying directly on the bottom in water that is in the upper 50s. When over sand or silt, suckers rest in small depressions that they make on the lake's bottom. Because at these depths there is no wave action to disturb these sucker-made depressions, they persist for a long time, marking the resting places of these fish.

Patrolling these depths are solitary specimens of large northern pike, which prefer colder water as they get older. These top-of-the-line predators primarily eat suckers, ciscoes, and whitefish. Like most fish, their optimum prey size is one-quarter to one-third of their body length. Thus, for a 36- to 40-inch pike, a 2-pound sucker or whitefish makes a perfect meal. Interestingly, while studying the lake with an underwater camera, I have never seen a walleye in the deep waters below the thermocline, although the finding of walleyes caught in deeply set experimental gill nets shows that in the summertime walleyes do make occasional forays into deeper water.

As one descends into the greater depths of the lake, animal life on the bottom becomes less frequent but is not absent. I have directly observed whitefish in Ten Mile in water as deep as 110 feet and have seen what are probably whitefish tracings on fish finders in even deeper water. The deepest waters of some north country lakes are inhabited by a reclusive member of the codfish family, the eelpout, or burbot (fig. 2.10). In the summertime these fish seem nonexistent, and their habits

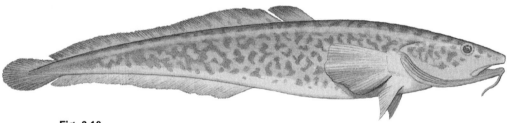

**Fig. 2.10.**
. . . . . . . . . . . . . . . . . . . .

*Eelpout, or burbot.*

are almost unknown to biologists. Eelpout become more active in the wintertime and can be caught while ice fishing. One of the major winter social events in Walker, Minnesota, is the annual Eelpout Festival on Leech Lake, where great honor, but less reward, is given to the angler who pulls the largest of these slimy creatures out of the frozen lake.

### The Pelagic Zone

In Ten Mile Lake and other deep lakes, much of the activity takes place in the open water and is unrelated to the bottom. The surface of the lake is teeming with life. Flocks of gulls and terns rest on the water between forays for dead or dying fish. Loons, permanent fixtures on the lake, spend their time socializing or fishing. Toward the edges of the lake, female mergansers and mallard ducks herd their broods of newly hatched ducklings as they strengthen their swimming muscles and learn how to obtain food for themselves.

Depending upon the day and time of year, the surface can be covered with insects, ranging from large mayflies in late June and early July to caddis flies later in the summer. These insects, which spend the majority of their lives as larvae living on or in the bottom of the lake, respond to some unknown signal and emerge in large numbers for a brief orgy of mating before they fall spent onto the water. Such hatches attract a large number of fish, from panfish to walleyes and even whitefish, as they gorge themselves on this protein-rich feast.

Just go out in a slowly moving boat on a perfectly calm day, and you can get some idea of the fish life that abounds just beneath the surface film. Every few hundred feet you can see patches where the surface is dimpled by the movements of schools of minnows or recently hatched fish. Occasionally, groups of frantically jumping small fish betray the presence of predators that are attacking them from below. Pelagic fish, as these are called, almost always congregate in schools, most likely for protection. Without the benefit of cover, these small fish would, individually, be easy prey for a predator, but dense schools, which can turn on a dime—as if controlled by a single brain—provide an evolutionary advantage that protects the greatest number of individuals by confusing the predators through their irregular movements.

The middepths in Ten Mile are alive with activity, and the entire food chain is represented in figure 2.11. At the bottom are the plankton—both plant (phytoplankton) and animal (zooplankton). Phytoplankton, which include microscopic diatoms encased in beautiful silica shells and barely visible specks of floating green algae, are at the absolute bottom of the chain, a link below the zooplankton. The green algae must be in the upper zones of water (40 feet or so) in order to effectively engage in photosynthesis. The phytoplankton serve as food for myriads of zooplankton, creatures that either are microscopic or look like specks to the naked eye. Most of the species of zooplankton are herbivorous, but a few of the larger varieties are carnivorous and feed on the smaller specimens of zooplankton.

Zooplankton are basically defenseless and must resort to camouflage in order to escape being something else's meal. This is accomplished, in part, by their having almost transparent bodies, making them difficult to see. During the bright daylight hours they congregate in deep waters where the dim light adds to their invisibility. Every evening the zooplankton undertake an amazing vertical migration toward the surface, where they encounter the phytoplankton, their main food source. Prominent among the zooplankton community are the rotifers, a group of animals that have a crown of tiny, nearly submicroscopic hairs called *cilia* that create miniature water currents, almost whirlpools, that sweep the even tinier phytoplankton into their open gullets.

In Ten Mile Lake the zooplankton are, in turn, beset by swarms of small ciscoes—a dwarf strain of a species in the whitefish family, unique to Ten Mile, that does not grow much over 4 to 5 inches long (see chapter 4). During the day the dwarf ciscoes range about in massive schools in water from 60 to 90 feet deep and at about 46 degrees. These fish feed almost exclusively on plankton, and they do so by swimming with their mouths open and letting the water flow through their mouths and out their gill openings. Any plankton in the water are strained out by fine gill rakers on the concave side of their gills and are swallowed. In the evening as the plankton rise toward the surface, the schools of ciscoes rise with them and go on a feeding binge.

When the ciscoes rise to the higher levels of the water column, however, they become the prey of suspended walleyes and northern pike looking for an easy evening meal. But the food chain is not complete, as anglers troll the midwaters, hoping to catch a few walleyes for their evening meal.

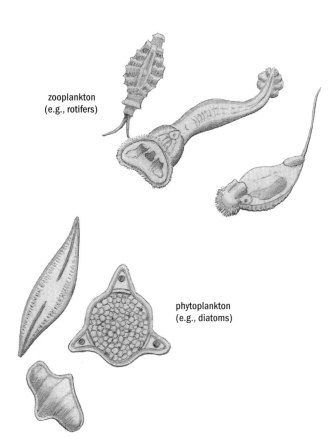

zooplankton
(e.g., rotifers)

phytoplankton
(e.g., diatoms)

**Fig. 2.11.**
. . . . . . . . . . . . . . . . . . .

*Aquatic food chain, from microscopic phytoplankton to the patient angler waiting above the water's surface.*

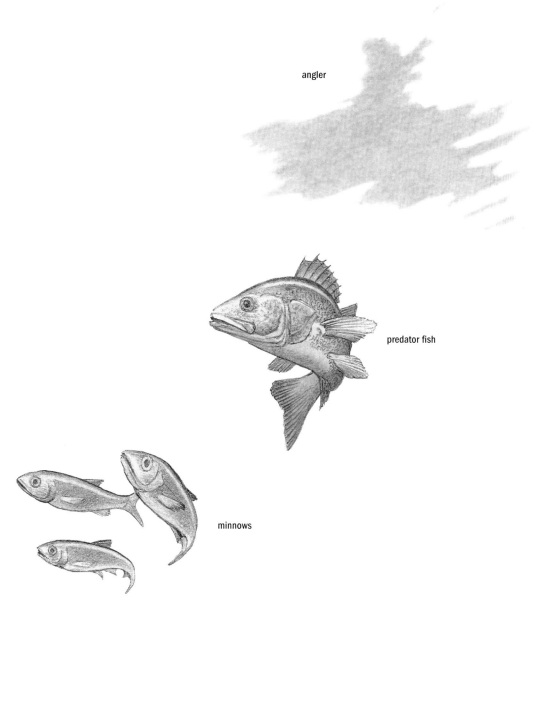

angler

predator fish

minnows

## 3 THE LAKE ON A SUMMER'S NIGHT

*T*he sun has set, and the warm summer sky has turned dark red above the western horizon. Venus is visible as a bright spot in the evening sky, and if you concentrate, you can see a few stars twinkling in the dark eastern sky. The jet skis have landed, and most of the recreational boaters have also left the lake. The last to arrive at the dock are greeted by a cloud of midges creating a steady high-pitched hum with the beating of their wings. A batch of mosquitoes makes life miserable as the boat is unpacked. For most folks this is the end of the day, a time to return to the cabin for a late snack, a look at the evening news, and a good night's sleep.

Some folks also have their late-night snack but then pack up their boats for a round of night fishing for walleyes. Those who engage in this activity are thought by most to have a screw or two loose, but the intrepid night angler finds himself immersed in a completely different world.

The human eye does not work well at night, so from the start night anglers are largely deprived of their most valuable sense. Therefore, much of what happens in a lake after dark is experienced indirectly, through sound and touch or from instrument readings. The general sensation at night is that the world has closed in, so one must extrapolate a picture of the whole from small bits and pieces. Over several decades I have spent most or all of about twenty-five nights a summer out on the lake. This chapter reconstructs my experiences and combines them with data obtained from scientific studies.

Though we may sleep all night, the lake does not. Patterns of activity at night differ greatly, however, from those during the day. Some animals also shut down for the night, but others are more active after dark than during the day.

## Creatures of the Night

. . . . . . . . . . . . . . . . . . .

For campers and those out on the lake, the deepening evening darkness means relief from the bites of black flies and deer flies, but mosquitoes soon pick up the slack and torment anyone outside until deep into the night. Especially early in the summer, swarms of insects fly around lights on or near the lake. Most of these insects have just emerged from the water, where they have spent the previous months or even years as aquatic larvae. When large numbers of such insects emerge at the same time, it is called a *hatch*. During hatches the air may be thick with mayflies, caddis flies, or midges (chironomids), with a smattering of mosquitoes, as well. Even though they don't bite, caddis flies, in particular, can be a nuisance as they are attracted to any light. Fortunately, their numbers tend to decline after midnight, so the late-night hours are much more merciful. In fact, the very late night is essentially insect free.

Many aquatic insects, especially mayflies, are indicators of good-quality water. Their larvae, which live at the lake bottom, need oxygen, so if the water is polluted, they will no longer be present. In fact, their reappearance in lakes and rivers is proof that pollution control is working. Around some lakes and large rivers, mayflies can be so numerous that they need to be removed with snow shovels. In 1996 an enormous mayfly hatch blew from Lake Erie into Toledo, Ohio, and almost paralyzed the city due to the masses of slippery creatures that covered the roads. I once parked a car under a light pole behind our cabin late in June, and the next morning it was covered with mayflies that had also completely packed the ventilation system. In addition, caddis flies had somehow gotten into the supposedly hermetically sealed instrument panel—and remained there for the duration of the car's life. Although I spent several hours picking mayflies out of the vents with a long forceps, the car smelled of dead mayflies for several years when it rained.

### Mayflies

Most mayflies are associated with clear streams and rivers, but a few species inhabit lakes as well. The most prominent mayfly in our northern lakes is one of the largest species, *Hexagenia limbata*, commonly called the *fishfly* or the *giant Michigan mayfly*. The adults, which can reach 1½ to 2 inches from the top of the head to the tip of the tail, are among the largest of all the species of mayflies. To most people living near water and to lake anglers, mayflies are most noticeable in their final adult stage, when they lie spent on the water or collect below lights on land. But, like so many animals, the bulk of a mayfly's existence is spent as a feeding larva hidden in a burrow in the lake bottom. This is all preparation for the final flurry of its life cycle—the brief period when it emerges as a mature winged mayfly whose entire brief existence is devoted to reproduction.

The life cycle of the giant mayfly begins when the female drops her 4,000 to 8,000 fertilized eggs onto the surface of the water, usually just after dark in the late spring or early summer. The eggs are heavier than water and sink to the bottom. There, their sticky surface coat attaches them to rocks or aquatic vegetation, where in two to four weeks, depending upon the water temperature, they hatch into larvae (nymphs), which are initially less than a millimeter long. Mayfly nymphs live in 6- to 12-inch U-shaped burrows under silt or sand bottoms in lakes. They spend much of the daytime in their burrows and come out at night or during periods of very low light, when they feed upon various particles of organic detritus that they run across. During the two to three years that they spend as nymphs, they both grow in size and develop new body parts through a succession of as many as 40 to 50 molts. With each molt they shed their exoskeleton and then grow a new covering as their overall structure becomes more mature (fig. 3.1). Biologists call each stage between molts an *instar*. Actual molting may take 5 to 10 minutes. The new instar is pale and somewhat larger than the former one and remains inactive for a few hours after molting to let the new exoskeleton harden. When in their final stages, the larvae are about 1½ inches long. Alongside the abdominal segments are feathery gills, which in addition to a respiratory function, create water currents in the burrow through regular pulsations.

Responding to signals that are still incompletely understood, large numbers of nymphs in the same lake undergo a rapid series of major changes that bring them from their long period of larval life to their mature winged form. The most visible external change is the development of wingpads, which presage the ultimate emergence of the wings of the adult form. Internally, even more striking changes occur. The most sweeping change is the degeneration of the entire digestive system, including mouthparts, since the adult mayfly does not eat. While losing their digestive tract, the late instars gradually develop genitalia in anticipation of the reproductive functions of the adults. The body cavity remaining after degeneration of the digestive tract often becomes filled with gas, which facilitates the rise of the emerging larvae from the bottom sediments to the surface film, often tens of feet higher in the water column. These same gasses also enable more efficient flight by reducing the specific gravity of the adult mayflies. The final stages of mayflies' emergence is the stuff of trout fishing lore because at these stages, especially in streams, mayflies are especially vulnerable to predation by fish, which often go on wild mayfly-feeding binges. Large hatches also occur in lakes, and in very infertile northern lakes many of the predatory fish,

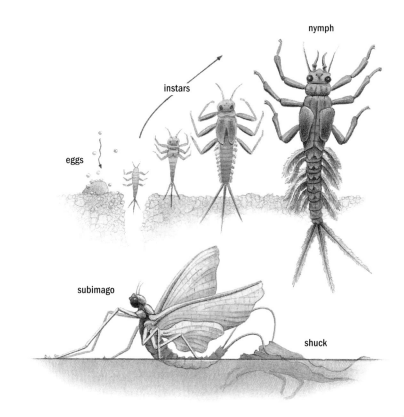

nymph

instars

eggs

subimago

shuck

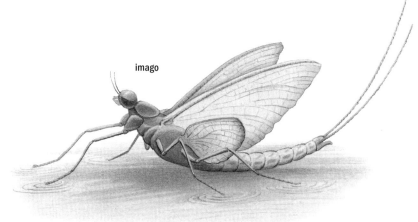

**Fig. 3.1.**

*Stages in the life
of a mayfly.*

imago

such as walleyes, move in on the mayfly hatch and absolutely gorge themselves on emerging mayfly larvae and adults to the virtual exclusion of other foods.

During their metamorphosis from larva to winged adult, the mature nymph, which has already undergone many of the changes leading to adulthood, rises to the surface of the water during the late evening. There it undergoes another major metamorphic change (fig. 3.1). Its hard outer casing splits longitudinally down the back (thorax), and out from the larval casing emerges a sexually immature winged mayfly called a *subimago* (or *dun* by the trout angler, because of its dull color). Through the split emerge first the wings, followed by the thorax, head, abdomen, and finally the three-pronged tail of the dull-colored, but otherwise adult-looking, subimago. The nymphal casing, which is left floating on the water and is very visible during mayfly hatches, is called the *shuck*.

Lacking in mouthparts and a digestive system, the newly hatched mayflies must be careful to preserve body moisture during the precarious few days of their adult existence. The newly emerged subimagos fly from the surface of the water to shaded vegetation near the water, where within two to four days they undergo a final molt to their sexually mature adult form (imago). A prominent change is the transformation of the dull-colored wings of the subimago to the glassy transparent wings of the imago. The sexually mature *Hexagenia* is yellow to tan in color with brownish markings. Cabin owners alongside lakes that have mayfly hatches may notice shed casings of the subimago skin on porch screens. Mayflies are the only insect forms to undergo a second molt once they have developed wings.

Once a full-fledged adult, a mayfly may have only hours of precious existence in which to perpetuate its lineage. At this stage its only remaining function is to reproduce. How they do so is fascinating. For most species of mayfly, the males fly around in swarms above the water, and then the females are somehow attracted to these swarms. How this attraction occurs is a mystery, however. Some biologists think that there is a behavioral element (a male dance), but I suspect the males secrete a pheromone (a chemical attractant that can be detected over great distances) that encourages females to enter the swarm. Once within the swarm, the female is seized by a male, and the two copulate in midair.

Mating is facilitated by huge eyes that take up much of the facial profile in the males. The eyes of females are of more usual dimensions. Upon fertilization the biological usefulness of the males is over, and they fall exhausted onto the water, where they are easy pickings for hungry fish. Spent mayflies may still flap their wings for a while and are called *spinners* by trout anglers. After copulation the females retreat to shaded vegetation for a short time while the fertilized eggs inside them begin to ripen. Then the females fly over the water and deposit their eggs, initiating the next cycle in the mayflies' multimillion-year history.

*Caddis Flies*

In contrast to mayflies, which have been found as large fossils hundreds of millions of years old, caddis flies are more recent insects closely related to moths, even looking like small moths as adults (fig. 3.2). For the lake dweller, caddis flies are most visible as small brownish insects that swarm around lights on boats or docks on summer nights. They don't bite, but they can be extremely bothersome flying into one's face when turning on a flashlight in a boat at night. Hundreds of species of caddis flies inhabit North American streams, and they are of considerable interest to trout anglers, who try to mimic both adult and larval patterns with their flies. Despite their preponderance in streams, a number of caddis fly species live in clear northern lakes.

Although the adults are distinctive because of their numbers, the larvae represent in many respects the most interesting stage of this insect's life cycle. In both lakes and rivers, some caddis fly larvae are net builders. They construct small nets made of silk that catch tiny bits of detritus or small animal forms that are swept into them by the currents

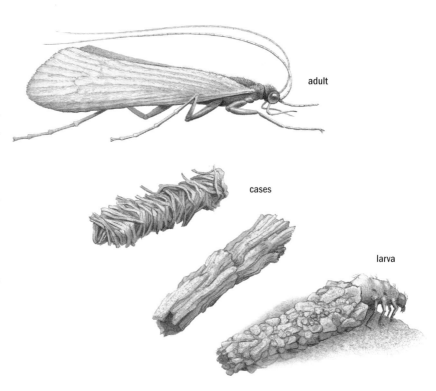

**Fig. 3.2.**
. . . . . . . . . . . . . . . . . . .

*Caddis fly. The aquatic larvae construct and live in cases made from tiny pieces of organic material or sand. They metamorphose into brownish, soft-winged adults; most are a bit over a half inch long.*

adult

cases

larva

of rivers or the waves in lakes. Other types of larvae make exquisite cases around their bodies for both protection and camouflage and wear them like shells. The nature of the case depends upon the species and the available materials. Some caddis fly cases, which are usually less than one-half inch long, are perfectly rectangular cylinders made of wood chips, whereas others are made of grains of sand or tiny pebbles. If you look carefully at rocks pulled up from the shallow water at the beach, you may see tiny caddis fly cases (6 to 10 millimeters long) stuck to them.

The female caddis fly may deposit her eggs on the surface of the water or may actually dive into the water and deposit them on objects at the bottom. Typically, only one generation is produced per year. The eggs hatch into tiny instar larvae, but in contrast to mayflies, the larvae go through only five instar stages. The larva has three pairs of legs located not far behind the head and a long abdominal segment that it surrounds with its characteristic case. With each molt the larva must build a new case to accommodate its larger size. Caddis flies end their larval phase of life by becoming a pupa. Within their pupal case, which is often just a sealing off of the larval case, they undergo a metamorphosis lasting up to three weeks that takes them from the larval to the adult form. When ready to emerge, the pupa swims to the surface in a motion that has been described as a breaststroke effected by a long pair of their legs. While on the surface, the pupal case cracks and the adult emerges. Caddis fly adults spend only a few seconds on the water before flying off. Because of this, emerging adult caddis flies do not constitute a significant food source for fish. Adults may live for one to two months and can take nourishment from plant juices. Although the adults form mating swarms, actual mating commonly occurs on the ground or vegetation near the shore. Like most aquatic insects, caddis flies fall spent onto the surface of the water after laying their eggs, usually within a year after their birth.

## Midges

One of the most impressive things about midges is their numbers. This is readily apparent to anyone who has seen thick clouds of midges gathered about the edges of a lake on an early summer's evening. Even more impressive is the number of midge larvae inhabiting the bottom sediments of a lake. It has been estimated that various lake sediments may contain from 1,000 to 9,000 midge larvae per square foot. The number of midge species is equally impressive. There are over 2,000 species of midges in North America, and a single lake may host as many as 200 species.

Like most aquatic insects, the adult phase, which is the one apparent to most of us, represents only a small part of the overall life cycle of a midge. Most of their existence is spent as larvae in the bottom sediments of a lake, sometimes as long as seven years in Arctic lakes. Many life cycles last a year, but some midges, such as bloodworms, may go through six generations in a single year. No part of a lake is too deep to contain midge larvae. I was recently on the boat that carried the scientists who have probed the depths of Loch Ness in Scotland looking for Nessie, the Loch Ness monster. The captain said that numerous midge larvae were found in core samples of bottom silt taken in 700 feet of water.

Like the usual aquatic insect, the female midge deposits her eggs on the water, and they drop to the bottom where they hatch into larvae. The midge larvae dwell in the bottom sediments of a lake, often in the deepest parts, where they eat detritus and small algae, mostly of the blue-green type. Their numbers are so great that a substantial proportion of the silt that makes up the bottom sediments of the deepest lakes consists of fecal pellets of midge larvae. It has been suggested that this may be the origin of much of the oil shale deposits that are widespread in the western plains of North America.

Midges are very sensitive indicators of water quality. The larvae of most species require abundant oxygen and thrive only in clean lakes. Certain groups of midges, however, contain hemoglobin, which stores oxygen, in their body fluids and have a body metabolism that allows their survival in poorly oxygenated water, such as is found in the depths of highly eutrophic lakes or in polluted waters. These midges, often of the genus *Chironomus,* are typically bright red from their hemoglobin and are commonly called *bloodworms.* Bloodworms are very important in the dynamics of sewage-settling ponds, where large amounts of algae are important in the treatment of the sewage. Huge numbers of bloodworms live among the algae and eat the dead algal matter. If they did not do this, the dead algae would consume much of the oxygen needed for the aeration of the sewage.

The deep bottom sediments of oligotrophic lakes contain large populations of species of midge larvae that require abundant oxygen. In addition to processing detritus, they serve as food for larger organisms. A substantial component of the diet of Lake Itasca whitefish, for example, consists of midge larvae.

Many midge larvae live in small tubes or silk-lined cases within the bottom silt. There, like the larvae of most aquatic insects, they grow and undergo periodic molts, but typically, they undergo only three or four molting cycles as larvae. Typical midge larvae are about one-half inch long and look quite worm-like. They have a recognizable head and a pair of thick leg-like structures in their first body segment (fig. 3.3). At the very back of their body, midge larvae typically have tufts of hair-like or gill-like structures and projections that may allow them to hold to their

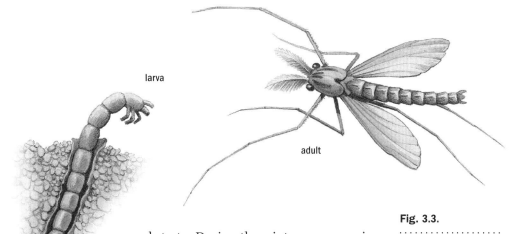

larva

adult

**Fig. 3.3.**

. . . . . . . . . . . . . . . . . . .

*A midge spends the majority of its life as a larva that lives in a lake's bottom sediments. As an advanced insect the midge goes through a pupal stage before metamorphosing into a nonbiting adult.*

substrate. During the winter some species build silk cocoons and remain dormant until the water warms. Midges are members of the order of flies and mosquitoes, Diptera, and like other members of that group, they go through a pupal stage during which the wormlike larva becomes transformed into a delicate winged insect. During this metamorphosis the larval body essentially liquefies and becomes replaced by an adult body that is derived from some undistinguished-looking masses of cells called *imaginal disks*. Through exquisitely controlled developmental processes, individual imaginal disks form wings, legs, or other specific components of the adult body. Once the adult emerges from the pupal case, it enters the frenetic short-lived existence of a typical nonfeeding aquatic insect. The adults gather into immense swarms and breed before dying. It is fortunate that the adults do not feed on blood as do mosquitoes, as it would be almost intolerable to live by a lake at certain periods of the year.

*Mosquitoes*

Mosquitoes are the insects that everyone loves to hate. Nobody who has spent any time at a lake has escaped the onslaught of hungry mosquitoes along the shore as dusk approaches. Yet despite their frequent association with lakes, they have quite a different life history from that of most other aquatic insects. There are about 150 species of mosquitoes in North America. Three genera are most commonly known—*Culex,* the ordinary biting mosquito of the north; *Anopheles,* which carries malaria; and *Aedes,* which is a vector for yellow fever. West Nile virus, a recent arrival in North America, is transmitted through bites of members of the ordinary *Culex* genus.

Although mosquito larvae are aquatic, they are much less commonly found in lakes than in marshes, swamps, or even small temporary pools of water. Another difference is that mosquito larvae live near the surface of the lake rather than at the bottom. Almost all mosquitoes begin their lives as eggs that have been deposited singly or in rafts on the surface of the water. There the eggs develop into larvae. The posterior segment of the body contains a siphon, which serves as a breathing tube so that the larva can take in air (fig. 3.4). Because of their need to breathe air, mosquito larvae spend their life just beneath the surface film and hang head down so that the siphon at the tail end has access to the air. The larvae feed on floating detritus and microorganisms. *Culex* larvae hang head down, perpendicular to the surface, whereas *Anopheles* larvae remain parallel to the surface. When disturbed, they jerkily dive from their normal position, which is why the larvae are commonly called *wrigglers*. In as short a time as a week, the larvae enter the comma-shaped pupal stage, still just beneath the surface of the water. Upon emergence from the pupa, male and female mosquitoes go separate ways. Only the females are bloodsuckers, a requirement for reproduction, whereas the males feed on plant juices. Mosquitoes are diurnal, and most people who frequent the woods or lakeshores can testify that they bite very readily in the evening and early morning or in the dull light before and during storms.

**Fig. 3.4.**

. . . . . . . . . . . . . . . . . . . .

*The early part of a mosquito's life is spent in small puddles as a larva suspended from the surface of the water. It takes in air through a breathing tube that reaches the surface. It also pupates at the surface before turning into the adult form.*

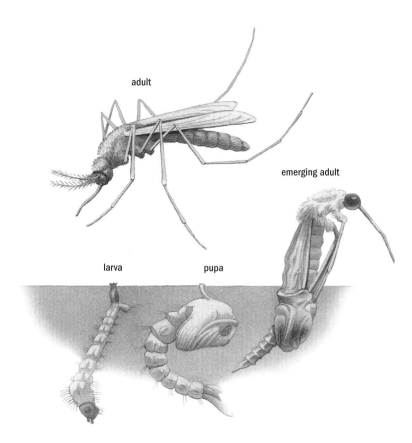

adult

emerging adult

larva          pupa

Early in the summer cabin dwellers often notice what are usually described as "giant mosquitoes" on their screens. These are crane flies, which can reach over two inches in length. Their larvae can be either aquatic or semiaquatic, and like the mosquito, they require air for breathing. Fortunately, they do not bite.

*Bats*

The other dominant flying creature at night is the little brown bat, which feeds exclusively on flying insects. Even though I know the scientific theory behind bats' powers of echolocation, I never cease to be amazed at their ability to capture tiny swiftly flying insects on a windy night. They do this by emitting sounds in the 40 to 100 kilohertz (kHz) range (well beyond our range of hearing) that bounce off the insects. The returned sound then enters their large ears and is processed within their brain to tell them the exact location of the insect. Bats are said to catch insects by scooping them into their broad tail membrane and then flipping them into their mouth. This is a most efficient process, and on a good night a bat eats up to ten insects per minute. In one night a bat may eat up to half of its weight in insects.

A few years ago I switched from trolling with monofilament line to one of the new superlines, which are much thinner than monofilament lines and do not stretch, thus increasing their sensitivity. I began experiencing very faint taps on my line and at first thought that they came from fish that were barely mouthing my lure. On one moonlit night I discovered the real cause. Bats were attacking the segment of my line that was above the water. Apparently, the composition and diameter of the new line registers as an insect on the bat's radar, and they dive in for what turns out to be a very unpalatable meal. Bats keep their distance from the boat, and I have never had a close encounter with one at night.

Bats are very sensitive to temperature, and their own body temperature fluctuates with the temperature of the air. On very cool nights they go into a state of semihibernation. I still remember a seminar that I attended in the 1970s where a bat expert took a bat that he had been keeping in a 39-degree room and passed the inert hibernating creature among the forty members of the audience before it began to stir. On very cool evenings they remain semidormant rather than flying, because they might not catch enough insects to satisfy their very high metabolic needs (their heart beats as many as 1,300 times per minute when they are flying). Bats are legendary for their ability to squeeze through small cracks as they look for places to sleep during the day. In the fall bats migrate toward southern caves, where they spend the winter. I have heard that the little brown bats around Ten Mile Lake winter in caves near Stillwater, Minnesota.

*Other Night Creatures*

On top of the water, most birds rest for the night. The calling of the loons at night creates one of the strongest impressions of a north country lake. Only when the boat approaches a resting loon does it emit its nervous cry and then swim out of the boat's path. The gulls and terns typically roost in flocks at night, but sometimes the ducks are actively paddling around. Canada geese, although not common on Ten Mile, often engage in noisy social activity at night, especially in moonlight. Although not strictly connected with the lake, the "hoo-hoo-hoo" of great horned and barred owls calling to one another is one of the more memorable night sounds that carries across the water.

One of the busiest creatures of the dark is the beaver. After resting in their lodges during the day, beavers emerge in the late evening to forage for their favorite meal, alder and poplar branches. Beavers' nighttime forays can take them amazing distances from their lodge. One summer a beaver came to the front of our cabin every night for about two weeks to harvest branches of alder bushes, leaving the cut branches in the water by the beach as a calling card. This destination was about two miles from the nearest beaver house. The loud slap of a disturbed beaver's tail on the quiet evening water is one of the truly memorable north woods sounds. More than one angler has mistaken a tail slap for the sound of a fish of a lifetime jumping near the boat. In the swampy bays muskrats silently swim along the surface as they go to and from the patches of vegetation that they use both for food and, later in the summer, for their houses.

## Nightlife below the Surface

Beneath the surface of the water, the typical pattern of daytime activity has changed. This change is dramatic enough that I can look at a tracing from a fish finder for a given area in Ten Mile and tell whether it was made during the day or the night. One of the most dramatic changes in the littoral zone is the disappearance of the schools of perch that figure so prominently over weedy flats during the day. The eyes of perch are not adapted for night vision. This puts them at a distinct disadvantage after dark, so their response to darkness is to scatter and bed down in the weeds to make themselves as inconspicuous as possible. In the main lake basin the ciscoes drop to the very bottom in over 100 feet of water within an hour after sunset and remain there until dawn. For the most part pike reduce their activity considerably at night, but this is not an absolute rule. Like the perch, their eyes are not as well adapted for functioning in dim light as those of some other fish. This doesn't completely prevent them from feeding at night. Especially on moonlit nights, it is not uncommon to catch northern pike on artificial baits. On several occasions I have caught northern pike in more than 30 feet of water on moonless nights. At that depth the amount of light that penetrates from the stars is negligible, and it illustrates the accuracy to which pike and other fish can home in on sound and vibration to strike a lure. The human eye also adapts to darkness, but it is a relatively slow process, taking about 20 to 25 minutes to fully equilibrate to night vision.

For a fish like the walleye, nighttime is its element, and much of its feeding is done at night. The reason for this is that the large eyes of a walleye have an anatomical adaptation that concentrates available light and makes night vision much more efficient. It is basically the same adaptation that allows your cat or a deer to function so well after dark. If you shine a flashlight into the eyes of a nocturnal animal, chances are that you will see a strong reflection coming back to you. Something that I never tire of is seeing the orange reflections from the eyes of a hooked walleye swimming in the water as I bring it toward the boat. In the springtime some anglers shine a searchlight into the shallow water to locate walleyes through the reflections from their eyes. This light coming back at you is from what is called the *tapetum lucidum*. Located behind the retina of the eye (see fig. 9.1), the tapetum lucidum is composed largely of a layer of reflecting crystals. In normal vision light rays enter the cornea of the eye, pass through the lens, and then hit the retina. Within the incredibly complex structure of the retina are photoreceptor cells called *rods* and *cones*. The rods are responsible for black-and-white vision, and the cones detect color. Not all light hitting the retina is taken up by the rods and cones. Much of the light passes through the retina and is absorbed by other tissues. In walleyes and other animals that have a tapetum lucidum, the light that passes through the retina is bounced back off it much like light reflected off a mirror. That reflected light hits the rod and cone cells again, allowing them to process the same light twice, thus making their eyes much more efficient in dim light.

Although walleyes are the most prominent night feeders in the lake, they are not alone in feeding at night. Both largemouth and smallmouth bass are very active after dark and will readily take an artificial lure even on a moonless night. Among the panfish, rock bass will strike a bait without hesitation at any time of the day or night. In fact, on more than one night when the walleyes were not hitting and I was wondering if it was too dark for anything to see my bait, I was heartened by the pull of a rock bass on my line and figured that if a rock bass could see my bait, a walleye should have no trouble. Crappies also feed actively after dark. Some of the largest that I have caught have been taken late at night. Another fish that feeds at night is the whitefish. On dark nights early in the summer when the mayflies are hatching, whitefish can be seen swimming just beneath the surface, most likely looking for a juicy meal. Because the light is so dim at the depths that they often inhabit, their level of light in 100 feet of water during the day probably isn't much more than that of the surface of the lake at night.

Because eating is the main reason why many fish are active at night, it makes sense that predators will be found where there is food. Some fish, such as rock bass, don't change locations much at night because much of their food (crayfish and insect larvae) also lives in the rocks where the rock bass hang out. Crayfish feed much more actively at night than during the day, and mayfly larvae are most active at night. Others, such as walleyes, typically move to distinctly different feeding locations at night. During the day in the summertime, walleyes commonly congregate at the base of drop-offs, where the water temperature and light levels are more to their liking. After the sun has set, they begin to move toward their after-dark feeding positions. One of their favorite nighttime haunts is the tops or sides of underwater islands where schools of minnows gather. The minnows are easy pickings for hungry walleyes, which move in on the minnows. This pattern is so regular that many walleye anglers anchor along the edges of underwater islands and still-fish for them with leeches or minnows for bait. On particularly nice nights, the lighted boats of walleye anglers neatly outline the periphery of popular underwater islands. Some anglers shine bright lights into the water, which attracts minnows. The walleyes then follow to feed on the minnows. Other walleyes move from the bases of underwater bars to the tops of the bars as the night wears on. An important fishing technique for giant walleyes in deep, infertile Canadian Shield lakes is to cast large minnow-shaped baits over the tops of underwater islands at night. In many lakes walleyes move into very shallow water (2 to 3 feet) late at night, especially in the fall, but for some reason this rarely occurs in Ten Mile during the summer. Other walleyes cruise the deep, weedy flats, sometimes in the same general regions as largemouth bass, which also feed actively at night.

The habits of minnows can make it easier for both walleyes and anglers. Long after the ciscoes have dropped to the bottom of the lake for the night, well out of the reach of their chief predators, many of the pelagic minnows gather in dense schools and move toward underwater structures like bars and underwater islands. The walleyes follow, and so do the anglers. One very unusual nighttime pattern is the aggregation of immense schools of tiny fish, possibly a pelagic minnow called the *emerald shiner*, over a very narrow vertical zone, usually 10 to 12 feet from the surface during the last weeks of August. These schools range from several hundred feet to almost a quarter mile in diameter, and in the early morning hours they move in over the deep flats, where they make it easy for a hungry predator to find a meal.

The intensity of light hitting the water at night is about $\frac{1}{100,000}$ of that in the middle of the day. Even at night there are striking differences in the intensity of light. On a clear night with a full moon, I can see well enough to clean off hooks and do minor repairs without a flashlight, but on a dark night I can hardly see my hand. This corresponds to a 100- to 1,000-fold diminution of the light on a dark night compared with that of a full moon (see table 2.1). Night-feeding fish are able to find food even in the darkest of nights through a combination of sight, sound, vibration, and smell. Despite that, I have found that their activity level varies considerably with seemingly minor changes in light level. When a strong display of the aurora borealis comes out, fishing often picks up. Nighttime ecologists who are concerned about light pollution have found that urban lights can increase light levels on water almost to those of a full moon—50 times greater than that on a rural lake on a moonless night. On cloudy nights the light bouncing off the low clouds increases levels of incident light by 2 to 3 times. This light pollution significantly disrupts the migratory activity of some species of zooplankton and correspondingly alters the behavior of fish.

I always try to be out on the water on the nights before, during, and just after the full moon. More than once I have excused myself from attendance at a summertime scientific meeting because of "other pressing matters," which astute observers might have noticed were coincidental with the full moon symbol on the calendar. One night, when there was a full eclipse of the moon, the walleyes stopped biting during the duration of the eclipse and then began again when the eclipse was over.

Angling lore is full of theories concerning when in the nightly moon cycle the fish bite best. According to some, you shouldn't miss either moonrise or moonset, and there are also the staunch devotees of the moon overhead–moon underfoot school. My guess is that most lakes have their own nighttime rhythms, some of which are determined by local factors. Certainly, in Ten Mile the evening cisco rise and fall is a dominant factor. In that lake I have found by far the best night fishing on shoreline flats to occur well after midnight. Most of those who still-fish off underwater islands do so, however, before and around midnight. One possibility is that the walleyes move from the open waters, where they have been gorging on ciscoes, to the nearby underwater islands, where they move on to the minnow course. They might not get to the shoreline flats for dessert until late in the night.

## Some Tips on Baits and Retrieves

One of the issues that perplexes many anglers is how a fish can detect an artificial bait at night. The quick answer is, easily, but some baits are easier to detect than others. More than any other type of fishing, success in night fishing is based upon the ability of a fish to sense its environment in many different ways. For walleye fishing this means using bait that takes advantage of their ability to see and hear and to feel vibrations. Their sense of smell comes in a distant fourth. All of these senses working together allow a walleye to detect your bait and to home in on it for an accurate strike. Which of these senses first attracts a walleye to your bait is a matter of conjecture. It may be a function of the level of darkness, as well as how close the fish is to your bait.

Sound, which travels well through the water, could initially attract the attention of a walleye. Imagine a walleye on the other side of a boulder or a stand of weeds from your trolled bait. It hears a soft regular clicking that alerts it to the presence of something moving. Under most circumstances the amount of sound need not be great, and some highly successful night lures emit no sound. I have found that a bait that emits a simple dull click when it is retrieved is as effective as anything. The clicks come from a small metal ball placed inside a chamber within the plastic body of the lure.

Vibration is another sense that is important not only as an attractor but also as a trigger to elicit striking behavior. Vibration does not have to be fast to be effective. One of the best patterns is just the slow side-to-side rolling motion of a trolled crankbait, especially one with flat sides. At another extreme are the rattlebaits, which are reeled in or trolled very fast and which give off tight vibrations, as well as strong sound in most cases. These attract fish from a long distance, and even after dark the fish strike them savagely.

Vision is a critical sense much of the time at night, and certain patterns are more effective than others. For fishing walleyes after dark, most experienced night anglers prefer a bait that has silvery sides and a dark back. The light sides catch whatever light is available, and the dark back provides contrast. With the rolling of the bait, the sides catch the moonlight or even light from the stars and on a bright night give off a surprisingly pronounced flash. Some walleye anglers have advocated using black baits at night, but in my experience they are nowhere near as effective as lighter-colored ones for deep trolling at night. Around dusk, conversely, a black bait can be very effective. Many anglers believe that chartreuse is an effective color at night. On Ten Mile I often use a bait with a blue back at night. Whether or not a walleye can see color at all at night is not known, but certain color patterns are definitely more effective than others. My preference for blue baits at night may be explained by the Purkinje shift (see chapter 9), by which a fish's eyes become more sensitive to colors at the blue end of the spectrum when it becomes darker. It may be, however, that they don't see the color as blue but just as a more visible shade of gray. It's hard to say.

The topic of luminescent accents on baits has been discussed a great deal in fishing publications over recent years. Some excellent night anglers put a few dabs of luminescent paint on their baits and swear that it substantially increases their catch rate. A few bait companies have put out models that are completely luminescent. To activate the luminescence, one is supposed to shine a light on the baits for a few minutes before putting them in the water. Over time the luminescence fades. The general consensus is that a small bit of luminescence probably helps, and at least it doesn't hurt. It may give just enough of a faint visual cue to enable a fish to home in on the bait. Too much luminescence may actually scare fish, however, because they don't normally see a completely lighted 5-inch fish in the lake. Although I have put luminescent patches on many of my night baits, I must say that I haven't noticed any difference between baits with or without added luminescence.

For nighttime bass fishing, almost everybody agrees that black is the best color by far for surface baits such as Jitterbugs. The black makes the profile of the bait stand out against the night sky regardless of the amount of moonlight. I even find that black is the most effective color for spinnerbaits after dark.

Other issues of importance in night fishing are size of bait and speed of retrieve. Under most circumstances, for walleyes it is appropriate to use baits a size or two bigger at night than you would use during the day. On Ten Mile Lake many of my night-fishing baits for walleyes are 6 inches long, with some at 5 to 5½ inches and a few longer than 6 inches. Fish, in general, are bolder at night and probably don't discriminate size or shape as well as they do in the daytime. A larger bait seems to give the fish a better target. The best nighttime retrieve is usually relatively slow and steady, but a deadly technique for casting is to use suspending minnowbaits and pause during the retrieve. Sometimes the motionless bait suspended in the water is irresistible to a large walleye. There are some inklings that sometimes nighttime walleyes will fall for a very fast retrieve in conjunction with a vibrating bait. This idea needs more experimentation before it can be presented as a fact.

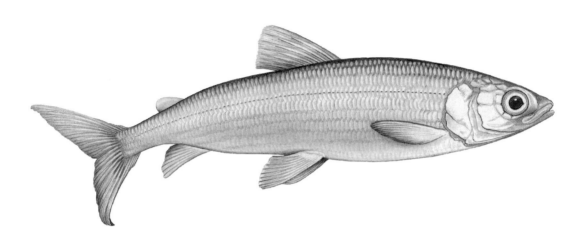

*4* DWARF CISCOES AND WHITEFISH

## Dwarf Ciscoes

. . . . . . . . . . . . . . . . . . .

Far beneath the surface, in the deepest reaches of Ten Mile Lake, the waters teem with literally millions of a unique fish. These fish are dwarf ciscoes, a member of the whitefish family. Most folks have never seen a cisco unless they have gone to one of the small smoked fish stores scattered around the northern Great Lakes and seen packaged foot-long fish usually labeled as *lake herring* or sometimes *cisco*. In Minnesota they are often called *tullibees*. These fish represent a species that is called *Coregonus artedi* by fish biologists. Regardless of what they are called, the dwarf ciscoes, more than any other fish, are the dominant species and define the character of Ten Mile Lake.

Ciscoes are the little cousins of whitefish—leftovers from the glacial times. They require very cold water, and the only lakes that still contain them are those that are deep enough to have cold, well-oxygenated water throughout the summer. Lakes that are marginal habitats characteristically have cisco die-offs in warm summers when the water temperatures rise above the tolerance limits of these fish. Whereas whitefish weigh typically 2 to 4 pounds in most inland lakes (although the world record is 42 pounds), a cisco over 1½ pounds is a large one. In addition to being much larger than a cisco, a whitefish has an overhanging snout, whereas ciscoes have a lower jaw that protrudes slightly beyond the upper jaw (fig. 4.1).

For some reason that scientific research has not yet been able to explain, Ten Mile ciscoes are dwarves, averaging less than 5½ inches long and weighing only ½ ounce when mature. Yet a transplantation experiment showed that this

. . . . . . . . . . . . . . . . . . . .

*Dwarf cisco.*

**Fig. 4.1.**

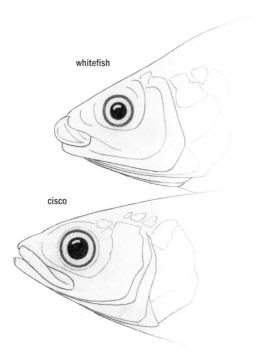

whitefish

cisco

*Mouth of a whitefish and a cisco. The mouth of a whitefish is strongly turned down, in keeping with its bottom-feeding habits, whereas that of the cisco is oriented straight ahead so that it can capture plankton more efficiently as it swims with its mouth open.*

small size is not permanently ingrained into their genetics. In 1976 and 1977, almost 40,000 of these fish were transplanted into several Minnesota trout lakes on an experimental basis in order to provide forage for trout and serve as decoys for their predators. During the two-year study period, the transplanted Ten Mile ciscoes doubled in length to almost 8 inches and increased their weight sixfold. Although this fact suggests that Ten Mile Lake ciscoes are undernourished, they do not have the relatively large heads and ultrathin tapering bodies that are characteristic of undernourished fish. Why these ciscoes could grow larger but do not is a mystery. Two possibilities were brought out in a 1990 doctoral thesis by Ted Halpern. One relates to the amount of zooplankton in Ten Mile, which is only one-tenth as abundant as that in Lake Itasca, a lake with normal-sized ciscoes. The second possibility relates to the cold temperature in which Ten Mile ciscoes live. They spend most of the year in water less than 46 degrees, whereas most ciscoes prefer water of 53 degrees. Fish need less nutrition and grow more slowly in cold water, and Halpern suggests that, since there is apparently less food for them in Ten Mile Lake, these ciscoes choose the cold water to minimize their nutritional requirements. The bottom line is that at this time nobody really knows why most of the Ten Mile ciscoes are dwarf fish. Regardless of theories, the lake is awash in bite-sized food for a variety of predators, ranging from walleyes and northern pike under the water to gulls, terns, and loons descending upon them from above.

During the daytime dwarf ciscoes inhabit the midwaters of the lake in massive schools numbering in the millions. Most schools of ciscoes are found between 60 and 90 feet from the surface in water between 100 and 200 feet deep. They drop down to these levels as soon as the ice goes out and remain there all summer. In the summertime the water temperature at their preferred depth is usually 46 degrees or less, and the water is well oxygenated. At that depth they are located 30 to 50 feet below the lower limits of the thermocline in water that is well below the comfort zone of walleyes and northern pike, their main predators. In October, when the oxygen concentration in the deepest water sometimes becomes very low, the main schools rise into better-oxygenated water.

Ciscoes and most pelagic (free swimming) fish make use of a remarkable method of camouflage that is not intuitively obvious to those of us who inhabit land. Most people are aware that many aquatic animals are more darkly colored on their backs and tend to have silvery bellies. The same goes for inhabitants of the sky—birds and sometimes even military planes. When one looks up at individuals toward the light, whether in the water or in the air, the light belly serves as a camouflage, as does the darker back if they are observed from above. Some South American catfish that swim upside down have dark bellies and light-colored backs. Many of the small fish that swim in schools in both lakes and the oceans are very silvery over all their sides. In nature that silveriness acts like a mirror. If one places a mirror vertically in a lake and a fish (or human) looks toward it from below, it reflects light in a manner that makes it absolutely invisible. The same principle applies to silvery-colored fish like ciscoes. When swimming normally in the water, their silvery scales reflect the light just like a vertical mirror, making them much harder for predators to see. Some fish go to seemingly extreme lengths to maintain the mirror effect. Certain members of the herring family have their scales arranged so that when the body contours taper, the scales stick out a bit, thus preserving the verticality. In addition, many pelagic fish, such as alewives in the Great Lakes, have a sharp keel on their belly rather than a rounded contour. Freshwater shad have a similar contour. This sharp edge reduces the bottom profile of these fish, as would be seen by a predator from below. These adaptations are not always effective, because ciscoes still get eaten, but a lot of these small fish are still swimming because their camouflage protected them from hungry predators.

While protected from most of their predators, ciscoes are busily feeding on zooplankton, their main source of food. The arrangement of their mouth, with a protruding lower jaw, is ideal for their style of eating, which consists of swimming forward with their mouth open and engulfing the tiny plankton. Both plankton and water stream through the cisco's open mouth and into the area of its gills (fig. 4.2). The water passes through the gills, providing life-giving oxygen to the soft red filaments on the outside of the gills, which serve the same purpose to the fish as our lungs do for us. On the inside of the gills are harder white gill rakers, which act as strainers. The water passes through, but the plankton get hung up on the closely spaced gill rakers and are swept into the fish's gullet. Ciscoes in many lakes also eat larvae of chironomid midges, which inhabit the silt in unimaginable numbers even in the greatest depths.

Dwarf ciscoes are important predators of zooplankton, and like any predator, they can be found where the food is. When the zooplankton undertake their daily evening migration toward the upper waters of the lake (see chapter 3), the ciscoes follow (fig. 4.3). What the ciscoes do depends heavily upon the water temperature. Early in the summer, when the water temperature ranges from the upper 50s to the mid to upper 60s, masses of ciscoes rise toward the surface starting about an hour before sunset. Although most of the fish don't get much closer than 30 to 40 feet from the surface, some smaller groups of ciscoes swim all the way to the surface as long as the water temperature isn't too warm. Their presence is revealed by their frantically jumping out of the water as they are chased by small walleyes looking for an evening meal. For the angler this behavior is very important because keying in on jumping ciscoes clues them in to where to be trolling for walleyes. Larger walleyes and northern pike also gorge themselves on ciscoes in the evening, but they typically occupy deeper water—at least 15 to 20 feet below the surface. Later in the summer, when the water temperatures get into the 70s at the surface, the ciscoes are less likely to come all the way to the surface, and in warmer summers jumping ciscoes are rarely encountered. Nevertheless, the larger predators still try to make the evening

**Fig. 4.2.**

. . . . . . . . . . . . . . . . . . . .

*Location and structure of a cisco's gill. The gill filaments on the outside edge are richly supplied with capillaries and, therefore, red in color. The long white filaments on the inside are gill rakers and are used for straining out food. The fish sucks in water containing plankton through its mouth and then expels the water through the gills. The gill rakers strain out the plankton, which are then swallowed.*

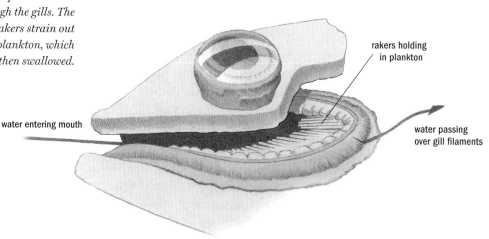

water entering mouth

rakers holding
in plankton

water passing
over gill filaments

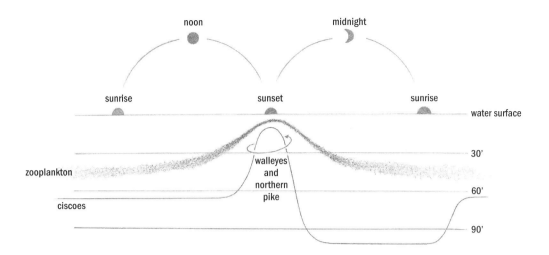

noon

midnight

sunrise

sunset

sunrise

water surface

30'

zooplankton

walleyes
and
northern
pike

60'

ciscoes

90'

cisco connection, although by late summer the perch in the shallower waters have grown to the extent that many of the walleyes move closer to shore to feed on perch and seem to feed less on ciscoes.

You can tell if walleyes have been eating ciscoes by watching them carefully as you are about to net them. Very commonly, walleyes disgorge their stomach contents into the water by the boat. For the angler it is very important to know what they are eating, and checking out the kinds and size of fish spit up can provide a valuable clue as to what bait to use. On a couple of occasions, I have caught walleyes that have spit up dwarf ciscoes so fresh they were still quivering.

There is a definite correlation between the presence of large predators and the densest schools of ciscoes. This relationship became apparent one summer evening when I encountered a very dense mass of ciscoes that had risen close to the surface of water that was between 100 to 120 feet deep. Within an hour I had caught five or six walleyes and northern pike. The next night I went back to the same place and didn't get a bite, but about a quarter of a mile away, I again got five walleyes in less than an hour. The dense schools of ciscoes had left the spot where they were the previous evening and were now in the area where I was catching walleyes. This pattern continued on successive nights, and for almost two weeks I followed the dense schools of ciscoes and invariably caught walleyes when I found them (fig. 4.4). Because it was a warm summer with water temperatures in the mid 70s for many feet below the surface, the large cisco schools were rarely found in water less than 100 feet deep. Although I have no scientific proof, my guess is that the enormous schools of ciscoes deplete the zooplankton population in a particular region and then keep moving into areas where they haven't been for a while in order to get a fresh food supply. After a few weeks the populations of zooplankton recover to the point where they can support

**Fig. 4.3.**
. . . . . . . . . . . . . . . . . . .

*Daily vertical migration of Ten Mile ciscoes. They spend most of the day about 80 feet below the surface. An hour or two before sunset, the plankton, upon which they feed, rise toward the surface, and the ciscoes follow. Within an hour and a half after sunset, the ciscoes drop down to the deepest areas of the lake basin, where they spend the night. Around sunrise they then move up to their daytime depths.*

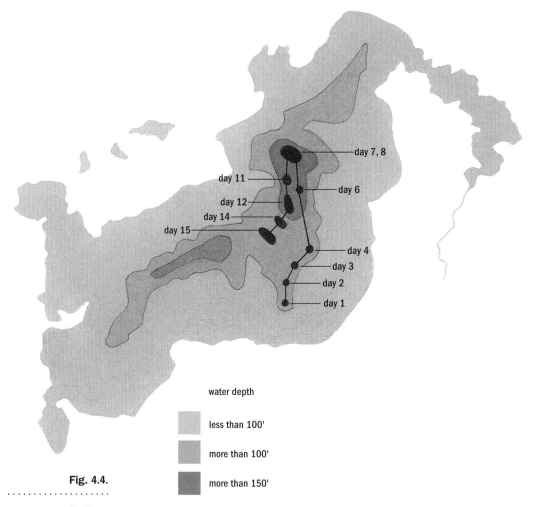

day 7, 8
day 11
day 6
day 12
day 14
day 15
day 4
day 3
day 2
day 1

water depth

less than 100'

more than 100'

more than 150'

**Fig. 4.4.**

Movements of a dense
school of ciscoes over
a two-week period.
Walleye fishing was
best when the boat
was over the densest
cisco schools.

huge schools of hungry ciscoes, and the ciscoes can return to their former location, repeating the feeding-depletion cycle.

The hour before sunset is the time when ciscoes are located at their
highest point in the water column. Starting shortly after sunset, the
cisco schools reverse their upward migration and begin dropping
quickly toward the bottom of the lake. I have often taken continuous
sonar recordings of cisco schools as nightfall approaches. About a half
hour after sunset, the dense masses of ciscoes split into two distinct
groups. Some of them remain 40 to 60 feet below the surface, but others have already moved down to 80 to 100 feet below the surface. By an
hour or so after sunset, almost all of the ciscoes have dropped down

close to the bottom, and a good fish finder shows a seemingly solid mass of ciscoes in the bottom 10 to 20 feet of the water column, almost always at depths greater than 100 feet. There they remain for the night, protected from their enemies. When the sun rises in the morning, the ciscoes also rise in the water column to assume their daytime positions 60 to 90 feet below the surface.

Ciscoes spawn in the fall, usually late October to mid-November. Relatively little is known about their spawning habits, but it appears that the main spawning activity occurs at night. According to the report of a year-round resident on the lake, during their spawning time you can hear them splashing in the waters off sandy beaches during the dark of night. Even during the morning shimmering schools of spawning ciscoes can be seen swimming in almost circular routes close to shore. Unlike panfish, ciscoes don't make nests, so after fertilization the eggs drop to the bottom, where they develop very slowly over the winter and hatch the following spring. Although my university duties have not allowed me to visit the lake during the spawning period of the dwarf ciscoes, I strongly suspect that any angler who is intrepid enough to locate cisco spawning sites at this late time of the year would find some excellent fishing for large walleyes and northern pike. Fieldwork conducted during the 1970s suggested that many ciscoes die shortly after spawning. Dying ciscoes, in particular, are easy pickings for predators. One northern pike netted during the cisco spawning season contained 37 ciscoes in its stomach!

Little is known about the habits of dwarf ciscoes under winter ice, but under the ice they swim freely throughout the water column from the surface to the bottom. Even in the early spring the bulk of cisco schools spend most of their time in the deep waters of the lake. The cold water temperatures do not confine the ciscoes, however, to the deep water, and when there are early hatches of insects, some of the ciscoes rise to the surface, where they inhale midges. This is one of the few times during the year when they deviate from their normal diet of zooplankton or insect larvae.

## Whitefish

The other major deepwater fish is the whitefish (fig. 4.5). Despite their commercial importance, whitefish are rarely seen or caught and are little understood or even recognized by the average lake resident. Like other deep north country lakes, Ten Mile has a large population of whitefish, which go almost unnoticed by local anglers. Until a few years ago, when I decided to figure out how to catch whitefish in the summertime, I was similarly ignorant about these beautiful fish. Since then I have spent many hours not only fishing for them but also directly observing them with underwater cameras and checking their locations with fish finders.

The whitefish of Ten Mile Lake have been described as dinosaurs. A 2005 survey of northern Minnesota whitefish conducted by the U.S. Geological Survey sampled the whitefish population in Ten Mile. The sizes of the whitefish were not remarkable—the largest sampled was only 23 inches. What was remarkable was their age. Out of a sample of 134 fish, 31 were more than 30 years old, and 2 Methuselahs of the fish world were more than 50 years old. In northern lakes normally only

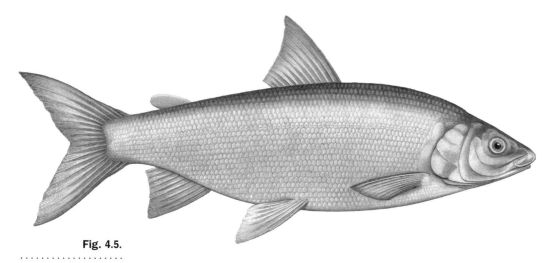

**Fig. 4.5.**

*Whitefish.*

sturgeon and possibly lake trout can be expected to live that long. These age statistics indicate that the Ten Mile whitefish population is largely unexploited by humans and that once they attain a certain size they are relatively protected from all natural predators in the lake. Interestingly, the oldest fish sampled (over 52 years old) was only 17.6 inches long. This example illustrates the inaccuracy of the common belief that the largest fish are the oldest. In fact, gerontologists have long recognized that, statistically, the smaller members of a species tend to live longer than the larger ones.

The time when an angler is most likely to accidentally encounter a whitefish is the early spring when trolling for walleyes. The first time I caught one was while trolling in the early 1990s. I felt a gentle tap on my lure but then had a whale of a fight on my hands. It felt like a 6- to 7-pound walleye, but the fish fought with slashing runs that were more reminiscent of a lake trout. When the fish finally surfaced, the first thing that I saw was the iridescent violet back and bright silvery sides of a whitefish that weighed a bit less than 4 pounds. This whetted my appetite for more. The question was where to start. I was told that a few local anglers sometimes caught whitefish on crappie-sized minnows in about 90 to 100 feet of water, but since much of Ten Mile Lake is deeper than 100 feet, that didn't help much in locating them. This information provided a couple of clues, but the two big questions were still where to find them and what to use to catch them.

The biggest breakthrough on the second question came early one summer when almost everyone who fished had caught one or two whitefish, and I had gotten a couple of them accidentally on the standard 5- to 6-inch minnowbaits used for walleyes. It was obvious that there was no way a whitefish could swallow a bait that size, because a whitefish has a very small, turned-down mouth with smooth, leathery lips (fig. 4.1). The reason for the turned-down mouth is that, in contrast to ciscoes, which are plankton feeders, whitefish feed mainly off the bottom, where a mouth facing downward is a real advantage.

Since whitefish feed at or near the bottom, it made sense to place a bait in that area, but for exploration purposes it also made sense to use a bait closer to the size of the mouth of a whitefish. This led to my trolling a three-way rig with a 3-ounce sinker keeping the bait on the bottom and a 4- to 5-foot leader pulling a panfish-sized artificial minnowbait about 2½ inches long (see fig. 5.7B). After investigating lots of different areas, I found that, when I caught whitefish that early summer, they were typically at the base of drop-offs in 30 to 40 feet of water—just below the thermocline—or at the edge of deep flats just above steep drop-offs. Interestingly, one place that I found purely by accident was a spot about the size of a living room floor that has ever since been the most consistent location for finding whitefish. That spot has been my outdoor laboratory for testing different baits for whitefish. Once I worked out some consistent methods for catching whitefish on artificial baits, I was then able to more effectively figure out their locations and movements in the summertime.

It soon became apparent that trolling a three-way rig wasn't a very efficient way to catch whitefish, once they had been located. Although they are sometimes solitary, it is very common for whitefish to travel in schools, so once you have found one or two, there are likely to be more. Under these circumstances, you want to be able to get a bait to them quickly and accurately. The best way to do it is to drop a marker as soon as you catch a whitefish and then concentrate on the area around it. Since whitefish usually live in relatively deep water—from about 30 feet in the early summer to 50 feet later on—heavy jigging lures of the type used in ice fishing are a good choice. One of the best bets is the Cicada, a metal vibrating lure that has a curved fin which causes an intense vibration when the lure is raised in the water (fig. 4.6). A quick

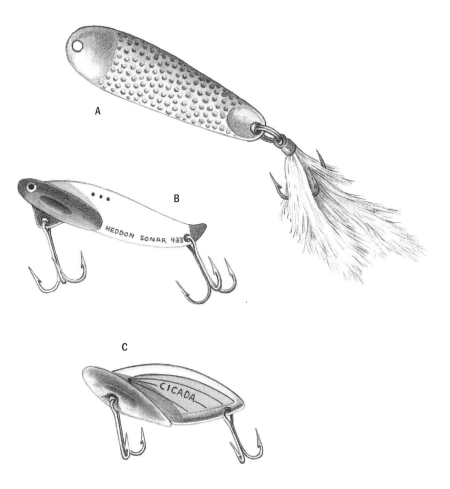

**Fig. 4.6.**

. . . . . . . . . . . . . . . . . . . .

*Excellent baits for whitefish.* **A***, Jigging spoons should be sharply raised 1 to 2 feet and then allowed to settle on a taut line. Sometimes whitefish will even pick them off the bottom.* **B***, Sonar and,* **C***, Cicada are all-metal baits that vibrate rapidly when sharply lifted. Whitefish often hit them as they are settling back to the bottom.*

lift of 1 to 2 feet followed by a gentle drop is often highly effective for whitefish. More recently, I have tried using one-quarter-ounce jigging spoons, oblong pieces of silver-covered metal that look like flattened fishing sinkers (fig. 4.6). When lifted and dropped close to the bottom, these lures fall irregularly and give off reflections of light like a dying minnow. The first time I tried this method, I caught and released about 100 pounds of whitefish in the first hour.

Another method that is sometimes effective is a technique called *drop-shotting* (see fig. 7.9). For this method one places a sinker at the end of the line and attaches the hook (size 8 to 10) some distance above the sinker—in this case about 1½ to 2 feet. This rig works because whitefish usually cruise a foot or two above the bottom. One could put a small minnow on the hook, but I have found that it is much more convenient to attach a tiny (1 to 1½ inches) plastic curly-tail grub onto the hook and either slowly troll or drift within the very tight area where the fish are located. With any of these fishing methods, it is necessary to concentrate in order to feel a bite, because whitefish will, at best, barely tap the bait. Most of the fish are caught when you lift the line and feel a weight on it. Because of this, I prefer to use the newer nonstretch superlines, and there is no need to use over 6-pound test for whitefish.

A couple of times when I caught reasonable numbers of whitefish, I kept them so that I could see what they had been eating. It turned out to be a real surprise. Their stomachs are very thick and gizzard-like, and much like some birds' stomachs, most of theirs contained small stones or bits of gravel. The stones and gravel may aid in grinding their food. A number of the whitefish had 1- to 2½-inch fish, mainly young-of-the-year perch or darters, in their stomachs. The other common food was the remains of aquatic insect larvae, often mixed with bits of organic debris. Their choice of fish closely resembled the small metal jigging baits that I had used, and the tiny plastic grubs were close in size to the insect larvae.

Catching a whitefish is a real experience. Considering their weight, they fight as hard as any fish in the lake, making slashing runs and sometimes boring straight down into the deep waters. Because of their soft mouths, there is little need to set the hook, but since their lips are also leathery, there is little danger that the hook will be pulled out. One characteristic feature of catching whitefish is the stream of bubbles that they often emit during the fight. Almost all fish have swim bladders, white balloon-like bags that parallel the underside of the backbone. More primitive fish, like members of the trout and whitefish family, have an anatomical arrangement by which a thin tube acting as a pneumatic duct connects the swim bladder to the digestive tract (fig. 4.7). Such fish are called *physostomatous*. When fish rise in the water column, the gas in their swim bladder expands because of the reduced pressure. Physo-

**Fig. 4.7.**

. . . . . . . . . . . . . . . . . .

*Source of the bubbles when a hooked white-fish comes to the surface. Air in the swim bladder expands with the decreasing water pressure as the fish is pulled toward the surface. The excess air passes through the pneumatic duct and into the digestive tract, from which it leaves through the mouth as a stream of bubbles.*

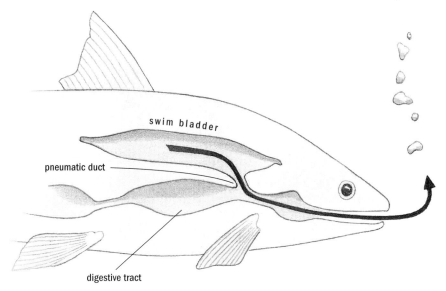

swim bladder

pneumatic duct

digestive tract

stomatous fish are able to quickly relieve the pressure by expelling excess gas through the pneumatic duct into the digestive tract and backward out their mouth. This is the source of the bubbles that one sees when fighting a whitefish. More advanced fish—those with spiny fin rays (e.g., perch, walleye, bass, and panfish)—don't have a pneumatic duct and are called *physoclistous*. They have a much more complex method of regulating gas pressure through a specialized gas gland, but it doesn't work so rapidly, which is why some swell up and float on the surface when they have been taken from very deep water.

For reasons discussed at the end of this chapter, I rarely keep the whitefish that I catch unless it is for scientific purposes. Whitefish are very delicate fish when brought to the boat, and after much experience in handling them, I now unhook them while they are still in the water, which reduces their mortality rate to almost zero, whereas if they are netted and taken into the air for even a short period, a significant percentage of them die when they are released. In the water they can be grasped by clamping your hand over the back end of their gill covers and holding firmly enough to remove the hook.

With this information catching whitefish should be no problem, assuming you can find them. Since whitefish are denizens of large, deep lakes, there is usually a lot of water, both vertically and horizontally, in which to look for them. Knowing their natural history makes life a lot easier for the angler and for those interested in hunting them with underwater cameras. Three main characteristics determine where whitefish can be found. First of all, they are cold-water fish and therefore prefer temperatures in the mid to upper 50s, although they can be found in much colder water as well. Second, their turned-down mouths are adapted principally for bottom feeding. Third, in my experience they prefer to be near steep slopes, although this is not always the case.

In the early spring, when the surface water is still in the 50s or less, all bets are off concerning whitefish locations. I have seen and caught them in water as shallow as 2 and as deep as 100 feet, but with the melting of the ice and the warming of the surface waters, many whitefish move into quite shallow water to stock up on food, principally insect larvae and small minnows. Virtually all fish, except for the dwarf ciscoes, tend to follow a similar pattern. One of my big fishing surprises occurred on an early June day when I was speed retrieving a vibrating bait while fishing for smallmouth bass and caught a 4-pound whitefish 10 feet from shore. Under similar conditions, with water temperatures in the upper 50s, large schools of whitefish may bite vigorously on walleye-type lures trolled in 20 to 30 feet of water.

One of the most unusual early season patterns for whitefish occurs when insect hatches cover the lake early in the spring, with the surface water temperatures in the low to mid 50s. On mirror-calm days one can go out to the middle of the lake over water 150 feet deep and see large numbers of whitefish feeding at the surface on floating insects, just like trout. This is one of the few times when you can take lake whitefish on dry flies. A bright red ant fly retrieved just beneath the surface is also effective. The whitefish are constantly moving, so you often have to anticipate where a fish is going once you have seen it suck up an insect. Sometimes the schools are dense enough that blind casting can produce fish.

As spring turns into summer and the water warms up into the 60s, the whitefish drop down into the region of the newly forming thermocline. This is a period when they are likely to be concentrated at the edges of deep flats, just above a steep drop-off. Here they can gorge on larvae of mayflies and midges or pick off small fish. In such locations they feed voraciously, and if you find them, they are easy to catch. This is the period when there are also large mayfly hatches in the evenings. Although I have not done stomach analyses of whitefish caught at this time, I would predict that these juicy insects or their emerging larvae constitute a major portion of their diet. While trolling at night through areas with dense concentrations of spent mayflies on the surface, I have seen whitefish swimming within a foot of the surface, and I would bet that they are feeding on mayflies at night.

As summer wears on and the water temperatures rise into the 70s and a strong thermocline forms, many whitefish position themselves below the thermocline in water that is in the mid to high 50s. By late July and early August, this means that they are in 40 to 60 feet of water and are commonly located at the bottom of drop-offs at the ends of points or along the upper edge of deep drop-offs. There seems to be no lower limit to their distribution other than the availability of food and oxygen. I have seen whitefish in water as deep as 110 feet. At this time of the year, one can still catch whitefish with the methods outlined above, but I have found that they don't bite as well as they do earlier in the summer.

With the cooling of the water in October and November, the whitefish begin to concentrate on spawning, which is done in the late weeks of the fall before the lake freezes over. Many lakes in Minnesota have a fall whitefish netting season, usually beginning in mid-November. In most lakes this is the only time when they are subjected to any significant fishing pressure. Although in Michigan and Wisconsin fresh whitefish fillets are considered a delicacy in restaurants, they are less highly regarded in Minnesota where most of the whitefish that are netted are taken to the smokehouse.

Unfortunately, many of the whitefish in inland lakes are heavily infested by a very unsightly parasite called *Triaenophorus crassus*. Ten Mile Lake is no exception. This worm forms large, ugly yellow cysts in the muscles of whitefish. Like so many parasites of fish, *Triaenophorus* has a complex life cycle (fig. 4.8). The main host of this parasite is the northern pike, which acquires the worm by eating infected whitefish. In the pike the worms live in the intestine. These worms lay huge numbers of eggs that pass into the water and are eaten by a species of zooplankton called *Cyclops*. Within the *Cyclops* the eggs develop into larvae (procercoids). When an infected *Cyclops* is eaten by a whitefish, the larvae migrate to the muscles and develop into the yellow cysts, thus repeating the cycle. Because of these parasitic infestations, whitefish from most smaller inland lakes are officially considered unfit for human consumption, and commercial fishing for them is not allowed. Nevertheless, this parasite does not infect humans. In Ten Mile Lake about one out of five whitefish is free of the parasite. When cleaning a whitefish, it is very easy to see if the fish is infected. The cysts are commonly 1 to 2 inches long and are very easy to see if you hold a fillet to the light.

**Fig. 4.8.**

. . . . . . . . . . . . . . . . . . .

*Life cycle of* Triaenophorus, *the parasite that infects the flesh of many whitefish.*

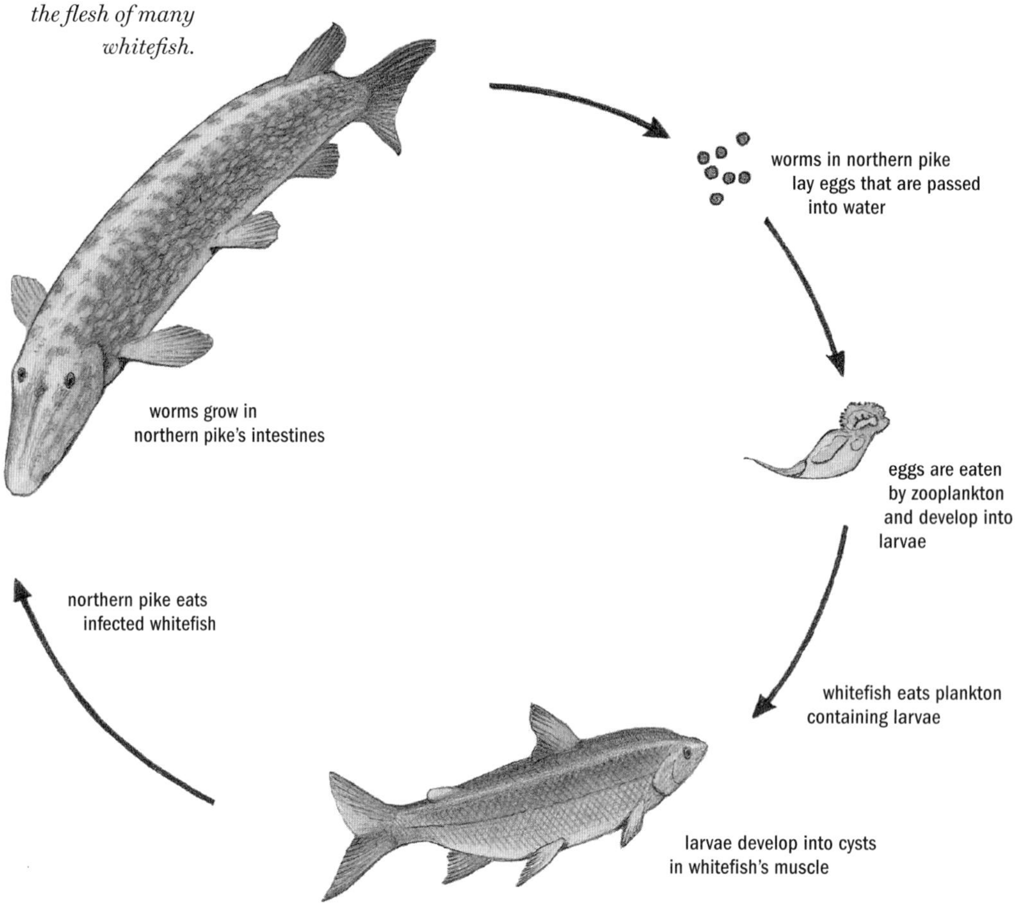

worms in northern pike lay eggs that are passed into water

eggs are eaten by zooplankton and develop into larvae

whitefish eats plankton containing larvae

larvae develop into cysts in whitefish's muscle

northern pike eats infected whitefish

worms grow in northern pike's intestines

An experiment on fisheries management may have a significant effect on the incidence of infected whitefish. In a number of northern Minnesota lakes the Department of Natural Resources has imposed special regulations on fishing for northern pike in the hope of restoring populations of trophy-sized fish. Such large pike are the natural predators of whitefish, and it would not be surprising if the presence of larger numbers of big pike reinforces the life cycle of *Triaenophorus* because the larger pike will eat more infected whitefish, which will consequently result in more eggs of the parasite being shed into the water.

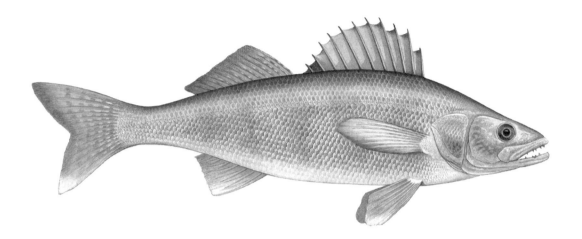

## Walleyes

. . . . . . . . . . . . . . . . . . .

The walleye has a special status in the north country. Along with the first day of deer hunting, the opening of walleye season in mid-May is the closest thing that Minnesota has to a state holiday. As someone who has always worked in Michigan that weekend, I have taken comfort in thinking my marriage has likely been saved by geography. Since almost all opening weekends take place Mother's Day weekend, I would have either been in agony or long divorced had I lived closer to our cabin during that time. In its infinite wisdom, the State of Minnesota has declared that mothers may accompany their walleye-fishing spouses without a fishing license on Mother's Day. I shudder to think of the casualties inflicted upon the institution of marriage in Minnesota during wet, cold, and windy Mother's Days. Opening weekend aside, the walleye is a dominant factor in the economy and psyche of northern Minnesota and some of the other north-central states.

Walleyes are complex fish that can at times make even professional anglers shake their heads in frustration, whereas on other rare occasions it's hard to keep them out of the boat. Many years ago I was speaking with a biologist who was doing creel census work on a lake in Minnesota's Arrowhead region that was absolutely loaded with walleyes. In the previous few weeks almost no walleyes had been caught by anybody, but that afternoon everyone who went out caught their limit within an hour. These extremes aside, it is still challenging to catch walleyes regularly. Many of the statewide fishing surveys have shown that on average it takes 8 to 9 hours of fishing effort to catch a single walleye that averages slightly over a pound in weight.

. . . . . . . . . . . . . . . . . . .

*Walleye.*

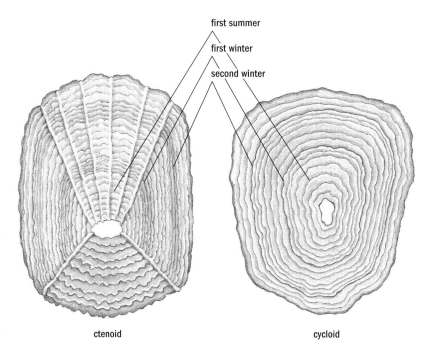

first summer

first winter

second winter

ctenoid

cycloid

**Fig. 5.1.**
. . . . . . . . . . . . . . . . . .

**Left**, *ctenoid and,*
**right**, *cycloid scales.*
*The areas on the*
*ctenoid scale where*
*the rings are close*
*together are winter*
*marks and were*
*made in the winter,*
*when the fish was not*
*growing as quickly.*
*Members of the perch*
*and sunfish families*
*have ctenoid scales.*
*Cycloid scales are*
*found in more prim-*
*itive species such*
*as ciscoes, whitefish,*
*and pike.*

Walleyes are top-of-the-line predators in most lakes, and even a quick look at one shows how well adapted they are for this role. They have a long, streamlined body and a good-sized mouth studded with long teeth. Their name, *walleye,* describes their most characteristic feature— very large eyes set high in their head that glow orange in the dark if a light is shined on them. The eye of a walleye is an amazing structure that is adapted for night vision (see chapter 3), making the walleye the most fearsome nighttime predator in the lake.

Walleyes and perch are evolutionarily advanced fish characterized by hard, sharp rays in their fins and scales with rough outer edges. Such scales are called *ctenoid scales,* in contrast to the smooth-edged cycloid scales of more-primitive fish like members of the whitefish and pike families (fig. 5.1). Because of these characteristics, it is possible to tell what kind of fish a fillet comes from if only a small amount of skin remains attached to it, thus the law that requires transported fish to have a square inch of scaled skin remaining on them. Like the rings of a tree trunk, scales tell a lot about the life of a fish. Magnified, scales show series of concentric rings that at regular intervals come closer together. By counting the numbers of these regions of close-together rings, biologists can accurately determine the age of a fish. Sometimes scales have large empty centers that are devoid of rings. These are regenerated scales, and their presence usually indicates that the fish was wounded by a predator earlier in life but managed to escape.

Walleyes are not extremely colorful fishes. Their overall color is slightly yellowish, with gray and brown overtones toward the top (dorsal side) of the body and a whitish belly. Two characteristic features typically used to identify a walleye are a white section at the tip of the bottom lobe of the tail and a small black patch at the back of the spiny dorsal fin where it meets the body. Walleyes in different lakes may vary somewhat in their overall coloration, especially the amount of yellow in the background. In many waters the background has more of a whitish or grayish cast, and in Lake Erie there used to be a subspecies of walleye, called the *blue walleye*, that had a distinctly bluish cast. The blue walleye may be extinct in Lake Erie, but there are periodic reports of a few specimens being caught in some southern Ontario lakes. Fishery biologists are interested in the possibility of restoring this species not only because they want to maintain the genetic diversity of walleyes but also because, in the days of heavy commercial fishing for walleyes in Lake Erie, blue walleyes were reputed to have a better flavor than that of the standard variety.

A close relative of the walleye, the sauger, is usually smaller with blotchy coloration and without the characteristic white patch at the tip of the tail (fig. 5.2). Their dorsal fins sometimes look almost spotted. Saugers are even better adapted than walleyes to functioning in dark or turbid water. They are more commonly found in turbid rivers where they seek the deepest channels, but in certain lakes and in reservoirs, walleyes and saugers coexist. Saugers are usually found in deeper water and on softer bottoms than are walleyes. Sometimes saugers hybridize with walleyes, giving rise to fish called saugeyes. This hybrid can be difficult to distinguish from the two parent species.

**Fig. 5.2.**

*Size comparison between a walleye and a sauger. As well as being larger, the walleye has a characteristic patch of white at the bottom tip of the tail and a black blotch at the back end of the spiny part of the dorsal fin. Saugers have a more blotchy appearance on their bodies, and their fins are often full of black spots.*

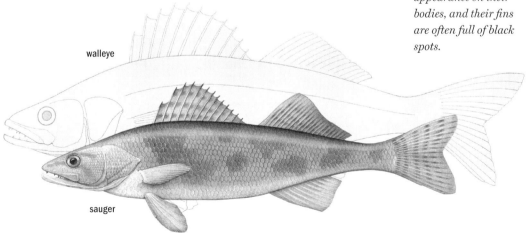

walleye

sauger

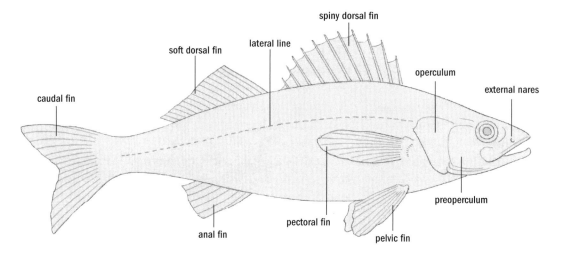

External anatomy labels: caudal fin, soft dorsal fin, lateral line, spiny dorsal fin, operculum, external nares, anal fin, pectoral fin, pelvic fin, preoperculum

**Fig. 5.3.**

. . . . . . . . . . . . . . . . . .

*External anatomy of a walleye. These designations apply to almost all lake fish.*

One anatomical feature of practical significance to the angler is the cheekbone, called the *preoperculum* (fig. 5.3). The back edge is razor sharp, and I have received countless deep cuts in my hands from trying to grab 4- to 6-pound walleyes by the back of the head while unhooking them. With smaller fish it is easier to grasp them firmly so that you don't get cut. Actually, with larger walleyes the best way to handle them is to slip a hand under a gill cover and lift the fish while you are unhooking it, taking care that you don't get impaled by other free hooks on your bait.

In contrast to bass and pike, which are principally ambush predators with well-defined home bases, walleyes are wanderers whose domain is the entire lake. Several years ago I conducted an intensive tracking study of three radio-tagged walleyes in Ten Mile Lake, sometimes following them throughout the 24-hour daily cycle. Getting the study under way was an adventure in itself.

The first step was catching three decent-sized walleyes in the first days of my summer vacation. This involved fishing at night, which meant that around midnight I was in a small boat in the middle of the lake performing surgery under the beam of a headlamp. Note that surgery under such conditions is not for the inexperienced. Fortunately, I had operated on many thousands of animals, ranging from fish to mammals, before undertaking this study, which was approved by the Minnesota DNR. Fish are very sensitive to the effects of chemical anesthetics, so the technique of choice was to completely wrap a 4- to 5-pound walleye in a wet towel and turn it over on a V-shaped wooden "operating table." The wet towel technique was borrowed from a colleague who used it for surgery on salamanders. He told me that when salamanders receive an overload of sensory input (e.g., being surrounded by cotton balls in that case), their sensory systems become overloaded and they don't respond to painful stimuli. The wet towel technique worked like a charm on the walleyes, and it took only a few minutes to make a slit in the body wall and insert a transmitter about the size of a small cigar into the belly. Then the incision was closed with a few sutures, and five minutes later the walleye was again swimming in the lake. All survived the surgery, and within a day I could detect them swimming around the lake.

Detecting them and determining their exact location was a much more daunting job than I had anticipated. Each of the three implanted transmitters emitted its own characteristic pattern of beeps, which could be heard through headphones connected to a cone-shaped receiver attached to a 5-foot stick. The stick was lowered into the water and turned until I could hear the pings of one of the walleyes. Then I would follow the beeps in the direction from which they sounded the strongest and, when I got close to the fish, use triangulation to determine its exact location. Since it was usually hard to hear the fish more than a half mile away, I spent a lot of time trying to pick up even the first faint beeps on a lake whose main basin is 2 miles by 4 miles. Following these three fish occupied a surprising amount of the day, and on more than one occasion I followed them throughout the 24-hour day. The batteries and fish remained alive for more than a year, so they could be followed for two summer vacations, plus a few sampling periods at other times throughout the year, including some observations made under the ice by Buzz Converse, an intrepid Ten Mile Lake resident. One evening about a year after the experiment began, I got a phone call from a remorseful resident on the lake who was cleaning a freshly caught walleye and found one of the transmitters in its belly. Other than having been caught, it was no worse for the wear for its extended contribution to science.

Each walleye exhibited its own pattern of behavior, which was described in three articles in *In-Fisherman* magazine (March 1995, 79–86; December and January 1996, 106–12; March 1996, 146–52). Rarely were they in the same area for more than a few days at a time (fig. 5.4). Among these three fish major changes in weather systems seemed to trigger their most extensive excursions, often clear across the lake in less than a day. On a longer time scale and in larger bodies of water, walleyes tagged in other studies have been shown to undergo pronounced seasonal migrations—related primarily to their spawning and to water temperatures. In very large lakes, especially those connected to open river systems, seasonal migrations in the 50- to 100-mile range are not uncommon.

Their innate urge to migrate is most closely tied to spawning. Despite their usual lake habitat, walleyes are descended from river-based fish that relate to currents. This trait continues to be manifest in their spawning habits. The ideal and preferred spawning site for walleyes is a stretch of river lined with small rocks and rubble, and if a lake has an inlet or outlet that meets these criteria, the walleyes will swim into these areas to spawn. In larger lakes and those that don't have such river connections—Ten Mile Lake being a good example—walleyes will also spawn on rocky shoals in the lake itself.

Many fish anticipate the upcoming spawning season by staging in areas near their future spawning sites. Walleyes spawn in the early spring, and in very large systems, such as the Great Lakes or the Mississippi River system, populations of heavy egg-laden females begin to shift toward spawning areas by the late fall or early winter. Shortly after the ice goes out, typically mid-April to early May in the northern states, the walleyes migrate into their spawning areas. Spawning takes place at night, and

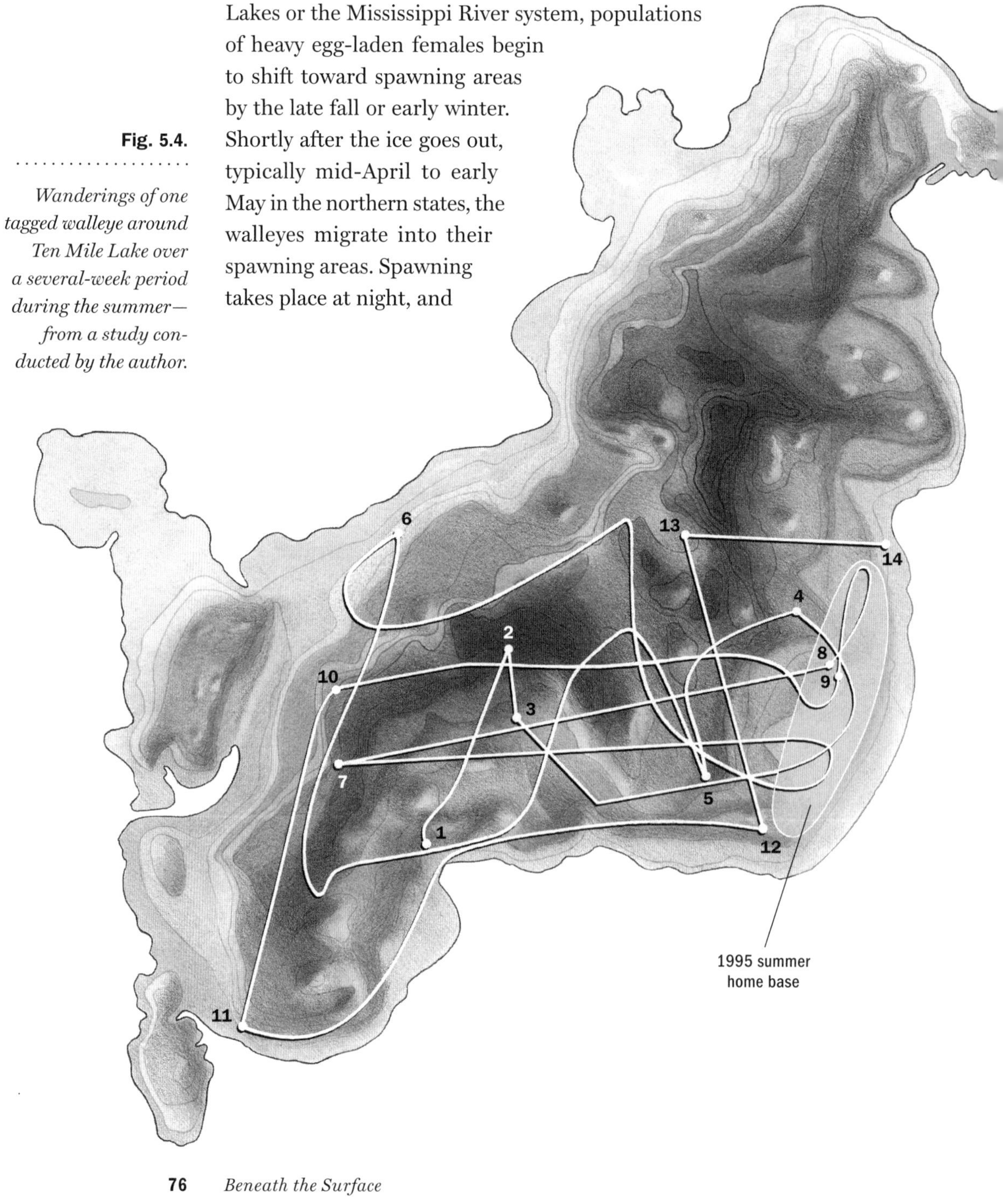

**Fig. 5.4.**

. . . . . . . . . . . . . . . . . . .

*Wanderings of one tagged walleye around Ten Mile Lake over a several-week period during the summer— from a study conducted by the author.*

1995 summer
home base

whether in a river or in the lake itself, you can locate spawning walleyes by shining a light into the water and looking for the orange reflections from their eyes.

During spawning, larger females are typically accompanied by several males, which are much smaller. Both females and males just release their eggs and sperm (milt) directly into the water, and it is a matter of chance if an individual egg gets fertilized. Like most fish, walleyes show a pronounced size dichotomy between the sexes. Males don't often get longer than 20 inches or 2 to 3 pounds. Anything larger is almost certainly a female, and the larger the female, the more eggs it can lay. Fishery biologists estimate that an 8-pound female can lay up to 500,000 eggs, whereas a 2- to 3-pound female lays only about 50,000 eggs. This is why it is so important to practice catch-and-release fishing when you land large walleyes. Quickly take a picture, enjoy the moment, and then return her to the water.

The time of spawning is strongly determined by water temperature, usually taking place when the water warms to the low 40s. At this time the water temperature in the main basin of the lake, where walleyes usually spend the summer, is still much colder than the walleyes' preferred temperature, so they will remain in the shallower, warmer waters of the lake until the deeper waters warm up.

After the eggs are laid, they fall randomly to the bottom, where they receive no parental care while the walleye embryos develop for 2 to 3 weeks before hatching. Only a small percentage (1 to 25 percent) of the eggs actually hatch. The eggs that fall in cracks between stones have the best chance to survive. If they land on mud or silt, they do poorly because of the lower oxygen content. The lucky walleye larvae that make it out of the egg face a daunting road to survival and growth. Only about 1 out of every 1,000 newly hatched walleye fry will survive the first year. For the first few days after hatching, the walleye larvae carry with them their own personal food supply in the form of a small sphere of yolk that remains from the egg, but once their intrinsic yolk supply has been exhausted, they need to find food to grow, while at the same time trying to avoid becoming the meal of some other fish. At first the newly hatched walleyes eat zooplankton, but within a few weeks they are large enough to begin the fish-eating habits that will characterize their diet for the rest of their lives. This is a very precarious time of their lives because the supply of springtime plankton is highly dependent upon the water's warming up sufficiently for them to reproduce. In a very cold spring, the mortality of newly hatched walleyes is tremendous because the cold lake waters do not produce enough food for them to survive. In a normal spring, after the perch have spawned later in

May, the young-of-the-year walleyes are normally large enough to eat the newly hatched perch, starting a predator-prey relationship that lasts the rest of their lives. This predator-prey relationship is not always one-sided, however. During the first year of a walleye's life, larger perch are one of its main predators.

While the newly hatched walleyes are making their way in the world, the adults go their own way after spawning season, but with food rather than reproduction being the main drive that governs their behavior. Right after spawning, the females leave the spawning grounds and head for nearby deeper water for a few weeks to recover from their reproductive efforts. During this period they are notoriously hard to catch. The males, on the other hand, remain closer to the spawning site, feed more, and are easier to catch. Temperature remains a main determinant of walleyes' location because in all but the shallowest lakes the waters of the main basin are still much colder than those of the bays. Walleyes, like other fish, are highly sensitive to temperature, and water even a couple of degrees warmer than that of the lake basin will attract them during the early spring. In Ten Mile Lake the great depth of the main lake deters the early spread of walleyes, so until early June many walleyes are concentrated in Long Bay or some of the smaller shallow bays. Springtime walleyes commonly enter trap nets set just off shore in less than 4 to 5 feet of water in Long Bay.

As a lake begins to warm up during the spring, a thin layer of surface water can warm up relatively rapidly on calm, sunny days even though the deeper water remains very cold. This provides a thin layer of thermal comfort for fish, and it often concentrates them in a narrow surface zone and provides an avenue for them to spread. This is one time when trolling Rapala-type baits right on top is a very effective method of catching walleyes. I stumbled onto this pattern in 1962. During the previous year I had spent some time in Finland and bought a couple of funny-looking long light baits called *Rapalas*. One bright, sunny June morning I was kayaking across the lake and decided that it wouldn't hurt to drag a fishing bait behind the kayak. The bait was the Rapala, and by the time I had reached the other side, I had caught three 2-pound walleyes. That led to further experimentation and the identification of a regular pattern of walleye behavior. Although in June it was possible to catch walleyes on the surface at most times of the day in wavy conditions, by far the best times were the hours just before and after sunset. For a number of years, I would troll very fast—almost half speed with a three-horse motor on a small boat. During the early years people thought I was crazy fishing for walleyes on the surface in the middle of the lake at a high speed. The walleyes hit the bait like a ton of bricks, but most were on the small side—from about 1½ to 3 pounds. In experimentation during subsequent years, it turned out that larger fish could be taken by adding weight to the bait and trolling a bit more slowly.

As the water warms up a bit more so that surface temperatures are in the low to mid-60s, the walleye-cisco connection picks up full steam, and trolling for suspended walleyes in the evening becomes the most effective way to catch Ten Mile walleyes until the water warms further. This fishing connection is based upon the regular evening rise of ciscoes from the depths to the limits of the thermocline (see fig. 4.3). During the late spring and early summer, the temperature of the surface water is still cool enough that some of the huge numbers of rising ciscoes come all the way to the surface where they are very vulnerable to predation by walleyes. At this time of the year, the perch are small enough that they are not as attractive prey as the densely concentrated ciscoes in the middle of the lake, and it is much more efficient to fish for walleyes over the open lake basin than over the deep shoreline flats.

The most effective way to catch open-water walleyes is to troll crankbaits with long lines. The amount of line depends upon the depth of the bait. For surface trolling I usually let out 100 yards of line so that the fish have a chance to return to a feeding mode after having been disturbed by the boat. Those who use larger boats for open-water trolling often find that the use of planer boards, which take the baits off to the side of the boat's path, is a more effective method. I personally like to use a small boat and hold the rod in my hand because I prefer the direct feel of the strike, which tells a lot about the mood of the fish on a given evening. For deeper trolling it is not necessary to let out so much line, but I still like to have my bait 150 to 200 feet behind the boat. The type of line makes a huge difference in this type of trolling. Ordinary monofilament stretches considerably, and with the length of line that is used for open-water trolling, sensitivity is considerably reduced. In addition, it is harder to make an effective strike when a fish hits because the stretch of the line attenuates the force of the strike. For a number of years, I have used the newer no-stretch lines, particularly Fireline, for trolling, and I wouldn't go back to anything else. It allows for an exquisite sensitivity that enables you to detect not only the most tentative of bites but also the fouling of your lure with small floating objects such as leaves or bits of aquatic plants. With these new lines there is no need to strike very hard; in fact, doing so may tear the hook out of the fish's mouth. Because this type of fishing is done in totally open water, heavy line is not necessary; 6- to 14-pound test, which has a much thinner diameter than that of monofilament, is all you need.

The most commonly used baits for open-water walleye fishing are long minnow-shaped lures. Although most anglers use baits about 4 inches long, larger lures in the range of 6 inches long often take not only

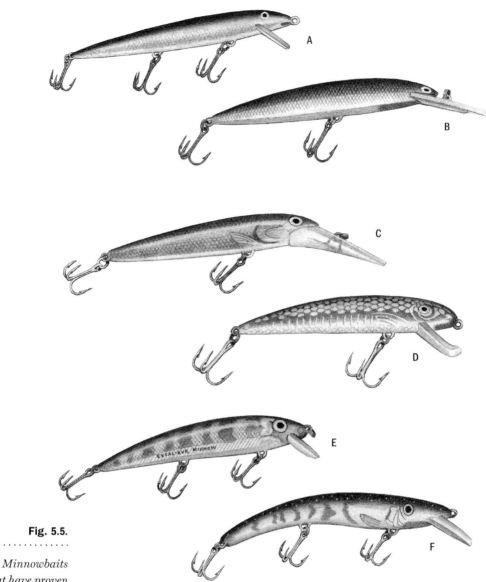

**Fig. 5.5.**
. . . . . . . . . . . . . . . . . . . .

*Minnowbaits
that have proven
effective for walleyes.*
**A**, *Rapala;*
**B**, *Deep Bagley's;*
**C**, *Deep Thunderstick;*
**D**, *Grandma;*
**E**, *Bomber Long A;*
**F**, *Red Runner.*
*Those baits with
long lips are designed
to swim from 10 to
20 feet below the sur-
face when trolled
without any weight.*

larger but more fish (fig. 5.5). The correct size of lure usually needs to be determined by experimentation. I have found that some years are large lure years and that other years are characterized by the walleyes' preference for smaller baits. If there is more than one angler in the boat, each person should initially use a different bait, and all should fish at a variety of depths. The depth is controlled by a combination of the length of line and the weight of sinkers that are commonly attached to the line about 4 to 5 feet ahead of the lure. If someone catches a fish, that should provide a clue to the walleyes' preference for that evening. When I am fishing alone, I routinely change baits and depths every 15 minutes until a pattern develops. During that 15-minute period, it is also good to change your trolling speed from quite slow to fast at periodic intervals to see if that makes a difference. Different lures work most effectively at different speeds, so it is best if everyone in the boat is using baits that function at the same range of speeds. This represents a lot of variables, but paying attention to such things significantly increases your fishing success.

One general rule of thumb, which doesn't always hold true, is that as the season progresses, one should use larger lures in trolling for walleyes. The theory behind this is that the walleyes' preference for lure size parallels the growth of the fish upon which they feed. To some extent this holds true for open-water trolling, but there is relatively little change in length of the mature dwarf ciscoes, although this is certainly the case for the schools of perch that inhabit the inshore flats. I have actually found that annual cycles of preference for bait size are stronger than seasonal cycles when it comes to open-water trolling.

For those anglers on lakes other than Ten Mile, a pattern similar to that described above may very well hold true. Most deeper lakes in the north have cisco populations, although they are not likely to show the pronounced dwarfism found in Ten Mile Lake. A number of these lakes also have an evening walleye bite over open water, but in many lakes it has hardly been explored. In addition to ciscoes, the open waters are often home to large schools of minnows such as emerald or spottail shiners or, farther south, to huge schools of shad. In these cases some local experimentation will be needed to determine the best times of day and the best conditions for an open-water walleye bite. Certainly in the Great Lakes, especially Lake Erie, Saginaw Bay in Lake Huron, or the Bays de Noc in northern Lake Michigan, open-water trolling is presently the hottest thing going for catching large fish. Once you determine a general pattern, spend some extra time fine-tuning it. Sometimes the exact depth or speed can be very important, and even slight variation away from the ideal results in far fewer fish in the boat.

Late in the spring and early summer is the period when hatches of aquatic insects are at their peak. The mayfly hatch is of particular importance to walleyes. Both mayfly larvae and mayflies themselves are relatively large and nutritious. Trout anglers live to be on a stream during a mayfly hatch because the trout often go on unbelievable feeding binges. The same can hold true for walleyes in northern lakes. Walleyes normally feed almost exclusively on fish, but in many north country lakes, especially the infertile ones in the Canadian Shield, they often aren't able to find enough small fish to fill themselves up, which is one reason why walleyes in that region are often much smaller than they are in more fertile lakes. When the mayflies hatch on such lakes, the walleyes gorge themselves on mayflies to the point where their stomachs are crammed with the juicy morsels. Such periods are maddeningly frustrating to anglers using conventional methods because often the walleyes refuse to go after the normal baits. This is one time when it would be useful to match the hatch as trout anglers do and troll flies the size and shape of emerging mayflies in areas of the lake where they are concentrated. One technique that I have never seen used in this country is called *harling* in New Zealand, where it is used very effectively for catching trout in lakes. Harling basically consists of trolling with a fly rod and a sinking fly line plus a long leader that takes a fly as much as 10 to 20 feet below the surface. This could be just the ticket for walleyes during their mayfly-eating binge. Another option might be to set up a three-way rig, but instead of trolling live or artificial bait, attach a fly to the end of a thin leader.

As summer settles in, walleyes in Ten Mile and other northern lakes gravitate to classic locations such as the slopes of underwater islands or the tips of bars. Their temperature preference must be kept in mind in order to have the best chance of finding them. All things being equal, walleyes prefer water temperatures from the mid 60s to the low 70s. The best way to find walleyes in the summer is to take a temperature profile of the lake so that you have defined the thermocline and the gradients of water temperature leading down to it. There are now some very efficient and reliable digital water temperature gauges that allow one to take a temperature profile of a lake as deep as 100 feet in just a few minutes. Once you know the depths at which the water temperature is between about 66 and 72 degrees, look at a contour map of a lake and identify bars and other underwater irregularities that are located in the preferred temperature range. With that information you'll be able to connect with the majority of the lake's walleyes.

Underwater cameras give some fascinating insights into both the locations and behavior of summertime walleyes. The first generalization is that there are a lot more walleyes in a lake than most anglers would guess. Very often there is little correlation between abundance of walleyes and fishing success. A second generalization is that if you know where to look for walleyes, they are easy to find. If you just drift randomly across a lake, you will see few or no walleyes. This can be extrapolated to fishing. The more you know about the habits of walleyes, the better your fishing success will be, because no matter how good your equipment or techniques are, they will do you no good if you are fishing where there are no walleyes.

Many hours of peering into underwater cameras on Ten Mile Lake have greatly clarified the habits of summertime walleyes in this lake, and I suspect that many other north country lakes follow a similar pattern.

First, a negative observation: I have never seen a summertime walleye in water below the thermocline. This is not to say that they are never found in the deeper waters, especially in the open water where the ciscoes swim, but under normal circumstances it would be rare to find them in the deep, cold reaches of the lake. Walleyes tend to congregate at the upper side of the thermocline, and although they may make feeding forays below it, statistically, your chances of finding walleyes in this cold temperature zone are poor.

The classic daytime walleye habitat in the summer is the end of a sloping bar that ends at a depth where the temperature is in the mid to high 60s. In Ten Mile this is typically a region where coontail is the dominant plant and where the bottom is changing from sand or silt to rubble with scattered boulders (fig. 5.6). Here they feed on crayfish, as well as small fish. Small aggregates of walleyes slowly cruise 2 to 6 feet above

**Fig. 5.6.**
. . . . . . . . . . . . . . . . . . .

*Classical deep habitat scene for walleyes.*

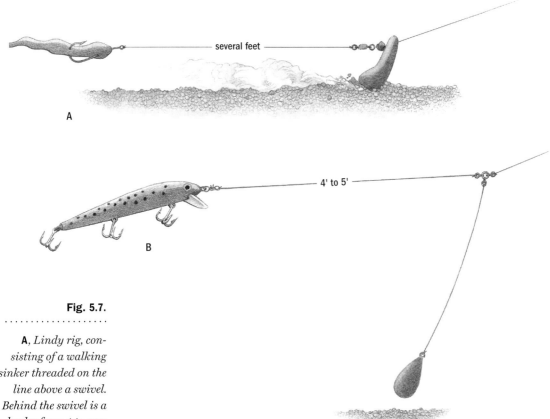

several feet

A

4' to 5'

B

**Fig. 5.7.**

. . . . . . . . . . . . . . . . . .

*A, Lindy rig, consisting of a walking sinker threaded on the line above a swivel. Behind the swivel is a leader from 4 to over 8 feet long tipped with a simple hook and a leech. When a walleye bites, it can pull the line through the sinker without feeling any resistance. B, Three-way rig with minnowbait. For the weight of the sinker, use 1 ounce per 10 feet of water depth.*

the bottom, sometimes in the company of isolated suckers or northern pike. Another observation of mine is that regardless of the weather conditions, I have never seen a walleye resting directly on the bottom in Ten Mile. Although this is known to occur in some lakes, especially after the passage of strong cold fronts, a number of highly experienced anglers are beginning to reconsider the supposition that cold-front walleyes automatically sink down to the bottom in deep water when a front passes.

When summertime walleyes are associated with such textbook structure, they can often be best taken by anglers using the time-honored method of slow back-trolling with a Lindy rig or something similar. This consists of a slip sinker (fig. 5.7A) followed by a several-foot-long leader and a single hook attached to a leech or night crawler. Another method that can be equally effective is trolling a three-way rig (fig. 5.7B) with a minnowbait or a spinner and night crawler or leech combination attached. If you are bothered by lots of perch or rock bass nibbling, try using some of the new soft plastic night crawler or leech imitations. These are now impregnated with scents that seem to attract fish about as well as the real thing. Another method that remains highly effective is the venerable technique of jig fishing. For this to be effective, it is important to know that you are fishing above fish, or you can spend a lot of time exercising your wrist with little to show for it. Most walleye anglers tip the jig with a leech, part of a night crawler, or a minnow. Jig fishing is an art—and there are many ways to do it effectively—because the angler supplies all of the motion. The most effective method for a given day depends upon the mood of the walleyes. Some days, especially after the passage of cold fronts, the most subtle jiggle is the best motion, whereas on others the fish respond to a strong upward jerk and a slow fall of the jig. For jig fishing, it is important to have a slow fall. Therefore, it is usually best to use the lightest jig that will get to the bottom at the depth you are fishing. A common mistake by beginners is to use a much too heavy jig.

Walleyes in real life seem less committed to classic behavior patterns than many articles in fishing magazines would suggest. On calm sunny days I have seen walleyes on the tops of drop-offs, say 18 to 20 feet deep, as often as in the 40-foot waters at the base. One common place for walleyes to hang out is on small weedless rocky ridges that top out at 25 to 30 feet below the surface. On broad, deep sandy flats that are close to the bottom limit of weed growth, walleyes are sometimes found associated with small patches of *Chara*. A likely reason for this is that the *Chara* also attracts perch, and where there are perch, one has a good chance to find walleyes.

The deep weedy flats of Ten Mile Lake are home to numerous massive schools of perch, typically 4 to 5 inches long. Perch this size are ideal eating size for 3- to 4-pound walleyes, and it is very common for walleyes and also small northern pike to accompany schools of perch. There is a very interesting relationship between the schooled perch and their predators. The schools of perch are often dome shaped, extending from as deep as 25 feet to within 5 feet of the surface. Walleyes and other predators hover just off the sides and near the base of a school of perch. For relatively long periods they simply accompany the school without showing any signs of aggression, and the perch don't seem excessively bothered by their presence. They may pick off sick or dying perch at this time. For some unexplained reason the walleyes will at times move into a feeding mode and slash into the densely packed perch. On two occasions when observing fish with an underwater camera, I have seen large schools of walleyes wade into masses of perch, causing the perch to scatter to the winds. One sunny afternoon I was drifting along a broad weedy bar about 22 feet deep and noticed a number of perch dashing about just inches above the bottom. I then raised the camera and saw dozens of walleyes swimming back and forth 3 to 5 feet above the bottom in what was undoubtedly a feeding frenzy.

Toward the end of a very hot summer, the warm water may drive the walleyes into much greater depths than would be the case in a normal summer. Every year as summer wears on, the water above the thermocline continues to warm up, and there is often little difference between the temperature at the surface and that at 30 feet. If this temperature approaches the mid-70s or above, the cool-water-loving walleyes will drop down to a more comfortable temperature, which is sometimes below the lower limits of weed growth. The anglers who continue to follow their normally productive pattern of fishing for walleyes in shallower water will often come up empty. Under these conditions either deepwater trolling with live or artificial baits on three-way rigs or concentrating on the deep slopes of bars is likely to prove most effective. It may also be that in Ten Mile, at least, the walleyes move out into the main lake basin and concentrate more on hunting for ciscoes, but this has hardly been explored.

In the summertime much of the walleyes' feeding activity takes place at night when they change their locations and their feeding behavior. As the sun sets and the levels of light penetrating the water drop dramatically, walleyes' feeding activity rises because, with their specially adapted eyes, they can see better than their prey, especially the perch, which begin to disband their schools and drop toward the bottom for the night. Fishing for walleyes during the dark is a special proposition (see chapter 3).

With the approach of autumn, the water begins to cool and the walleyes, especially the larger ones, become more active as they begin to store up on food for the coming winter. At first they can still be caught in their summer locations, but when the water has cooled significantly, they change their behavior dramatically. A good rule of thumb for late fall walleyes is that they can be found at almost all depths, but their most dramatic and consistent pattern is to move into deep water and frequent steep slopes. After the lake turnover (see chapter 12), walleyes can be found hanging out at depths as great as 60 to 80 feet in many lakes. The standard way of fishing for these walleyes is to put a large minnow (e.g., a redtail chub) on a jig and fish vertically, placing your bait in front of the fish's nose. Ten Mile Lake sees very little fall fishing of any sort, so effective fishing patterns have not been well worked out for this time of the year. Given the nature of the lake, however, it is a good bet that fall walleyes would head deep.

Other lakes show quite a different pattern of behavior for fall walleyes. As the shallow waters cool to a more comfortable range, large walleyes move very close to shore at night. Starting in early September, it is not unusual to take 8-pound walleyes in trap nets set up in less than

2 feet of water, especially in areas associated with reed beds. A classic fall walleye pattern is tied to the annual migration of frogs into shallow soft-bottom bays where they will hibernate at the bottom for the winter. This pattern is rapidly becoming a thing of the past because for reasons unknown the numbers of amphibians worldwide has been declining disastrously in recent decades. Pollution, increased ultraviolet radiation, and being squashed by cars have all been blamed for this decline, and all of these may be factors. Regardless of the cause, each year fewer frogs head for the lake. In full force, the fall frog migration is a very impressive sight. The grass leading to the lake can be literally alive with frogs, mainly the irregularly spotted leopard frogs, during the daytime. Then toward evening they enter the lake and prepare to burrow into the mud. Somehow the walleyes sense this frog migration and stack up in the shallows, waiting for the frogs. If you are at the right place on the right evening, you can find some of the best fishing imaginable for lunker walleyes.

Fall walleyes will, similarly, enter the shallows at night in search of smaller fish. The most effective technique for catching walleyes in shallow water is to wade out for them. Big walleyes are extremely wary, especially when they are in shallow water, and even though they are bolder after dark, it doesn't take much to spook them. A simple misstep or even waving of your rod on a moonlit night is sufficient to send a panicked big walleye racing for deeper water. The most effective lures for shallow-water fall walleyes are long minnow-shaped baits cast long distances. The prime time for this type of fishing is the period surrounding the full moon in late September or early October.

The fall pattern of walleye behavior continues until the ice begins to form. One variant, which has been little exploited by anglers, would be to fish at night in the places where dwarf ciscoes are spawning during late October and early November. At this time the walleyes are gorging themselves on the spawn-laden ciscoes and should be readily taken on long minnow-shaped baits either from shore or from boats. This kind of fishing could be a mighty cold proposition, but it probably represents one of your best chances to connect with a trophy walleye.

As the winter ice forms, the water temperature is pretty much the same from top to bottom, and the walleyes initially remain in their late fall locations. They feed actively during the early winter months, but in many lakes things slow down as winter drags on. Under-ice walleyes still respond to changes in light levels by feeding more at sunset as the light dims, but when the ice is covered by snow, there is considerably less variation in the amount of light that they see.

As winter merges into spring and the days start lengthening, the added sunlight acts on the walleye's brain, stimulating the production of reproductive hormones. With their spawning instinct strengthened, they move closer to their spawning areas, which on Ten Mile Lake means Long Bay. There they concentrate in the early springtime spawning season in order to once again generate a new batch of young walleyes.

## Perch
. . . . . . . . . . . . . . . . . . .

Perch are the little cousins of walleyes, and in lakes that contain both species, their lives are intertwined from birth to death. Perch have roughly the same shape as walleyes, with an elongated, streamlined body and a full array of spiny fins (fig. 5.8). They are very colorful fish with pronounced vertical stripes overlaying a yellowish background, and their pelvic fins are often bright orange. Two major features that distinguish perch from walleyes are their eyes, which are more normally proportioned and do not glow in the light, and their mouth, which is smaller than a walleye's and relatively toothless. Another major difference is size. Whereas an average walleye weighs a couple pounds, a one-pound perch is a whopper. In Ten Mile Lake most perch range from 5 to 6 inches long. Perch make excellent eating, and around the Great Lakes perch is one of the favored meals in seafood restaurants. Especially in the wintertime, perch rank among the most sought after species by anglers.

Despite their toothless mouth perch are carnivores that, after graduating from the plankton-feeding stage, eat both insects and fish. Although insects constitute a relatively larger part of the diet of young perch, even 3-inch perch will eat small minnows whenever they can. They are also among the main predators of young-of-the-year walleyes.

Perch are creatures of the daytime, and early in the morning they come together into large schools containing hundreds or thousands of fish. Members of the schools tend to be segregated by size. Like so many other kinds of fish, the very largest perch have somewhat more solitary habits, but they, too, will aggregate in areas where there is a lot of food. Schools of fish, like flocks of birds, exhibit amazing behavior. When undisturbed, almost all of the fish swim in the same direction and at the same speed, but when something frightens them, large numbers change direction almost instantaneously as if they were all connected to a common brain. What guides the near-synchronous behavior of both flocks of birds and schools of fish is still a mystery to scientists. In the case of schools of perch, what often frightens them are the feeding attacks of large predators that often accompany the schools.

Schooled perch are pack feeders that are most active around dawn and sunset, largely because a visual pigment in their retinas, called *porphyropsin*, is most efficient under these low-light conditions. Perch packs have several interesting modes of feeding. One is akin to herding, where a pack of perch will either encircle a group of minnows or pin them down next to some object. While the unlucky school of minnows is thus confined, some of the perch will dash right into the minnows to try to get the school to break up. When some of the minnows break rank, they are quickly captured by surrounding perch. Another method of group feeding is for a pack of perch to charge through a weedy area, scaring insects and minnows out from their cover into open water. These unfortunate creatures are then snapped up by other perch waiting in the wings. On an individual basis larger perch, in particular, will wait in weeds to ambush small fish passing by or even stalk their prey.

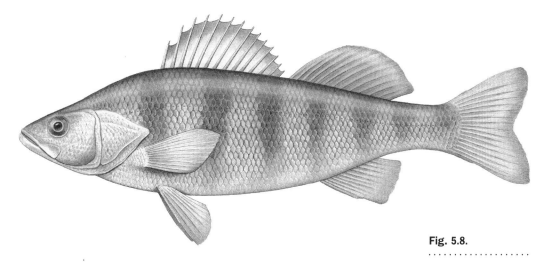

**Fig. 5.8.**

*Yellow perch.*

The latter strategy works best in somewhat murky water, and large perch prone to stalking behavior even seem to lose their bold striping to make them less conspicuous in the open water.

Although the time-honored way to catch perch is with a hook baited with a worm or a small minnow, an equally effective method is to use a quarter-ounce metal jigging spoon (the same size used to catch whitefish). Just lower a jigging spoon into the school, then lift it up sharply a foot or so, and let it drop on a taut line. In a very short time you can take a large batch of perch. If you do the same thing with a larger jigging spoon, you have a good chance at attracting one of the walleyes or pike at the edge of the school. A small jigging spoon looks to the perch like an injured or dying minnow, and a larger one looks to a walleye like a sick or dying perch.

A perch's life cycle begins with spawning, which takes place in the spring a few weeks after the walleyes have spawned—commonly in early to mid-May, depending upon the water temperature. In contrast to walleyes, perch spawn over beds of emerging aquatic plants. Although perch are purported to spawn in shallow water, typically less than 8 to 10 feet, I have seen large groups of spawning perch in water as deep as 25 to 30 feet with temperatures in the low 50s. In those spawning areas patches of *Chara* were completely covered with long strands of eggs surrounded by a whitish mucus coating. Spawning perch are quite preoccupied with their own breeding activities, but they are often not alone. Once walleyes have recovered from their own spawning efforts, they rest for a few days but then go on an early feeding binge. Many of them head for the perch spawning areas to feast upon the perch, which have let down their defenses because of their breeding activity.

When the eggs are laid, they are generally abandoned by the parents, and after a couple weeks they hatch. Like all fish, the newly hatched perch subsist on their built-in yolk supply for a few days while keeping a low profile near the lake bottom, which allows them to grow a bit and develop their swimming skills. After their yolk is absorbed and they become free swimming, the perch fry move to areas with a high density of zooplankton, usually near the surface in the open lake or close to shore. For most of the first summer, plankton is their main source of food. At the same time many of the perch fry become the food of the somewhat larger young-of-the-year walleyes that hatched several weeks before the perch. Like walleyes, newly hatched perch are very sensitive to dramatic changes in water temperature, and a stretch of very cold spring weather can be devastating to that year's class of fish. If the development of the young perch is not directly affected by the cold, they may die of starvation because of poor reproduction of the zooplankton upon which they feed. Larger perch are not squeamish about eating their own kind, and cannibalism is common. Those newly hatched perch that do survive the first few months begin to eat small insect larvae in addition to plankton. By their second year small fish are added to their diet. Young-of-the-year perch sometimes gather into schools that swim just beneath the surface of the water. On a calm day you can see them dimpling the surface as they feed on plankton, floating insects, or small minnow fry.

Adult perch spend most of their days looking for food, but they also have the unenviable task of trying to keep themselves from being eaten, in turn. Because of their elongated body, perch are a favorite food of virtually all predators, and by the end of the summer, the vast majority of perch of any size that started out the year have turned into some other fish's meal. Their populations are kept going by the periodic years when everything went right and large numbers of perch not only hatched but survived their perilous first year of life. When such year classes mature to the point where they are ideal food size for walleyes, fishing for walleyes often declines precipitously because the walleyes are stuffed with perch.

Perch have very poor night vision, and toward evening the schools break up and individual perch scatter to resting sites for the night. Only the pelagic young-of-the-year perch remain in open water over night. In the late evening, when the light level is declining rapidly, walleyes with their night-adapted eyes feed heavily on the visually disadvantaged perch. By the time it gets dark, most perch are hidden among the vegetation and resting on the bottom. Skin divers report seeing them with their fins actually touching the bottom at night. Whether perch actually sleep at night or are just inactive is not known. Most fish have some inactive periods during the 24-hour day, but the extent of their inactivity varies. In the ocean the colorful parrot fishes of the reefs actually secrete a cocoon around themselves at night as they rest at the base of the reefs. At the other extreme tunas and many sharks are obliged to move constantly because water must continually flow through their gills in order to provide them with sufficient oxygen.

## Darters

The majority of the members of the perch family are tiny but colorful fish, usually stream dwelling, called *darters*. Most darters measure only a few inches long and are rarely seen unless someone is looking for them. During their springtime breeding seasons, darters take on a rainbow of bright breeding colors that often match those of coral reef fishes.

In northern lakes one of the most common darters is the Johnny darter, a tiny dull-colored fish usually not much more than 1 to 1½ inches long. Johnny darters are usually a nondescript brown, but scattered along their sides are characteristic black W-shaped markings. Johnny darters live on the bottom, preferably in rocky areas, often very close to shore. On a quiet day if you look at the bottom off the shallow end of your dock, you will likely see them taking short hops, measured in inches, from one crevice to another. Despite their secretive habits, significant numbers of Johnny darters find their way into other fish's stomachs. They are often found in the stomachs of whitefish, suggesting that they live in deep, as well as shallow, water.

$6$  NORTHERN PIKE

*E*very couple years I catch a 2- to 3-pound walleye or whitefish that has fresh wounds extending in a slightly curved line on either side of its body. These fish have somehow survived an attack by a large northern pike, the top-of-the-line predator in most north country lakes. Northern pike are ambush predators that typically lie in wait for their prey, and when something edible swims by, they go after it with a seemingly jet-propelled lunge. What constitutes suitable prey can defy imagination. In addition to fish, biologists have found animals as diverse as birds, muskrats, and snakes in their stomachs. I once caught a 2-pound pike with an odd bulge in its belly and found that it had swallowed a large chromium-plated shower curtain ring. Pike are among the most important predators of young ducks, and it is not uncommon for a brood of twelve ducklings to be reduced to two or three by the end of the summer. Even humans are not exempt from northern pike attacks. Almost every summer there are newspaper reports of swimmers, usually wearing shiny bracelets, who have found themselves under attack. If the lake doesn't contain muskies, the culprit is almost certainly a large northern pike.

Even casual examination of a northern pike tells a lot about how they function. They have a highly elongated streamlined body that has a single dorsal fin positioned far back near the tail. If they have lived in shallow water, their color often takes on a greenish hue, which is accentuated by light oval spots scattered along the sides. A dominant feature is their enormous mouth, which is studded with teeth—long ones in the jaws and broad rows of smaller teeth running from front to back along the roof of the mouth. A pike has impressive jaw-closing muscles, and when it clamps down on something, it is beastly difficult to open its mouth.

. . . . . . . . . . . . . . . . . . .

*Northern pike.*

Another characteristic of pike is their slime, which is both abundant and smelly. Many walleye anglers contend that this smell scares away walleyes. If they catch a northern pike while fishing for walleyes, they will change baits or leaders, if live-bait fishing, so that the contaminated bait doesn't spook the walleyes. I have not noticed much of a negative effect when trolling artificial baits, but I do carefully wipe the bait off if it has contacted pike slime. This precaution may be more important when still-fishing with live bait, where the walleyes are more deliberate about approaching and inhaling the bait. With artificial lures the walleye usually strikes at the lure so rapidly that it wouldn't have much time to detect a pike odor.

The life cycle of a pike begins early in the spring when the first ice melts from the shallow dark-bottomed bays (like Lundstrom's Bay in Ten Mile) that have absorbed heat from the springtime sun even when the main body of the lake is still covered with ice. Large female pike, accompanied by two or three smaller males, move into the bay and head for the shallowest grassy areas that they can find (often flooded marshes) to lay their eggs, around 10,000 per pound of the female. The eggs are scattered randomly and adhere to the vegetation. They are immediately abandoned by the parents. After two weeks they hatch into miniature versions of the adults. Because of factors like rapidly dropping water levels and predation, mortality is extremely high, with as few as 0.2 percent (2 out of 1,000) of the eggs producing young pike that actually leave the spawning grounds. Recently hatched pike spend their first ten days in a quiescent phase, obtaining nutrition from their yolk. When they have reached close to one-half inch in length, they begin to feed voraciously on planktonic animals, such as water fleas and small aquatic insects, until they are 2 to 3 inches long; then they turn to eating fish. True to their instincts as ambush hunters, a young-of-the-year pike lurks suspended among aquatic plants in shallow water until a small fish passes by. It then shoots out to engulf its prey. If in a lake with an abundant food supply, young pike grow quickly, often reaching 9 to 10 inches by the end of their first summer.

During its first year or two, a young pike leads a precarious existence because its elongated shape makes it an ideal snack for a large fish. In fact, one of the favorite foods of a pike is a smaller pike, especially in infertile lakes or rivers where the supply of other fish is limited. On one such northern river, I once caught a 7-pound pike that spit up a 14-inch pike plus a smaller one. Although a good rule of thumb is that the preferred prey size is one-half to one-third of its body length, this doesn't deter a pike from becoming greedy and trying to swallow another pike almost as long as itself.

When a pike makes up its mind to go after a fish, it does so very deci-

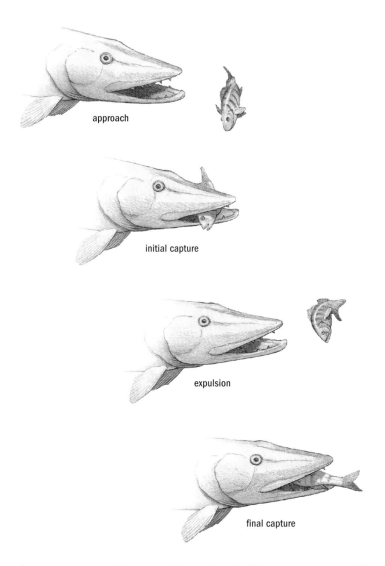

approach

initial capture

expulsion

final capture

**Fig. 6.1.**

. . . . . . . . . . . . . . . . . . .

*Northern pike
capturing a perch—
based on actual
observation.*

sively. I once saw such an attack in clear shallow water. A roughly 6-pound pike was stationed motionless just above a thick bed of *Chara* when a 7- to 8-inch perch swam past about two feet in front of the pike. With blinding speed the pike lunged at the perch and caught it from below at about the level of its pectoral fins (fig. 6.1). After briefly clamping down hard on its hapless prey, the pike then opened its mouth, allowing the stunned perch to float free. Opening its mouth, it inhaled the floating fish headfirst, with the tail sticking out its mouth. Then, in a third motion, it swallowed, and the perch disappeared down its gullet. Pike aren't as efficient predators as one might suspect. Observational studies have shown that the prey escapes a pike attack about 50 percent of the time.

The mode of capturing prey described has direct relevance to fishing and the design of fishing lures. Generally speaking, if a bait has multiple hooks, the front-most hook is the one that most often catches the fish. In fact, most lures could dispense with the last hook entirely and be none the worse. Interestingly, the design of most spoons, one of the most time-honored pike lures, is just the opposite; the hook is at the bottom end of the spoon. Anyone who casts spoons for pike on more than a casual basis has had the experience of a pike clamping down hard on the spoon and putting up a whale of a fight only to open its mouth at the boat or the shore and have the spoon drop out. Sometimes they even allow themselves to be brought into the boat without having been hooked. A Swedish spoon, called the ABU Atom, which unfortunately is not sold in the United States, is designed with a treble hook fastened toward the front end in addition to the usual one at the back and is the most effective spoon I have ever used for pike.

After spawning, adult pike stay in shallow water, often 5 feet or less, as long as the temperature remains cold—usually less than 55 degrees. As they recover from spawning, they often lie in these waters, which are still warmer than those of the main body of the lake, seemingly absorbing the warmth of the sun. They soon begin to feed, and when they are in this mode, it is one of the best times of the year to consistently catch large pike. In the northern states this period usually occurs before the opening of fishing season, but in northern Canada's lakes this period might not occur until sometime in June. During this period large pike can be caught on a wide variety of baits. At one extreme, dead baits (literally dead smelt or other such fish) can be fished on the bottom. Large pike are often scavengers, and in the early spring they will eat fish that have died throughout the winter. This shallow water habitat is ideal for casting for pike, and they can be taken on a wide variety of spoons or large minnow-shaped crankbaits. Springtime pike can be very moody. Sometimes they react best to a bait that is burned through the water. At other times a very slow retrieve works best. One highly effective method that is slowly catching on is fly casting for springtime pike in the shallows. When large flies up to 4 to 6 inches long are slowly twitched in front of a pike, they can be irresistible, and catching a large pike on a fly rod is an unforgettable experience.

As the waters of the bays warm to 55 to 60 degrees, large pike begin to leave the shallow bays and head for deeper, colder water, while the smaller ones tend to remain in the weedy bays. After this time large pike are as scarce as hen's teeth for the average angler, whereas smaller pike (less than 5 to 6 pounds) can often be caught throughout the summer. What happens to the larger fish during most of the spring and summer was a mystery until it began to dawn on a few anglers that large pike are completely different beasts from their smaller counterparts. It is becoming increasingly apparent that large pike are creatures of cold water and cannot readily tolerate the warmer temperatures of the shallower waters. Thus, from the standpoints of both their biology and angling for them, it is best to treat the two size groups separately. With not only pike but also a number of other species of fish, the younger specimens have greater tolerance of warm water than do the larger representatives of the same species.

Conventional wisdom has it that pike are creatures of shallow weedy water, and for the most part this is certainly true until they reach about 5 to 6 pounds. There is no question that one of the best places to find pike is around the edges of shallow weedy areas, especially those heavily populated by a pondweed called *cabbage* (*Potamogeton amplifolius;* fig. 6.2). Here they lie in wait, partially camouflaged by the weeds, until a suitable prey swims past. They also hang out around the edges of bars or underwater islands during the summer. Although pike don't really school, they sometimes aggregate over deeper rocky reefs as the water warms in the summer. Perch constitute the main food of these smaller pike and, like walleyes, 2- to 4-pound pike sometimes accompany the lower edges of large schools of perch, looking for stragglers or weakened fish. Much of the time these pike just seem to be hanging out alongside the school, and predators and perch seem to coexist peacefully. At other times they become very aggressive and slash at the schooled perch.

**Fig. 6.2.**
. . . . . . . . . . . . . . . . . . .

*Northern pike waiting in the weeds for an unlucky prey.*

Fishing for shallow-water summertime pike involves a number of conventional techniques. One of the classics is still-fishing with live bait—often a sucker weighing up to a pound or more swimming beneath a bobber. It is usual to fish just at the edge of a thick weed bed and wait for a pike to find the bait. Often if you see the bobber moving erratically, it means that the sucker has spotted a big pike and is trying to avoid it. Not long after this, the bobber is likely to go down with a swoosh, and the fight is on. In shallower water, casting plugs or spoons is always a safe bet for taking pike, but it is a good idea to let the bait sink for several seconds at the end of a cast to get it down closer to the level of the pike. Trolling over deep flats in up to 25 feet of water is a highly effective way to catch summertime pike, and generally, faster trolling is preferable to slower trolling as long as the bait stays deep in the water column. A good-sized bait for this type of trolling is commonly 6 to 8 inches long, and if the bait can go down to 15 to 20 feet while trolling, it will be in the range of many active pike.

A long-standing myth is that pike stop biting in the late summer because they are shedding their teeth. Fish biologists have found no evidence to support this assertion. It is much more likely that the fish are well fed during this period or that, because of the warm temperatures in shallow water, the pike become inactive or head to deeper, colder water.

Smaller pike bite voraciously, and it is usually not difficult to catch them. There are some times, though, when they go absolutely crazy. Such periods often occur an hour or so before a cold front comes through, and they don't affect only pike. Bass, in particular, react in much the same way, but often in an even more intense fashion. Walleyes may also bite more readily, but their reaction is usually more subdued. Although every serious angler has experienced this phenomenon and scientists have tried to understand it, the physiological basis for such feeding frenzies remains unknown. Despite our ignorance, however, it is a time when you want to be on the water if at all possible. When fishing for pike during such a period, you should go into overdrive along with the fish. If casting, you cannot retrieve your bait too rapidly, and if trolling, rev up your motor to what might seem a ridiculous speed. The pike will hit your lure hard, so hold tightly onto your rod. With speed trolling, it is easy for a pike to pull your rod into the water. If fishing with nonstretchable superlines, be especially careful because the lack of give in the line not only increases the intensity of the strike but also is likely to rip the bait out of the fish's mouth.

Once a pike is in the boat, unhooking a fish with a batch of treble hooks swinging outside its mouth can be a bit tricky. There are three ways to handle smaller pike. For fish weighing less than 5 to 6 pounds, one of the easiest ways is to tightly clamp down with your hand on either side of the back, just behind the gill covers. This immobilizes the fish, facilitating hook removal. One way to paralyze a pike is to press your thumb and forefinger into its eyes. This paralyzes the pike but also damages the fish. Do not use this method if you plan on releasing the pike. One of the best methods of handling larger fish is to slide a hand beneath a gill cover and lift the fish. Be careful, however, not to get hooked yourself. It's a good idea to hold on to the line close to the head at the same time to damp the shaking of the fish's head.

During the warm-water period of the late spring and summer, most large pike adopt a completely different lifestyle from that of their smaller counterparts. Large pike prefer cold water, preferably temperatures in the mid to upper 50s, and if the deep water of a lake is sufficiently oxygenated, the large pike are most likely to be found in the hypolimnion just below the thermocline. These larger fish are typically solitary creatures that either slowly cruise just above the stark, weedless bottom or actually rest on it. In Ten Mile Lake, at least, they are most likely to rest on silt or sand, rather than on rocks. These fish, which are typically larger than 7 pounds, have for the most part graduated from eating perch to hunting larger fish more suited to their own size. Two-pound suckers, ciscoes, or whitefish are preferred prey for these deepwater pike, and both whitefish and suckers frequent these same waters in the summertime. One major surprise from directly observing fish with an underwater camera was seeing schools comprising dozens of suckers hanging right on the bottom in deep water within the same temperature range as that preferred by large northern pike. These suckers are so tightly packed that they would be easy pickings for a pike that happened by. Cruising whitefish along the base of deep drop-offs are similarly vulnerable.

The tendency of large pike to go deep during the summer has been just recently recognized by anglers, and few techniques have been developed to take advantage of this behavior pattern. One of the most effective ways of covering ground while searching for large deepwater pike is trolling large crankbaits with three-way rigs equipped with a 3- to 4-ounce sinker. For this type of fishing, a relatively slow trolling speed is often very effective. Another technique that can be deadly if the pike are more tightly concentrated around underwater points, for example, is the use of vertical jigging techniques with large plastic grubs or minnow-imitating (thumper) plastic baits. A technique often used in ice fishing for lake trout, vertically fishing vibrating blade baits can also be highly effective at times. Simply lift the metal bait quickly enough to feel the pronounced vibrations, and then let it fall on a taut line.

When pike are taken from deep water, they frequently become bloated with air that has expanded within their swim bladder. That, plus the exhaustion from fighting, often puts the pike in a precarious position for survival if you plan to release it, which should be done for most large pike. When you have unhooked the fish, gently place it in the water while holding on to its back. If the fish shows signs of turning over, don't just let it go, because chances are the fish will not survive. Instead, continue holding on to the fish just behind the head and gently swish it back and forth in the water. Usually, after a few minutes, it will revive and, with a flick of its tail, shoot out of your hands and head back to the deep water. Sometimes you have to have a lot of patience. Once I had to do this for almost 20 minutes before a 9-pound pike that I had caught was ready to start swimming on its own.

Another effective summertime pike pattern on Ten Mile Lake and on any other lake with large numbers of suspended bait fish is rapid trolling in the open waters over the lake basin. Like walleyes, pike follow concentrations of bait fish, and in Ten Mile Lake they can be found anywhere in the lake basin where the dwarf ciscoes are concentrated. Although pike are usually taken by anglers who are trolling for suspended walleyes, you can increase your chances of connecting with suspended pike by modifying your trolling techniques. The ideal bait is one that travels between 20 and 40 feet below the surface at a medium-high speed. The baits should be at least 6 inches long. Suspended pike often hit the bait viciously and can actually hurt your elbow or shoulder with the force of their strike. At other times the opposite can happen. While trolling, you may feel some very gentle periodic tapping over a distance of as much as 30 to 50 feet. This is almost guaranteed to be a big pike nibbling on your lure. Sometimes the pike will end up grabbing the bait without your doing anything, but when you feel such nibbling, you can often provoke a strike by moving the bait forward with a sweep of your rod and then letting it fall back. In my experience, suspended pike tend to run between 7 and 11 pounds. Whether or not truly large pike follow this pattern remains to be seen.

As the lake cools in the fall and fish, in general, become redistributed, the larger pike often come up from the deeper water and go on an active feeding binge in preparation for the coming winter. Because the fishing season remains open during this period, fall is one of the best times to catch large pike. By midautumn some large pike have already moved back into the shallower bays, where they can be fished by bait casting methods, or by rocky points and reefs, where they can be taken by trolling. In a lake like Ten Mile, where there are late fall spawning runs of both whitefish and dwarf ciscoes, you can be sure that hungry pike will be there too, waiting to devour some of these preoccupied spawners.

Winter is the time when the large pike in a lake seem to mysteriously reappear, and many north country lakes sprout villages of fish houses. In many of them crouch ice fishers with spear in hand, waiting for a large pike to nose up to a decoy suspended below the hole in the ice. These spearing-oriented fish houses are usually set up in shallow bays. Even though the pike have the entire lake in which to roam, some mysterious call brings many of them to the places where they will spawn in the coming spring. The spearing of large pike is a controversial sport because of the selective harvest of large fish, and it is becoming more restricted on lakes that are managed for trophy hook-and-line fishing. Nevertheless, the practice of spearing has a small but devoted following which maintains that this is one way of harvesting a segment of the population otherwise unreachable by anglers. As knowledge of the habits of big summertime pike evolves, this is less likely to be the case.

Of all the fish in our northern lakes, pike are among the most vulnerable to overfishing, mainly because of their greedy nature. When I first came to Ten Mile Lake as a teenager in the mid-1950s, I heard old-timers telling tales of catching northern pike as long as a canoe paddle. The same story is true of most of our north country lakes. Those days are largely gone in all but a few lakes. Whereas 20-pounders were not uncommon even up to the mid-twentieth century, today a 15-pound pike is rare, and anything over 10 pounds is considered a trophy. Especially in smaller lakes, a combination of overfishing plus spearing has selectively removed most of the larger pike. Instead, a more common present-day situation is a lake with lots of hammerhandles—pike of 2 pounds or less (see fig. 13.1). When the pike population gets to this point, experience has shown that it is not easy to reverse the situation and restore a more balanced population.

In several Minnesota lakes, including Ten Mile, where there is an abundant food supply, the Minnesota Department of Natural Resources is experimenting with ten-year periods where catching pike over a certain length is prohibited. This is intended to allow some of the existing pike a chance to grow to full maturity and hopefully reach trophy size of over 40 inches. If this phase of the experiment is successful, then slot limits will be imposed. Typically, these size limits allow smaller pike as well as only one in the trophy class to be kept. This experiment is still under way, and we are not likely to know for another decade if it is really successful. Similar fisheries experiments are under way to try to preserve populations of walleyes and other major game fish. On some lakes these experiments are quite controversial, but in fisheries research it is often difficult to obtain predictable results on a given lake from an experiment designed on paper. There are still many natural variables that we do not understand. Catch-and-release fishing for pike is required by resort owners on a number of famous fishing lakes in Canada, and the practice seems to be working because large pike continue to be caught in some lakes that are heavily fished.

*O*ne of the enduring images of a northern lake is that of a solitary angler in a small boat casting a bait toward a bed of water lilies in the early morning mist. Seconds later, the water explodes as a bass with bait in mouth clears the surface and shakes its head in a futile attempt to throw the bait. This signals the beginning of a scrappy fight that has attracted sport anglers for well over a century.

Without question bass are the most sought after game fish in the United States. Through increasingly high-profile professional tournaments, excellent bass anglers have achieved celebrity status. Some have even achieved the pinnacle of sporting fame by having their pictures plastered on Wheaties boxes. Bass are uniquely American fish, but they have been transplanted into lakes throughout the world. In Japan interest in bass fishing has exploded, and on Japanese television one can now see the same types of bass fishing shows that crowd some of our Saturday morning TV channels.

Although there are several species of bass in the United States, the two most prominent are the largemouth and smallmouth bass—the only ones found in north country lakes. The natural range of largemouth bass covers the entire eastern two-thirds of the United States and a thin rim of southern Canada. That of smallmouth bass is quite similar, but its southern extent stops at roughly the border between Tennessee and the Gulf states. Their respective distributions relate to the temperature preferences of the two species. Largemouth bass are warm-water fish, which are quite comfortable when the water temperatures are in the 80s. Smallmouth bass, on the other hand, are considered cool-water fish, preferring temperatures in the high 60s to low 70s. At the cold end of the spec-

. . . . . . . . . . . . . . . . . . .

*Largemouth bass.*

trum, however, there is not that much difference between the species, which may partially explain why the distribution of smallmouths extends only a bit farther north than that of largemouths. In fact, in very cold water largemouth bass seem to be somewhat more active than their smallmouth counterparts. Nevertheless, both species thrive in cooler north country lakes, and in cases where they have been introduced to lakes by stocking, they often become the dominant species. Because of the short warm-water season in north country lakes, largemouth bass don't attain anywhere near the size of their southern cousins. A 5-pound bass that would be considered a trophy on a northern lake would scarcely raise an eyebrow on a Florida lake.

Ten Mile Lake has historically been home to a healthy population of largemouth bass, which occupy a distinct niche in the lake. Despite indications that smallmouth bass have been present in the lake for a number of years, in the many thousands of hours that I have fished the lake since 1955, I did not catch a smallmouth bass until 2002 when I hooked a 10-inch specimen while fishing for whitefish in 40 feet of water. By 2004 I often caught smallmouth bass while fishing for walleyes and frequently observed them with underwater cameras. It is apparent that as of this writing the lake's smallmouth bass population is in the midst of a major expansion. What is uncertain is whether there has always been a marginal population of smallmouth bass in the lake or whether a recent introduction has taken hold and the population is exploding.

## Largemouth Bass

Largemouth bass are interesting creatures whose dominant characteristic is their large mouth, which allows them to eat an amazing variety of food. One early spring day in Michigan, I saw what appeared to be an enormous dead fish on the shoreline. When I got over to it, the "fish" turned out to be a 20-inch largemouth that had tried to swallow a 21-inch largemouth. Of course, the larger fish had gotten stuck in the smaller fish's mouth, and both fish had died. I have also seen live largemouth bass dashing about the surface in obvious distress with prey too large to be swallowed flopping about in their mouth. In many parts of the country, largemouth bass are the dominant predator, but in north country lakes they must usually cede this position to northern pike. Large bass can fall prey even to larger pike. Nevertheless, in their own domain of the lake, they still act as if they were king. Of all the fish I have viewed with an underwater camera, largemouth bass are the only ones that routinely swim over to stare the camera down when it is first dropped into the water. Whether that signifies aggression or curiosity is hard to say, but it tells a lot about these fish.

The stereotypical image of a largemouth bass is that of a greenish fish lurking in the weeds in shallow water over a muddy bottom. There is nothing wrong with this image, but it doesn't come close to encompassing the varied behavior and habitat of this species. Bass inhabit a wide variety of habitats and exhibit an equally wide variety of behaviors.

In Ten Mile Lake I have caught largemouths in water 200 feet deep a mile from shore with large muskie baits, but I have also caught 5-pound-plus bass in water inches deep on sunfish baits. It is probably this diversity of habitat and behavior that has intrigued anglers to the extent that the largemouth bass remains our number one sport fish.

A typical adult bass is greenish on its back and sides, with a pronounced dark stripe running the length of its body along its lateral line. It can be easily distinguished from a smallmouth bass not only by its color but also by the length of its mouth, which extends behind the eye. A healthy largemouth bass is a stocky fish. The most common size in northern lakes is 1 to 3 pounds, and anything over 20 inches and 5 pounds is considered a trophy. Even though northern largemouth bass are much smaller than their southern cousins, they live much longer. Many southern bass don't live more than five years, whereas large northern bass are often nine or ten years old.

*Spawning*

The life history of a largemouth bass begins in a 3- to 4-foot nest that has been cleared over a shallow soft bottom by a male bass who begins the activity when the water temperature reaches about 60 degrees. The male bass scoops the surface debris away from the nest site with its fins and tail until the depression extends as much as 6 inches below the normal contour of the lake bottom (fig. 7.1). Ideally, the bottom of the newly made nest extends to a layer of sand, gravel, or small sticks. Bass nests are very easy to spot from either the shore or a boat, but they can sometimes be confused with the smaller sunfish nests that are made in similar areas.

**Fig. 7.1.**

*Largemouth bass on a nest.*

In northern lakes nesting usually begins from late May to early June. When the water gets just a few degrees warmer, female bass swim into the spawning area and pair up singly with males. Once the female has laid her eggs, however, the male is likely to allow another female to enter the nest for another bout of spawning. As soon as she has laid her eggs, the female exits the scene, leaving the male to guard the nest.

The eggs hatch in about a week, and for another week or so, the newly hatched bass rest on the bottom of the nest resorbing the yolk left over from the egg. During this period the male bass ferociously guards the nest against all comers; the main culprits are sunfish, which love to steal eggs or fry. The male bass doesn't eat while guarding the nest. In one experiment minnows and frogs were dropped onto bass nests. The male savagely seized the intruders and chewed them mightily before ejecting their remains away from the nest.

*Life History*

After the bass fry have resorbed their yolk, they stick together in dense swarms, still guarded by their father. At this stage they eat small invertebrates and even algae. As they grow over the next few weeks, they graduate to eating small insects, and the father loses interest in them and goes his own way to begin feeding again. By this time the young-of-the-year are about three-quarters inch long, and they begin to spread out from the swarms that characterized their early days. During their first summer and even into their second year of life, young bass are less solitarily inclined than are young pike, and they typically forage for food in small groups. By the end of their first summer, they may be from 4 to 6 inches long and have graduated to eating fish and even small crayfish in addition to insects.

Largemouth bass grow quickly during their first few years of life and much more slowly after that. They typically mature in their fourth year, when they have grown 10 to 12 inches long. Like many fish, the females grow larger than the males, probably so that their body can accommodate the large number of eggs that they produce each year. Submature bass are mainly denizens of shallow water, which they often patrol in small groups. Although they are voracious eaters themselves, such bass have to be very careful to avoid being eaten by a variety of predators, including pike, muskies, larger bass, and fish-eating birds such as ospreys.

For mature bass open-water activity begins shortly after the ice leaves the lake, when they become more active and seek the warmest water they can find. This is often extremely shallow water in protected bays on the north side of a lake, where the sun hits the water for the longest period and where there is the greatest protection from cold winds. On calm early spring days it is common to see bass suspended motionless just below the surface of such bays as they are absorbing the heat of the spring sun. Because they are highly vulnerable to predatory birds in that position, they are extremely wary and will flee from anything that even smacks of danger. It is not uncommon for a fishing bait cast into the air to spook a basking bass 20 to 30 feet away.

*Bass Baits*

The major categories of bass baits alone are numerous enough to make the novice's head swim. Add together all of the permutations across categories, and the possible bass bait combinations reach into the thousands. This is why bass anglers often lug around tackle boxes (or groups of boxes) that are heavy enough to dislocate their shoulders.

One of the fundamental types of bait is the crankbait, the classical "fishing plug" (fig. 7.2; see color illustrations between pages 116 and 117). Most of these have a plastic or metal lip, causing the tail to wiggle from side to side and the overall body to tip from upright toward its side during the retrieve. Many bass baits are short and fat with a tight wiggle, but long, thin baits of the type used for walleyes are also deadly for bass in shallow water. Crankbaits are designed to dive to specific depths and to have certain wiggle characteristics on the retrieve. Each kind of bait is usually available in different sizes and colors.

A variant of the crankbait is the vibrating bait, a compact, thin lipless bait made of plastic (fig. 7.3; see color illustrations). Most have varying numbers and sizes of metal beads placed into chambers within the body. These vibrating baits are excellent search baits because they are designed to be reeled in as fast as you can. They stimulate bites through the bass's senses of vision and hearing (the beads) and through the vibration. With these baits you can cover a lot of water quickly, and if you find active bass, you can then try other baits to see what works the best. Although most of the bass caught on fast-moving vibrating baits tend to be a bit smaller than average, this is not universally true. The largest bass I have ever caught was taken on a vibrating bait retrieved at a super-fast speed.

Surface baits represent one of the classic ways to catch largemouths, and there are about as many ways to fish them as there are baits (fig. 7.4; see color illustrations). At one extreme is a popper—a floating bait with a concave face that literally pops and gurgles when it is twitched. At the other end of the spectrum are improbable looking baits such as the Jitterbug or the classic Heddon Crazy Crawler, which are often most effective when reeled in steadily, leaving a broad trail of bubbles behind them. In between are cigar-shaped floating baits that can be coaxed to move in a huge variety of irregular patterns by deft twitches of the tip of your fishing rod. Many bass anglers savor the times when the surface bite is on because few things in fishing match the excitement of a bass blasting a bait pulled over the surface.

One of the most effective baits for largemouth bass is the spinnerbait (fig. 7.5; see color illustrations). They are so effective on bass that some anglers use them exclusively. The most common design for spinnerbaits features a bent wire with a spinner on the top limb of the wire and a hook surrounded by a rubber skirt at the other end. The variations on this basic design are enormous. In addition to size, there are several fundamental shapes of spinners, ranging from the broad Colorado to the thin willow-leaf spinners, with the Indiana type intermediate between them. At the other end of the spinnerbait, the skirts come in a variety of materials and hues that make a rainbow seem pale. To top it off, many bass anglers attach a plastic grub with a curly tail to the hook, making a combination that out of the water bears no resemblance to anything that a bass would normally eat. Yet when dragged through the water, spinnerbaits often prove to be irresistible to bass. One of the real advantages of spinnerbaits is that they can be retrieved through weeds with minimum snagging. Spinnerbaits are most effective when used in shallow water—usually 5 feet or less.

A deadly, but often neglected, variety of spinnerbait is the in-line spinner, which consists of a spinner, a small weighted body, and a hook—all on a straight piece of wire (fig. 7.5). The classic example of such a bait is the Mepps spinner, which ends with a treble hook dressed in a squirrel-tail skirt. These are much smaller than the bent type of spinnerbaits, but even large bass love them. A major disadvantage is the treble hook, which snags weeds and sticks much more readily than the single-hook bent spinnerbaits. Another interesting variant of the spinnerbait is the buzzbait, which, with one exception, has the same fundamental design. Instead of a spinner, it is equipped with a propeller device (fig. 7.5). Buzzbaits are typically reeled in on the surface with a fast, steady retrieve. The propeller creates an enormous commotion on the water. When bass are in an aggressive mood, they absolutely blast buzzbaits.

The jig, consisting of a single hook embedded in a lead head and usually surrounded by a skirt of rubber or hair, is one of the most versatile baits for taking all species of fish, from sunfish to pike (fig. 7.6). Jigs of various sorts have been used by anglers for probably thousands of years, and there is a very good reason for their popularity. They catch fish! A jig has no intrinsic action. That must be supplied by the angler, but there is almost no limit to the ways that a jig can be made to move. Jigs can be fished totally vertically with just small jiggles, or they can be retrieved rapidly in a straight line. Most commonly, they are cast out and allowed to settle to the bottom and then retrieved with a series of short

**Fig. 7.6.**
. . . . . . . . . . . . . . . . . . . .

*Various types of jigs used in bass fishing.*

jerks or lifts that give the jig a hopping motion. As with spinnerbaits, it is common to decorate the hook of a jig with something—usually a soft plastic imitation of something that a bass would naturally eat. One of the time-honored attachments is a chunky piece of pork rind with a couple of flaps—presumably imitating the legs of a frog—trailing behind. This combination, called a *jig 'n' pig* by bass anglers, often takes bass when nothing else can. Because they sink rapidly, jigs are highly effective for bass in deep water, but with a different retrieve they can also be used for fishing among bulrushes in two feet of water.

Another category of bait that can be so effective that some bass anglers use them almost exclusively is the plastic worm (fig. 7.7). From humble beginnings almost 40 years ago, when few people took them seriously, the plastic worm has gained literally millions of converts. Initially identified with southern bass fishing, worm fishing was slow to

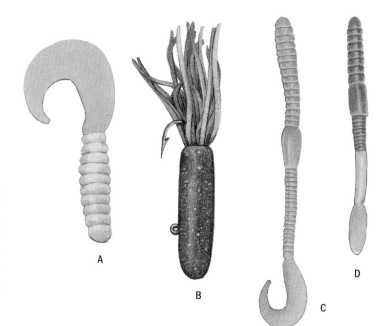

**Fig. 7.7.**

· · · · · · · · · · · · · · · · · · ·

*Various plastic worms
and other critters:*
**A**, *curly-tail grub;*
**B**, *tube jig;*
**C and D**, *worms.*

take hold in northern lakes, but now their place in the repertoire of bass anglers in all parts of the country is secure. Despite the existence of literally hundreds of models of plastic worms in an equal number of colors and shades, for the most part plastic worms are rigged and fished according to just a few basic patterns.

The most common way to rig a worm is the Texas style (fig. 7.8A). A bullet-shaped lead head is threaded onto the line before a specially shaped worm hook is attached. Most worm hooks have a couple of sharp bends near the eye that allow the worm to be skewered onto the hook without sliding off. The plastic worm, which is typically 5 to 7 inches long, is impaled by the point of the hook at the tip of its head end. After going through about ⅜ to ½ inch of the worm, the point of the hook is brought outside, and the head of the worm is threaded up to the eye of the hook past the first bend. Then the worm is slightly bent, and the point of the hook is embedded into the body until it gets to the circle of the hook. If done correctly, the worm can then be straightened out, with the straight point of the hook still completely embedded in it. Texas-rigged worms are virtually snagless, and they can be cast into dense weeds, lily pads, or tangles of brush without hanging up. They are most effective when fished on the bottom and retrieved slowly in sets of stops and twitches.

Another variant is Carolina-style rigging. Here the sinker is stopped on the line, usually with a swivel, some distance (12 to 18 inches) ahead of the worm (fig. 7.8B). With this mode of rigging, the worm floats above instead of on the bottom as the worm is being retrieved. A third method of rigging, called a *drop-shot rig,* is designed to keep the worm

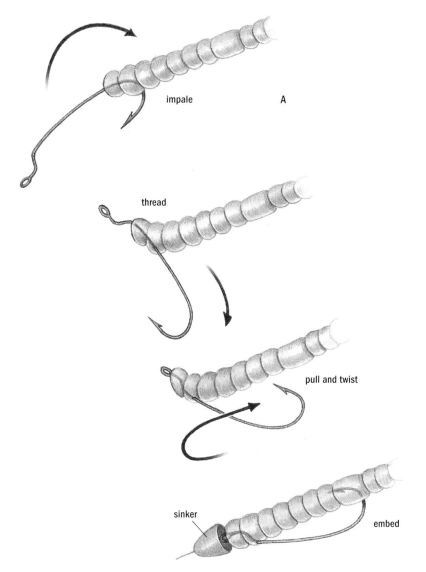

impale

A

thread

pull and twist

sinker

embed

12" to 18"

B

**Fig. 7.8.**
. . . . . . . . . . . . . . . . . . . .

*Two major types
of worm riggings.*
**A**, *Texas-style rig.
The bullet-shaped
sinker is slid onto
the line before the
hook is attached.*
**B**, *Carolina-style rig.*

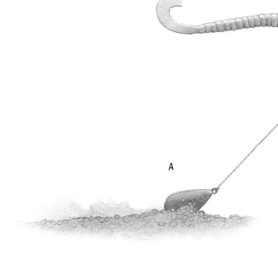

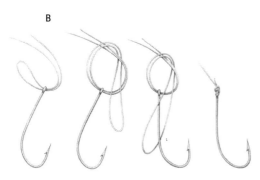

A

B

**Fig. 7.9.**
. . . . . . . . . . . . . . . . . .

**A**, *Drop-shot rig for bass.* **B**, *Palomar knot.*

at a defined distance above the bottom. In a drop-shot rig the hook is tied directly to the line with a special knot (the Palomar knot), leaving a tail of line of perhaps 1 to 2 feet. A sinker is then tied to the free end of the tail (fig. 7.9). The drop-shot rigging was relatively late to appear, but it was much ballyhooed. I became an instant convert to drop-shot rigs when my first cast with one resulted in a 22-inch bass.

For beginners, fishing with plastic worms is tricky because of the way bass go after them. Instead of feeling a whack as when using a crankbait, you are much more likely to feel only the gentlest tap or even to feel nothing but see your line moving a bit sideways. Then, when you reel the worm to the boat, there is no fish, but the worm is all bunched up around the eye of the hook. Successful worm fishing requires great concentration, quick reflexes, and a powerful hook set.

The reason for all this becomes apparent when you understand how a bass and many other fish usually take in food. Simply snapping at an animal in water is often ineffective because, with the incompressibility of water, the fish would send out a wave of water when it is closing its mouth and the prey would be swept out of the fish's mouth. Instead, fish have evolved a highly efficient strategy called *suction feeding*. The basic act of suction feeding is for the fish to closely approach its prey and, just before contact, quickly open its mouth and flare out its gill covers. This takes less than a second, and because of the rapid expansion of the mouth and gill area, water plus the prey are quickly sucked into the fish's mouth. The fish then closes its mouth. The water rushes out through the gills, but the white gill rakers, situated on the inside curve of each gill, keep the prey in the fish's mouth. Ideally in worm fishing, you strike the moment the worm has been sucked into the bass's mouth. Unfortunately, fish have a highly developed sense of what is or isn't a suitable meal, and if it decides the latter, it can expel the worm in the blink of an eye. Sometimes bass have streaks where they routinely reject the worm immediately, and more than once I have gone through six to eight takes—and crumpled worms on my hook—before actually connecting with a bass.

In a continuing quest both to attract fish and to get them to hold onto plastic baits longer, fishing tackle companies have devised numerous scents that can be either applied to the surface of the bait or mixed in with the plastic when the worm is manufactured. Many fish have a keen sense of smell. Among this group are bass, catfish, and trout. There is considerable debate concerning the effectiveness of such odors. Some anglers swear by them, and others feel that they make no difference. It's hard to know where to weigh in on this controversy, but a good rule of thumb is the following: For a fast-moving bait, vision and vibration sense are dominant in determining a fish's reactions, and smell likely plays little role in whether or not the fish takes the bait. The more slowly a bait is retrieved, however, the more likely odor will be either a turn-on or a turnoff. In the latter category, there is little doubt that a gasoline odor is a major turnoff for almost all fish, so if you spill gasoline on your hands, be sure to wash them well with soap before handling your bait. The same is true for insect repellents, which also repel most game fish. Another potential turnoff for fish is a natural secretion, called *L-serine* (an amino acid), that is found on the skin of many people. Some studies have suggested that people who consistently have better luck fishing are less likely to secrete this substance than their less successful counterparts.

Somewhere between jigs and worms is a category of baits that have jig-like heads but a variety of short plastic bodies, usually with a sickle-shaped tail that vibrates enticingly when pulled through the water. In contrast to worms, these baits are usually called *grubs* (see fig. 7.7).

Tube jigs are cylindrical soft plastic bodies with a rounded head and a fringed tail, all layered over a lead jig head attached to a hook. This type of bait is more commonly used in fishing for smallmouth bass and walleyes. It is also usual to fish these like regular jigs, especially in deeper water, but they can be effectively used in shallow water, as well.

These days spoons are a little-used way of fishing for bass, though one classic exception is the Johnson Silver Minnow—a highly weedless spoon with a single hook protected by a strong metal weedguard. When retrieved through dense weeds or rushes with a long strip of pork rind waiving enticingly behind, this combination can be deadly for shallow-water bass. One recent spring morning while pike fishing on Ten Mile with an ABU Atom spoon retrieved very rapidly, I caught fifty incidental bass in three hours.

Especially in north country lakes, live-bait fishing for largemouth bass is becoming a thing of the past, mainly because of the superabundance of highly productive artificial baits. Nevertheless, two live-bait strategies are particularly effective. One is fishing with frogs. When bass congregate in bulrushes or lily pads, it is hard to beat the simple rig of a frog hooked through the lips. If you drop a frog into a small indentation of the weed bed, chances are that it will be slurped up almost immediately by a hungry bass. Another highly effective bait is a still-fished golden shiner. Although rarely used in northern lakes, canny anglers in Florida have found that the largest bass are often taken on them.

One disincentive for using live bait is that the bass often swallows the bait and gets hooked in the stomach. In this era of catch-and-release bass fishing, the increased mortality of fish caught with live bait makes it a less than desirable method. But in recent years a special hook design, called the *circle hook,* has proven to be much safer when used with live bait because such hooks almost invariably hook the fish in the lips.

A last general category of baits for bass comes under the umbrella of fly fishing. Surprisingly few people fish for largemouth bass with a fly rod, and those who don't are missing an exciting sport. The classical fly fishing technique is to lob a small popper or hair frog near the edge of a weed bed and twitch the bait until a nearby bass can't stand it any more and blasts the popper. Another highly effective fly fishing bait is a thin, colored strip of rabbit skin fished underwater. When twitched gently during the retrieve, this bait attracts bass in much the same way as a plastic worm. A good-sized bass on a fly rod puts up a whale of a fight.

*Springtime Fishing*

Contrary to traditional belief, largemouth bass are quite catchable in the early spring, even within days of ice-out. By far the best time to find largemouths in a biting mood is during a warm-weather period, preferably sunny, so that local warming of shallow water can occur. Often they bite better late in the day due to the warming effect of the sun. Even a couple degrees variation in temperature can make the difference between the presence or absence of active bass in a given area. Water temperature readings are, therefore, invaluable for locating bass and for determining fishing strategy. In water up to the high 40s, many anglers find it most effective to reel in baits very slowly, often with a number of long pauses during the retrieve. By the time the water temperature reaches 50 degrees, largemouths enter a new phase of activity where sometimes retrieving a bait at almost top speed is the way to go. In a small lake in Michigan that I have fished a lot, by far the most effective cold-water technique is to use ultralight tackle and speed-retrieve tiny vibrating baits, like Rat-L-Traps, or to use a relatively rapid retrieve of

2- to 3-inch minnow-shaped baits. Paradoxically, sometimes the opposite strategy is the ticket: cast large, neutrally buoyant minnow-shaped baits toward shore in 1 to 4 feet of water, and after a short retrieve just let the bait rest suspended in the water before picking up your retrieve again. Some days this type of retrieve can increase the number of strikes by a factor of two or three. Then again, the next day it might be no more effective than a steady retrieve.

This contradictory advice provides one of the keys to successful bass fishing. Largemouth bass can be incredibly fickle. If you aren't catching fish on a particular bait or retrieve, the best thing to do is to try something else. Most of the time I change baits every ten casts or so until I hit upon a combination that turns them on. This fickleness not only occurs on a day-by-day basis but also can result in major changes in bait preference over the course of minutes. Sometimes changing baits can be as simple as a change of color, but much of the time it is good to change major categories of baits while you are trying to figure out what works at a particular time.

*Summertime Fishing*

Most northern lakes warm up to the mid-70s and even the low 80s in hot summers. These are ideal temperatures for largemouth bass, and at a practical level, it means that they can be found in water as shallow as 1 or 2 feet or as deep as 30 feet.

For the most part adult largemouths prefer to hang out near cover— often the denser the better. All sorts of things can constitute suitable cover. Near the shoreline, beds of lily pads or bulrushes provide excellent cover, as do fallen trees or brush piles. In deeper water, beds of cabbage (broadleaf pondweed) or coontail are preferred areas. Some lakes are infested with almost impenetrable masses of Eurasian milfoil. Beds of Eurasian milfoil are so dense that special fishing techniques have been devised to bring baits to bass that are lurking beneath these weeds. Unless the water is extremely warm, few largemouth bass will be found in water deeper than the lower limit of vegetation. There are notable exceptions to this rule, however, and water color and turbidity can play a role.

Unlike walleyes, largemouth bass are more stay-at-home types, with a relatively limited range. Within that range, however, they move around quite a bit. A common pattern is to stay in deeper water during the day and to move into the shallows during the early morning and evening. Some studies have shown that bass often follow regular routes from their deepwater refuges to their shallow-water feeding grounds.

One important characteristic of bass is that, even though they normally follow certain behavioral patterns, there are many variations.

One is a tendency to move into shallower water during cloudy or rainy days. Especially during an all-day rain, many bass can be seen patrolling shallow, somewhat weedy areas for hours. Such circumstances often make for excellent fishing with baits like Rapala minnows or spinnerbaits. Dark days (and dark, stained water, as well) often call for brightly colored baits. One of the most effective colors on a rainy day is bright fluorescent orange.

On bright sunny days, when the bass retreat to deeper water, it is usually best to use light-colored or silver baits, though black baits often work best regardless of the light intensity or color of the water. Bass show considerable variation in color preference from lake to lake. Under identical weather and atmospheric conditions, bass in one lake may show a strong preference for white, whereas in a neighboring lake chartreuse or green on exactly the same bait may be the way to go. No one has ever been able to account for such differences in color preference on a purely scientific basis, but there is no doubt that such preferences exist. For example, several years ago on a small lake that I fished regularly, I found that for several weeks from 8:15 to 8:45 AM the bass went wild over a bright blue crankbait. Before or after that time they ignored it. The next summer I tried the same thing with the same blue bait and never got a bite.

Certain summertime locations are almost certain to harbor bass. One of the most consistent is a pocket at the edge of a dense weed bed in 5 to 10 feet of water. Such a location is a perfect place to cast a Texas-rigged plastic worm or a jig and let it settle to the bottom. Often a bass will engulf the bait before it reaches bottom. Normally, the largest bass are found at the outside edge of a weed bed, but every once in a while, they will change their pattern and move to the inside edge. Such a change in pattern often means that they are more actively feeding, so it is a good one to identify. Some north country lakes are partially ringed by substantial beds of wild rice. If the water is deep enough, rice beds make an excellent habitat for largemouth bass, and a good way to fish for them is with spinnerbaits, which do a pretty good job of slithering through the rice plants.

Lily pads present an interesting challenge and opportunity for the summertime bass angler. I must confess to being rather unenthusiastic about lily pads. Much of the time they don't hold as many fish as one might suspect, but in bass fishing there is no such thing as always or never. A good example of this principle happened to me a couple of years ago. I was fishing a wilderness bass lake that was loaded with weed beds that just reeked of fish. The first few hours of fishing were singularly unproductive, with perhaps two small bass and a hammerhandle pike every hour. Nevertheless, I persistently fished these areas with every bait

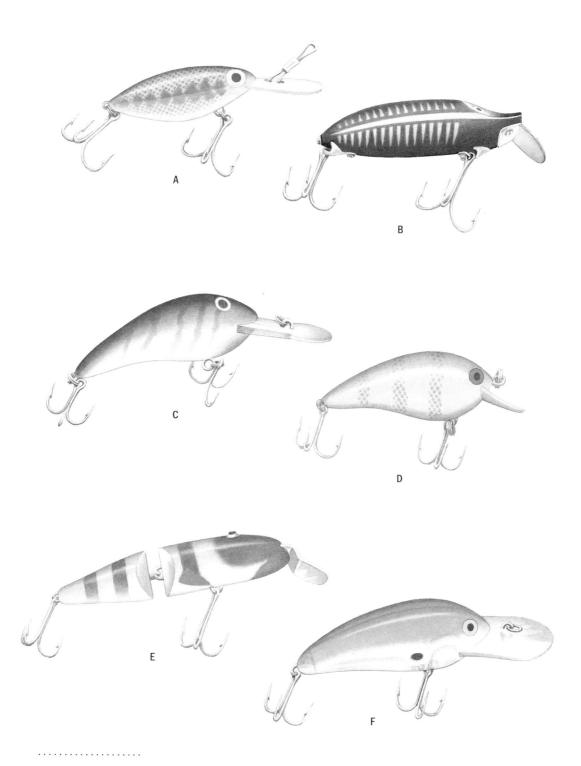

Fig. **7.2.** *Variety of common crankbaits used in bass fishing.* **A**, *Hot 'N' Tot;* **B**, *Big O;* **C**, *Grappler Shad;* **D**, *River Runt;* **E**, *Pikie Minnow;* **F**, *Bomber A. The River Runt and the Pikie Minnow are time-honored baits that are still highly effective.*

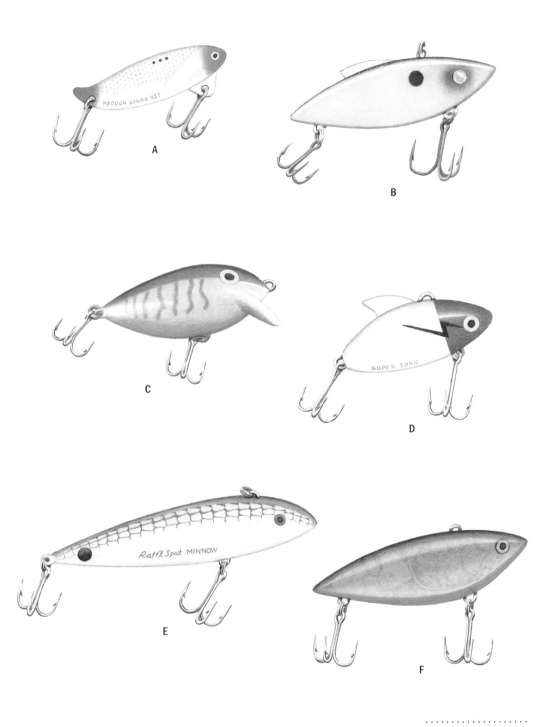

Fig. **7.3.** *Flat-bodied, mostly lipless vibrating baits or rattlebaits that are proven winners for bass.*
**A**, *Sonar;* **B**, *Rat-L-Trap;* **C**, *Thin Fin;* **D**, *Sonic;* **E**, *Ratt'l Spot Minnow;* **F**, *Spot Minnow.*

..................

*Fig.* **7.4.** *Some of the large variety of surface baits used for largemouth bass.* **A**, *Hula Popper;* **B**, *Jitterbug;*
**C**, *Tender Toad;* **D**, *Injured Minnow;* **E**, *Skitter Pop;* **F**, *Zara Spook. The Hula Popper and Skitter Pop are*
*popping-type baits. The Injured Minnow is a propeller lure. The Jitterbug is a venerable bait—but still*
*a winner.*

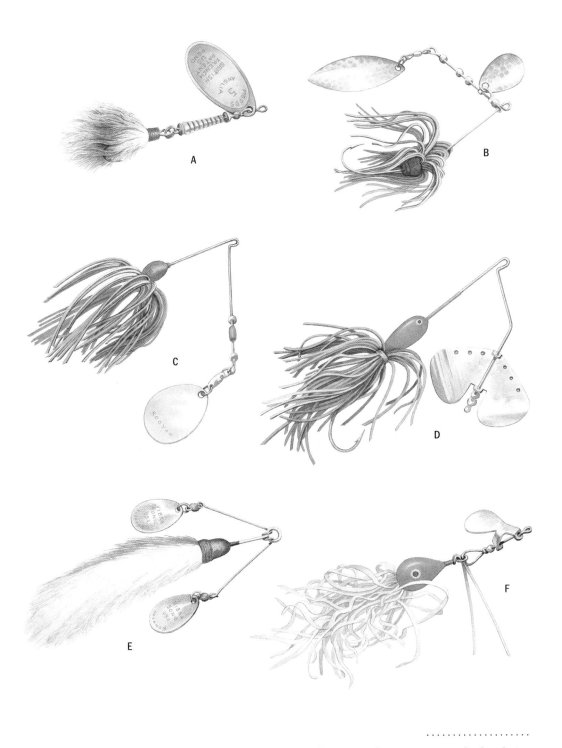

*Fig.* **7.5.** *Variants of spinner-type baits:* **A**, **C**, **and D**, *spinnerbaits;* **B**, *in-line spinner;* **E** *and* **F**, *buzzbaits.*

in my tackle box with no improvement in results. Then, in desperation, I headed for a nearby bed of lily pads and cast a Texas-rigged worm into the pads. Within 6 feet of retrieving the worm over the surface of the pads, a nice bass had charged up into a small opening between some pads and grabbed the bait. These lily pads yielded a bass every two or three casts, including one that was close to 6 pounds. The moral of this story is that, when bass fishing, don't get too set in your ways, because the bass aren't. Getting into a mental rut may cost you some excellent fishing.

Looking carefully at the color of the bass you catch can yield some important clues to the habits of the lake's bass. If the lake has clear water, the bass that live in shallow water typically have a pronounced greenish cast to their sides and back. Alternatively, bass in the same lake that have spent some time in deep water often lose this greenish cast and have more whites and dark grays to their color. Every once in a while when fishing in shallow water, I have noticed a fish that has more gray and white than green, which usually means it has recently moved into the shallows from its normal deep haunts, and typically when this happens, it means that these fish are on the prowl for food, since shallow-water fish of almost any species are usually feeding. Feeding fish are more aggressive than their nonfeeding counterparts, so it pays to adjust your fishing techniques to methods that are more appropriate for active fish. In some lakes, particularly those with muddy or stained water, all of the bass have lost their green color, so this color distinction doesn't apply. One lake that I often fish is fed by a small stream that runs through farmland. After a heavy rain the silt-laden stream, and soon the lake, takes on the color of coffee with cream. Biting bass are usually scarce for the first couple of days of such discolored water, but as the water begins to clear and the bass start biting again, they have all lost their green color and look very pale.

Particularly as lakeshore property is increasingly developed, boat docks are becoming an important bass habitat. They provide the conditions that bass desire most—shade, protection, cover, and food. In lakes that are ringed by cabins, some bass anglers concentrate almost exclusively on the waters under docks. Not all docks are created equal, however, and while some make ideal bass habitats, others are only marginal. Old docks with wooden supports are by far the best, since wood attracts both the insects and the small fish on which bass feed. The deeper the water at the end of the dock, the better the fishing, especially if the dock is close to a weed bed or a rocky bottom. And a large boat moored alongside the dock only improves the situation. Large bass will hang out beneath docks, even on the brightest of days. I have seen a bass jump out of the water and hook itself on a bait left hanging off the side of a moored boat. Bass prefer the shady side of a dock and at times can be in rather inaccessible locations. Effective dock fishing uses some highly specialized casting techniques that skip the bait underneath the dock. The key is to allow the bait to stay under or near the dock as long as possible, because bass often will not chase a bait very far from a dock.

Summertime bass can be very moody, and like walleyes, their moods are often strongly influenced by the weather. For some reason the passage of a cold front typically inactivates most of the bass in a lake, and even professional anglers may have trouble catching decent fish. It is suspected that strong light levels from the bright blue skies may be at least partially responsible, but there is little doubt that more than light accounts for the strong negative response. The most commonly given advice for fishing following cold front conditions is to fish deep, retrieve slowly, and use smaller baits. Some of my best cold front bass have been taken on panfish jigs.

Just the opposite response occurs just before a front moves in, especially on a hot, humid, hazy day. Under these conditions the bass can become supercharged and will bite on anything put in front of them. My best fishing advice for such conditions is to pick up the speed of your retrieve. Only four times in my life have I ever caught a *double*—two bass caught at the same time on the same bait. All four of these doubles occurred within the space of an hour one morning. For the previous two hours I had been catching small bass at the rate of about five per hour when, all of a sudden, the lake was boiling with bass. During the next hour I caught over fifty bass, including the four doubles, and lost about twenty more. This unusual event was not accompanied by a massive change in the weather, but a very inconspicuous band of loose clouds passed overhead at about that time. Whether that or any other weather-related phenomenon had anything to do with this intense feeding frenzy will never be known.

The moon is also reputed to have an effect on fish behavior. In 1936, John Alden Knight published a book, *Moon Up, Moon Down,* that laid out a persuasive argument in favor of a pronounced lunar influence on the behavior of both fish and land animals. He devised a system (solunar tables) for identifying periods of major and minor feeding activity based upon the phase of the moon and the position of the moon in relation to the earth during the day. These tables or variants thereof are still regularly published in newspapers and fishing magazines. Sometimes different sets of tables give contradictory advice. How well they predict fishing success on an hourly basis is up for grabs, but many experienced anglers, myself included, are convinced that fishing success is better a few days before and after a full moon or the new moon. Some anglers, especially those using live bait for walleyes, swear by the tables of active periods during the day; others don't notice much of an effect. Local weather can often be an overriding influence, especially the passage of fronts before or during the published periods of feeding activity. There is no doubt, however, that animals do have pronounced periods of increased activity. If I see an unusual number of woodchucks or deer alongside the road during the day, I try to get fishing right away, if I have the option, because the fish usually bite better during such periods, as well.

Although their eyes are not as well adapted for night vision as those of walleyes, largemouth bass are often active at night, even when there is no moon, and in Ten Mile Lake it is not uncommon to catch occasional largemouths while trolling for walleyes at night. Casting for nighttime bass is an exciting proposition. Two of the most effective baits are black Jitterbugs and black spinnerbaits. At night bass don't have to worry about being picked off by birds, so they often spread out over very shallow flats in search of food. Here is where the Jitterbug shines (see fig. 7.4). This surface bait has a large concave metal inverted lip that gurgles and creates a wide stream of bubbles when it is retrieved. The black color provides a well-defined silhouette against the night sky. The combination of noise and color makes the Jitterbug an easy target for a hungry bass looking up toward the surface. At night it is most effective to use a slow, steady retrieve. Hearing a bass blast a Jitterbug in the blackness of night is quite an experience. Bass are not boat shy at night, and sometimes they go after the bait just at the end of the retrieve. That definitely catches your attention.

Even at night many bass still relate to cover. Especially on clear moonlit nights, they prefer to remain near aquatic vegetation or in the shadows of shoreline vegetation. There in the shallows, they lie in wait for fish or any animal, such as a mouse, that might fall into the water from land. To catch bass in these locations, casting spinnerbaits near shore is usually the best way to go. One of the most effective methods of nighttime spinnerbait fishing for bass is to take a small boat within a few feet of shore and cast parallel to the shoreline only a few feet from land. This reduces the number of casts that land in trees or bushes, and it also keeps the bait in active fish territory most of the time. Again, a slow, steady retrieve is the way to go, and the bass are remarkably accurate in striking the bait.

### Fall Fishing

Once Labor Day approaches and the days start becoming noticeably shorter, bass begin to switch into their fall mode of behavior, which is dominated by their storing up enough food to get them through the winter. If the summer was a hot one, it means that they will move into shallower water once the nights begin to cool. Fall conditions also change the feeding habits of largemouths. Whereas in the summertime they are much more active in the early morning and evening, they tend to feed more actively throughout the day in the fall. This may be due not only to their greater overall level of feeding but also to the lower position of the sun, which doesn't strike them so directly from overhead.

As fall progresses and the water becomes significantly cooler, the bass again tend toward deeper water, especially at the base of strongly sloping banks. Here they feed heavily upon crayfish. As the weeds begin to die off, beds of dying vegetation are vacated, and the bass move to areas where the vegetation remains green. They still travel to shallow water for feeding forays, but when the water temperature drops into the 50s, their shallow-water excursions tend to occur late in the afternoon on sunny days when the sun's rays heat up the shallow water by a few degrees.

Late in the fall, when the water temperature has fallen into the low 40s and the 30s, largemouth bass congregate in deepwater havens where the water temperature is warmer than that nearer the surface. They remain in these locations throughout the winter. Contrary to earlier beliefs, largemouth bass do not become completely dormant in very cold water. Although much of the time they are inactive and their overall metabolism is greatly reduced, they still have periods of feeding activity, when they are occasionally caught by ice fishers.

One reason for the relative inactivity of cold-water bass in the late fall is that their bodies undergo some major adaptations for the winter, which is best illustrated by looking at their muscle tissue. Fish are cold-blooded animals (poikilothermic), meaning that their body temperature approximates that of the water. When the water gets colder, their overall swimming speed slows down because the enzymes that cause their muscles to contract function less efficiently at a lower temperature. Different fish prefer different temperatures and are adapted for such. The enzyme systems of a largemouth bass, which prefer water temperatures in the high 70s, are designed to function with maximal efficiency at a much higher temperature than, for example, those of dwarf ciscoes, which prefer water temperatures in the mid 40s.

If this logic was followed, one would expect that, at wintertime water temperatures (39 degrees), warm-water fish, like largemouth bass, would barely be able to move, which would probably happen if nature hadn't anticipated this situation. As water temperatures cool, many of the muscle proteins (both the proteins that actually cause contraction and the enzymes that power them) are replaced with similar proteins that function better at lower temperatures, allowing a fish to swim more strongly in cold water than it could if it had to use its summertime muscle proteins. To demonstrate this principle, take a fish that is adapted to warm temperatures and a fish that is adapted to cold temperatures and place both in an environment with an intermediate water temperature, say in the 40s. The fish adapted to the cold will be able to swim faster than the one used to living in warm water.

Most bass anglers pack up their rods after Labor Day, and their thoughts turn to football or hunting. Instead, they should spend more time on the water, because the fall is by far the best time of the year to catch a trophy bass. Being a scientist at heart, I keep meticulous records of my fishing. Not long ago I calculated how long it took me to catch a bass over 20 inches long on a small lake by our house in Michigan. Whereas in July I had to fish 17.8 hours to catch a bass over 20 inches, in October it took only 3.6 hours, and in early November, 2.2 hours. Over the years almost all of my 22-inch-plus bass have been taken in October.

Generally, bass prefer larger baits in the fall than they do in the summer. My personal experience is that during the fall large crankbaits are usually more effective than plastic worms or grubs. Also, the bass seem to show renewed interest in vibrating baits. In the warm summer waters vibrating baits are often less effective than they are in cooler water, either in the spring or the fall. Interestingly, one of my most effective fall big bass baits is a heavy (1-ounce), all-metal vibrating bait, such as the old Heddon Sonar bait. They cast a mile, and if they are retrieved at a high speed, large bass often attack them savagely. Unfortunately, these baits don't hook bass as efficiently as some others, and I have lost a number of huge bass on them.

Another effective fall fishing technique is to cast smaller sinking crankbaits toward surviving weed beds or along the edge of drop-offs. The retrieve is considerably slower than that used with vibrating baits, and as in summertime bass fishing, the key to successful fall bass fishing is experimentation. Largemouth bass never seem to follow only one pattern of behavior, no matter the season. Although for early to midfall fishing I normally prefer fast retrieves, there have also been periods when the most effective bait has been a plastic wormlike bait floated motionless in midwater. The bottom line on largemouth bass fishing is that, despite their large appetite and general aggressiveness, they are among the most fickle of all species of game fish. No single method will take largemouths all of the time, but there are very few occasions in which there isn't some bait that will take bass. This is probably why bass fishing has such a devoted following. Even the best bass angler still has a lot to learn about why bass do what they do. Nevertheless, largemouth bass are accessible to the novice angler because there is almost always a bass that is willing to bite.

## Smallmouth Bass

*Biology and Life History*

Smallmouth bass are often thought of as the little cousins of large-mouths, but in northern lakes they often grow as large as, if not larger than, their big-mouthed relatives. Although both species of bass have the same general shape, three principal characteristics distinguish one from the other (fig. 7.10). As their names imply, the most prominent distinguishing characteristic is the size of their mouth. The corner of a smallmouth's mouth stops ahead of the eye, whereas that of the large-mouth extends past the eye when the mouth is closed. Smallmouth

**Fig. 7.10.**

*Smallmouth bass.*

bass are sometimes called *bronzebacks*, and for a good reason. In contrast to the typically greenish shades of the largemouth, the skin of smallmouth bass is bronze colored or dark brown, and the belly often tends to be grayish instead of the white shade of the largemouth. Large-mouth bass have a single longitudinal stripe that runs along the middle of the body, but smallmouth bass often have faint, irregular vertical stripes. If specimens of the two species were arranged side by side, it would be apparent that the scales of the smallmouth are much smaller than those of the largemouth. This gives them a smoother feel when you handle them. Smallmouth bass have noticeably reddish eyes, in contrast to the darker eyes of largemouths.

One characteristic common to both species is that they become essentially paralyzed when lifted by the lower jaw, a convenient trait when removing hooks from their mouths. Many bass tournaments do not allow the use of landing nets, and the tournament anglers reach into the water and grab larger bass by the mouth in order to bring them into the boat. This works well when fishing with a single hook, like a plastic worm rig, but be careful landing them by the mouth when they are connected to a bait with multiple treble hooks.

Despite their close relationship, smallmouth bass occupy niches in lakes almost entirely different from those occupied by largemouth bass. Smallmouths usually shun the weed beds that are the favorite haunts of largemouths. Instead, they prefer rock or gravel bottoms and deeper water. Sunken logs or branches make for an even more desirable habitat. Smallmouth bass are cool-water fish and prefer water temperatures in the high 60s.

Paradoxically, in the early springtime, when the water temperature is below 50 degrees, smallmouths are less likely to be active than are largemouths. By the time the water has warmed to just above the mid-50s, groups of smallmouths suddenly appear in the shallow waters as they forage for food before spawning begins. By the time the water reaches the upper 50s, the mature males begin to make nests for the upcoming spawning season. They select areas with small rocks or gravel, usually in water from 3 to 6 feet deep, but sometimes they build nests in water as deep as 20 feet. To build their nests, which are almost perfect circles 3 to 5 feet in diameter, the males fan the bottom with their tails, displacing any sand or organic debris. They sometimes even remove larger pebbles with their mouths. Once the nest is completed, it is visible from a boat as many as 40 to 50 feet away on a calm day. Although the nests are not located right on top of each other, they are often concentrated in a given area, collectively called a spawning bed. Soon after the nest is constructed, a female enters the area, and spawning typically occurs when the water temperature reaches around 60 degrees.

In typical bass fashion, the female quits the nest immediately after spawning, leaving the male to guard the nest against all comers. The greatest threats to the eggs and newly hatched fry are larger minnows, but especially small groups of sunfish. Sometimes, one sunfish will enter the nest area and be chased away from the nest, leaving the unguarded nest vulnerable to predation by the remainder of the sunfish in the group, which feast on the eggs and young until the male bass returns to chase them away. Smallmouth eggs and young are very vulnerable to sudden drops in water temperature, and when this occurs, it is not uncommon for mortality to approach 100 percent. Sometimes the bass compensate for such occurrences by spawning a second time later in the summer.

Once the smallmouth fry have resorbed their yolk, they leave the nest and begin voraciously feeding on zooplankton such as *Daphnia* (water fleas). They soon graduate to eating tiny fish, which, along with insects, constitute the bulk of their diet during the first summer. Young-of-the-year smallmouths typically live in very shallow water, often over a sand or gravel bottom, where they can be distinguished by a dark vertical band at the back rim of the tail. They are less sociable than young largemouths, but they can still be seen in groups of two or three.

As the lake water warms after the spawning season, adult smallmouth bass retreat to deeper, cooler water, but early in the summer, in particular, they often make forays into the shallows in the early morning or evening to feed. Their deepwater haunts are preferably rocky slopes or ridges where they can feed on their favorite food—crayfish. Smallmouth bass are not great fans of bright light, and the reduced illumination of the deeper waters is also a plus for them.

*Fishing for Smallmouths*

One of the prime times for smallmouth bass fishing occurs just after they emerge from their long winter's period of semihibernation. As the slowly warming waters of the lake begin to arouse their near-dormant metabolism, they make their way from their deepwater winter resting places to the nearby shallow water, where the temperature approaches the mid-50s. At their spring awakening, smallmouths seek out areas where the bottom consists of a mixture of sand and small rocks, punctuated by a smattering of larger boulders. When they first arrive in the shallows, the smallmouth bass tend to aggregate into small groups or even schools of up to 20 to 30 individuals. After a winter of minimal food intake, they are hungry and are actively feeding. At this time their main food appears to be minnows and small fish, such as suckers and perch up to 3 to 4 inches long.

These early spring bass can be readily located visually if the water is calm and clear, and if you can locate a concentration of them, you will be treated to probably the fastest fishing of the year. It is common to catch ten or more bass per hour under these circumstances. Although they can be taken by a variety of means, I have found that the most effective method is casting tiny minnow-shaped baits with ultralight tackle. Since most of these bass congregate in depths less than 5 feet, using baits that dive 1 to 2 feet upon retrieve is one of the simplest techniques. Minnowbaits that are 2 to 3½ inches long match their springtime food, and I have found silver-colored ones work best during this period. For pure efficiency a medium to medium-fast retrieve allows you to cover the most water, and the bass react very positively to such retrieves. A little experimentation will determine whether a steady or a stop-and-go retrieve is most effective on a given outing. One of the problems with using ultralight tackle on spring smallmouths is that it is sometimes hard to properly set the hook with a limber rod. This is where the small minnowbaits shine. Most of them have very small (e.g., size 10 to 12) treble hooks, and they are so fine that the bass invariably hooks itself without a hook set when attacking these lures. There is no need to be nervous about using hooks this small. They are plenty strong to hold any bass if the fish is played properly. The larger the hook, the lower the percentage of fish that will make it to the boat when you are using ultralight tackle.

Early springtime smallmouths can on occasion be very fickle in their preference of baits. If small minnowbaits don't work, try different types of lures, such as tube or hair jigs. A disadvantage of these is that they are usually fished more slowly, and consequently, you can't cover as much territory as you can with minnowbaits. Sometimes spring smallmouths are in a highly aggressive mood and are best taken on vibrating baits retrieved as fast as they can be retrieved with an ultralight reel. Even then they can be very finicky. On one recent trip the bass refused even to nip at tiny Rat'L Traps, which are one of my favorite cold-water baits. Fortunately, in my tackle box I had a couple of one-eighth-ounce Heddon Sonic lures that I had success with on smallmouths in the 1950s. These baits vibrate, but in contrast to the Rat'L Traps, which are loaded with metal spheres, the Sonics make no sound. Within an hour I had hooked thirty bass and had brought over half to the boat. The remainder got off because of problems setting the hook with my limber rod.

After several days of intensive feeding, some of the male bass begin breaking off from the group and start constructing their nests, which, as mentioned, are readily visible in the water. As nest building nears completion, female smallmouths move in to join the males for their annual spawning ritual. On a quiet day you can see a pair of bass hovering over the nest as they spawn. During this period, as might be imagined, feeding is not high on their agenda, and if a line is dragged across the nest, they typically either ignore it or briefly swim away. Upon completion of spawning, the female departs, leaving the male to guard the nest while the eggs develop.

Male smallmouths are very susceptible to fishing pressure when they are guarding their nests. They are fiercely protective of the nest and will drive any intruder away. Fishing lures fall into the category of intruders, and if a lure is slowly dragged across the nest or dropped on it, the male will attack it. There is considerable discussion of the wisdom of catching male smallmouths that are guarding nests even on a catch-and-release basis. This is particularly an issue if there are large numbers of sunfish in the vicinity. Even during the time when the bass is being caught and unhooked, nearby sunfish can invade and devastate a nest. Studies have shown that when a hooked male bass returns to a nest that has had some predation, it is less likely to guard the nest with the same zeal that it would have had the nest remained undisturbed.

After the newly hatched bass have been left to fend for themselves, the adult bass gravitate toward deeper water as the lake continues to warm. During the early summer smallmouth bass feed particularly actively in the early morning and late evening. They frequently move into shallow water—often in areas containing bulrushes, if such are available—or into rocky shoreline areas. When they move into shallow water, they do so for one purpose—to eat—and shallow-water smallmouths can be readily caught by a number of different techniques. Their major shallow-water food is minnows and other small fish or insects, and the baits that work best on smallmouths are typically one or two sizes smaller than those that one would typically use when fishing for largemouths. Generally, shallow fish are in a feeding mode and an aggressive behavior pattern. Therefore, it is often most efficient to fish for them by casting baits that can be retrieved at high speeds. Shallow-water bass will travel many feet to intercept a lure, particularly if it emits sound or vibration during the retrieve. It is almost impossible to retrieve a bait too rapidly. The main limitation is the intrinsic action of the lure. As in fishing for largemouths, however, it usually pays to experiment instead of sticking with the same bait, even a tried-and-true one. If vibrating baits are not effective, try using tube jigs or small crankbaits.

For a complete change of pace, you can also try surface fishing for morning or evening smallmouths, especially early in the summer when insect hatches are most frequent. An exciting method of surface fishing is with a fly rod and popper, but small surface lures presented by spinning tackle are also highly effective. Although surface fishing would seem connected with shallow water, this does not always have to be the case. Smallmouth bass will rise from considerable depths, as much as 15 feet, to smash a surface lure. Many smallmouth bass anglers are so enamored of this method that they will sacrifice numbers for the thrill of explosive surface strikes.

As summer wears on and bass retreat to the rocky depths, much of their diet consists of crayfish and smaller bottom-dwelling fish such as sculpins and darters (fig. 7.11). Here they are most susceptible to fishing with live bait or with jigs. The subtle hopping action of a tube or hair jig or a vibrating metal blade bait can imitate the movements of these bottom dwellers. Because summertime smallmouths are often found as deep as 30 to 35 feet, drifting or slow trolling are often the most efficient way to get your bait down to their level. If you catch one, it is likely that others are in the vicinity, because they tend to congregate around good habitat.

Smallmouth bass can be very active night feeders. On Ten Mile Lake they are being caught with increasing frequency during after-dark trolling expeditions for walleyes, especially in water less than 12 feet deep. Smallmouths are not notorious migrators, so their nighttime hunting grounds are not far from areas where they can be caught during the day. Slim minnow-shaped baits 4 to 5 inches long retrieved at a steady rate are quite effective at night.

As fall moves in and the water cools after the turnover period, smallmouth bass move into deep water and congregate into extremely dense aggregations. Although they tend to be very sluggish in water less than 50 degrees, they can be caught with deep-jigging techniques. Because they spend the cold-water period in such a crammed-together manner, smallmouths are very vulnerable to angling pressure if their winter haunts are discovered. Because of the vulnerability, many bass anglers prefer not to disturb them at this time of the year. During the under-ice period smallmouths are almost dormant and are much less active then their large-mouthed cousins. Their metabolism slows down considerably, so they don't need much food during the winter. This, of course, brings their growth rate close to zero. As a result, the thin rings (annuli) on their scales are laid down very close together. By counting these bands of close-together rings, fishery biologists are able to determine the age of smallmouth bass and most other northern species of fish.

**Fig. 7.11.**

. . . . . . . . . . . . . . . . . . . .

*Crayfish in threatening posture warding off a hungry smallmouth bass.*

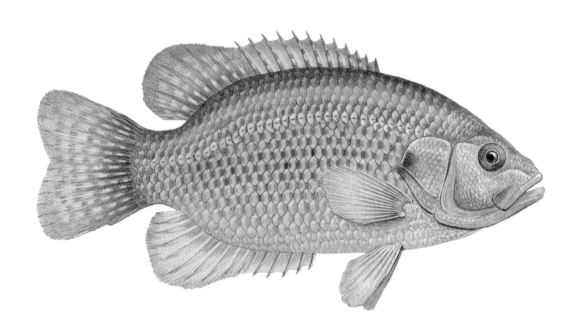

I still have vivid memories of catching my first fish at age four. My uncle and I were fishing with cane poles off the shore of Balsam Lake, Wisconsin, when a brightly colored sunfish tried to bite off too much of my worm. Seeing that pretty creature immediately set off in me a love of fish and fishing that hasn't diminished a bit over the years. For many of us, catching a panfish was our introduction to fishing, and this is likely how we will introduce our own children or grandchildren to fishing. Even for those who don't fish, panfish are often the most visible fish in a lake. Small ones congregate around docks and are often seen from pathways alongside the lake. Little children often have a wonderful time throwing small pieces of bread to sunfish and watching them slurp the bread off the surface.

For the serious angler, catching good-sized panfish poses as great a challenge as the larger game fish. In order to catch them consistently, you need to have a good understanding of their biology and adapt your fishing techniques accordingly. The three main panfish in north country lakes are rock bass, sunfish, and crappies. These are all members of the same family as bass, and their original distribution was limited to North America.

## Rock Bass

Rock bass are by far the dominant panfish in Ten Mile Lake. This is probably due to the abundance of suitable habitat—rocky bars with aggregations of boulders near drop-offs, as well as gentle, sloping flats with a mixture of rocks and sparse vegetation. As their name implies, rock bass really do like rocks, and that

*Rock bass.*

is where they congregate. Almost every summer weekend on Ten Mile, one can see a boat with an adult and several children anchored over a well-known rock pile in about eight feet of water. As soon as the anchor is dropped, schools of hungry rock bass gather under the boat and seem perfectly happy to exchange a sore lip for a juicy hunk of worm. Rock bass are utterly unsophisticated in their feeding habits, and to the delight of small children, they will rush to a baited (or even unbaited) hook. But, beyond this snapshot view, there is much more to rock bass.

Most adult rock bass run a bit larger than sunfish (in the 6- to 9-inch range), and they have very sturdy bodies that are covered with large scales. Their color ranges from brownish to olive on top, and almost all of their scales below the lateral line are punctuated with a black spot. Among their most characteristic features are their large, red eyes. Red eyes are common in fish that are active night feeders, and rock bass (along with smallmouths) are no exception. Rock bass are known to change their color very quickly, and some fish biologists have dubbed them the chameleons of the lakes. They have a relatively large mouth for a panfish, which gives them more flexibility in their choice of food.

Rock bass are normally shallow-water fish, but in clear lakes like Ten Mile, they can be found in water as deep as 25 to 30 feet. By far their preferred habitat is a highly irregular rocky bottom (fig. 8.1), but they

**Fig. 8.1.**
· · · · · · · · · · · · · · · · · · ·

*Rock bass in their preferred rocky habitat.*

also relate strongly to downed timber—both large trunks and branches or roots. In addition to liking relatively shallow water, rock bass are lit-

toral, meaning that they are found near the shore. In Ten Mile Lake, far from shore, there are some rock piles rising from relatively deep water that would make ideal rock bass habitat, but I have never seen a rock bass on them. Their preference for rocks corresponds with their preferred food, which consists of crayfish for adults and insect larvae for rock bass of all ages. Adult rock bass also feed voraciously upon minnows and small game fish, including members of their own species. They are often very aggressive in their feeding habits, and every year I catch several 5-inch rock bass on crankbaits that are over 6 inches long.

Like the other members of the sunfish family, rock bass scoop out nests near shore in the springtime. Rock bass nests, which are often located in the same areas as smallmouth nests, are more irregular in outline and are about 18 to 24 inches in diameter. Their preferred nesting temperature (close to 70 degrees) is warmer than that of smallmouth bass, so they spawn slightly later in the spring. Yet one can often see them on their nests at the same time as the smallmouth bass are guarding their young. Like bass, the male makes the nest and invites a female in for spawning. Once the several thousand eggs are laid, the female departs, leaving the male to guard the nest against predators. As an aside, the fact that members of the sunfish family construct and guard nests makes their spawning more efficient on a percentage basis. They can typically get away with laying several thousand eggs per female, whereas walleyes, which just broadcast their eggs and leave them to whatever fate awaits them, must lay eggs in the hundred thousand range in order to ensure perpetuation of the species. Regardless, it is sobering to think that of all these only a handful survive to adulthood. While on the nest, the male drives away any fish or crayfish that encroach upon the nest, and after three to four days the young rock bass hatch. On the nest the males exhibit striking jet-black breeding coloration on the edges of their pelvic and anal fins. Once the newly hatched fry have resorbed their yolk and have begun to feed upon plankton, the male abandons them, and the young-of-the-year rock bass move into very shallow water for their first summer.

Rock bass like relatively warm water, which allows them to remain in shallow water all summer. Only once, during an exceptionally hot summer when the water temperature was in the low 80s at 5 feet, have I seen the rock bass completely abandon their usual shallow haunts. They feed at all times of the day and night, and they are often caught more readily at night than during the day. Even the darkest moonless nights don't deter rock bass from actively feeding. When trolling at night for walleyes, it is usual to catch 10 to 20 rock bass per outing. In fact, the behavior of the rock bass gives valuable clues concerning the activity levels of the walleyes. Once in a while, I don't catch any rock bass, and on nights like these, I rarely catch a walleye either. Small rock bass, in particular, undergo a characteristic color change at night, leaving their bodies with a pronounced blotched appearance. One year, when removing paint from some baits that I had painted black as part of an unsuccessful experiment, I left some of the black paint on the baits in very ugly-looking blotches, and these baits outfished their unchanged counterparts.

Rock bass are rarely targeted for sport. Although they often strike hard at a lure, they quickly tire, so there is not the spirited fight of the sunfish. Nevertheless, on ultralight tackle, fishing for them can be an interesting diversion. They rarely go after surface lures, but small spinners, 2- to 3-inch sinking crankbaits, and even spoons are all effective baits.

As the water cools in the fall, rock bass move into deeper water and aggregate in specific areas. They are mostly dormant in the wintertime, and not until the water warms up to the 50s in the spring do they return to their shallow-water feeding grounds.

## Sunfish

Northern lakes contain several species of sunfish, but the two most commonly encountered by anglers are bluegills and pumpkinseeds. Bluegills are the quintessential panfish. They are usually abundant in shallow, weedy parts of the lake; they bite readily; and they are wonderful eating. Bluegills are among the most colorful fish in the lake (fig. 8.2). They typically have a dark olive green to dusky back and faint grayish vertical stripes along the length of their body. Their belly is usually pale yellow, but the area under the gills and the pectoral fins is often orange colored. Older males, especially around and somewhat after the breeding season, frequently have a pronounced violet hue to their skin, especially toward the head. Female bluegills are normally paler in color. Aside from their very small mouth, there are few distinguishing features of the head except for a somewhat saucer-shaped black mark at the tip of the membranous tab at the back end of the gill cover (operculum). A blackish smudge can sometimes be distinguished at the back of the soft part of the dorsal fin. These days any bluegill over 7 inches is considered big, and true one-pounders are rare.

Pumpkinseeds are even more brightly colored than bluegills. They are characterized by a bright orange belly and irregularly distributed orange spots along much of their lower abdomen. The most characteristic feature and the one that sets them apart from bluegills is a bright red crescent-shaped border behind the black spot at the back tip of the gill cover. Quite often the lower half of the head and gill cover is marked with very irregular blue and chestnut striping. They lack the prominent vertical striping along the body that is so often found in bluegills. Pumpkinseeds are normally a bit smaller than bluegills. Bluegills and pumpkinseeds frequently hybridize, and the progeny show characteristics of both species.

Like the other panfish, sunfish enjoy company. Where you find one, you are likely to find others. Nowhere is this more apparent than during their spawning season. Like all members of the sunfish and bass family, sunfish make nests. Sunfish are warm-water fish, and they don't start spawning until the water temperature approaches 70 degrees—

Fig. 8.2.
. . . . . . . . . . . . . . . . . . .

*Bluegill.*

considerably later than bass. The males clear off a circular area of shallow lake bottom about 18 to 24 inches in diameter so that small rocks and gravel line the nest. To clear the nest, they use their tails much like a broom, which results in the formation of a prominent rim of sand and smaller particles around the nest. In contrast to bass, whose nests often are loosely scattered in the same area, sunfish nests, especially those of bluegills, are often crammed right next to one another with only a thin rim between them. Each nest is guarded by a male who is either waiting for a female to join him in spawning or guarding eggs that have already been laid. During the breeding season sunfish, like many other nest-building species, take on a variety of dazzling colors, ranging from bright yellows and oranges to violets to blue greens. The breeding males are much more brightly colored than the females. Nesting male sunfish are very pugnacious, and they will drive away fish many times their size if they approach the nest. The males still tend the nest for a few days after the young have hatched, and they have been seen to pick up adventuresome fry that have strayed from the nest with their mouth and return them to the nest. Once in a while they seem to forget to expel the young from their mouth and swallow them. While the males are busy with housekeeping chores, the females have left the nest and begun to eat in order to replenish their bodies after losing a significant percentage of their weight in eggs.

Early in the season, both before and just after the breeding season, sunfish congregate in shallow waters. After ice-out, when the water temperatures have reached about 50 degrees, they break out of their winter aggregates and move inshore. Here they can be found near the remains of the previous year's vegetation, especially stalks of reeds or submerged sticks, where they feed heavily on insects. During the nesting season the males are usually too busy protecting the nest from intruders to eat, but after the young have hatched, sunfish are more than ready to eat. Sunfish have a tremendously varied diet that consists of anything from insects, snails, leeches, small fish, and crayfish to plant material.

Although sunfish feed throughout the day, they become especially active in the evening or at times when there are insect hatches on the water. It is not uncommon to see the surface of a calm bay dimpled with rings indicating the presence of sunfish sucking up insects that have fallen to the surface. Such times can be a paradise for the fly fisher. Feeding sunfish seem to be almost totally uncritical when it comes to taking a fly or small popper. Although they may show some preference for a certain color, they can be taken on the most miserable-looking flies in your box, and they don't seem to care much whether you messed up your cast or not. The beginner fly fisher could not find a better confidence booster than fishing for sunfish, as fly fishing is by far the most efficient method for catching shallow-water sunfish. I find that it is often ten times more effective than still-fishing with live bait. Besides being more effective, when sunfish are hooked on a fly rod, they put up a terrific fight. They use their wide body to great advantage, as they engage in what can best be described as a circular fight. If sunfish were as big as bass, their fight would put most bass to shame. Another fun way to fish for shallow-water sunfish is with ultralight spinning tackle. For this, use the tiniest jigs, spinners, or crankbaits that you can find, and don't be surprised if you periodically hook up with an occasional large bass in the bargain. It's amazing how often a good-sized bass will go after a tiny bait.

Come summer and warmer water, sunfish are not as easy to catch, and by August you may wonder if all the big ones in the lake have been caught. Smaller sunfish still tend to congregate in schools of 10 to 20 fish, but the larger individuals are more solitary or swim in groups of 2 to 4 individuals. The sunfish's preferred temperature is slightly above 80 degrees, and the smaller fish tend to remain in shallow, weedy water

**Fig. 8.3.**
. . . . . . . . . . . . . . . . . . .

*Sunfish in classic shallow, weedy habitat.* **Left**, *bluegill;* **right**, *pumpkinseed.*

throughout the summer (fig. 8.3). It is rare for a north country lake to get so warm that the small sunfish abandon the shallows. In contrast, it is very common for the larger individuals to be found in water as deep as 20 to 25 feet in lakes with clear water, like Ten Mile Lake. Even though sunfish tend to be homebodies and don't move much from their home base, they still move between shallow and deeper waters during the day. In summer for most of the day, the larger specimens will usually be in deeper water, but they are likely to swim into shallower water during the evening to feed. Because of the nature of Ten Mile Lake, the sunfish fall into two different patterns of behavior. In isolated bays like Lundstrom's Bay and Kenfield Bay, they behave more like sunfish in small, weedy lakes. In the main lake basin they tend to occupy deeper niches, and they are not as likely to be found in larger schools. In the main lake sunfish are seen in the greatest numbers on the tops of bars, where the water is commonly 15 to 25 feet deep. Here, the bottom consists of sand with areas of scattered rocks from 6 to 18 inches in diameter interspersed among patches of *Chara* and coontails.

Sunfish inhabiting the deeper waters are still mightily happy to eat worms, but interestingly, by late summer plant material may constitute a significant portion of their diet. They are definitely known to eat *Chara*, but that alone doesn't suffice to keep them going. They also eat the tips of larger, more luxuriant aquatic vegetation. For the angler who is looking to catch large sunfish, the best strategy is to fish deeper during the late summer period. Here, a tiny jig, sometimes tipped with a fragment of worm, makes an effective presentation, but just a worm on a hook fished at the proper depth is also very productive. In shallower bays or shallow lakes, in general, fly fishing in the evening is still a good bet. Even though late evening fishing is a great time to fish for sunfish, it is worth knowing that sunfish don't stop feeding when it becomes dark. Several studies have shown that sunfish can feed throughout the night. Every once in a while, I catch a sunfish, usually a pumpkinseed, when I am trolling for walleyes at night. This shows that they not only feed after dark but also can be amazingly aggressive in the dark. When I do catch a sunfish at night, it is usually a pumpkinseed that has gone after a Thunderstick lure that is 4½ inches long.

In many lakes sunfish, as well as rock bass, perch, and even northern pike, are infected with some parasites that are readily apparent when one looks at the fish. Probably the most common one, called *Neascus* or *black grub*, appears as tiny black spots that may be distributed all over the skin. Like almost all parasites, *Neascus* has a complex life cycle. The adult form is a flatworm, or fluke, which lives in the mouth of kingfishers. These worms lay eggs that pass into the water. The eggs hatch, and the free-swimming larvae, called *miracidia*, home in on snails. The miracidia reproduce in the snails, and their progeny leave the snails as free-swimming forms called *cercariae*. The cercariae enter the bodies of fish, where the larvae move into the musculature or the skin and turn into cysts, which look like black spots about the size of poppy seeds. When an infected fish is eaten by a kingfisher, the cysts develop into flukes, and the life cycle repeats itself. Although they look ugly, the black-spot parasite is completely noninfective to humans. Even if they are eaten without cooking, they cannot infect people.

Another similar parasite is the yellow grub *(Clinostomum)*. Yellow grubs, which are also seen in the skin and muscles of panfish, are several times larger than black grubs but have a similar life cycle. Adult yellow grubs, which are also flukes, live in the mouth of great blue herons. They lay numerous eggs, which find their way into the water and turn into the miracidia larvae and infect snails. From this intermediate host the next stage in the life cycle, a cercaria, gets into a fish and makes its way into the flesh, where it becomes encysted into the small, yellowish mass anglers see when cleaning fish. Like the black grub, the yellow grub is unsightly but is not infective to humans. When a heron captures an infected fish, the grubs find the environment hospitable and hatch into the adult form, and the cycle begins anew.

By the fall interest in fishing for sunfish almost disappears, and they are able to prepare for winter reasonably undisturbed. As the water gets colder, they move into deeper water and congregate into tight groups. Surprisingly, though, for a warm-water fish, sunfish actively feed during the winter, although their food intake is greatly reduced. In the summer a sunfish may consume up to 35 percent of its weight per week, whereas in the winter they may eat only 1 percent of their weight per week. Sunfish are one of the favorite quarry of ice fishers, and they readily take small live bait or tiny jigs. They remain in tight groups throughout the winter until the water warms up after the ice breaks out.

## Crappies

Crappies are one of the more mysterious members of the sunfish family. There are two species of crappie, the black and the white crappie, and they have different habits (fig. 8.4). Black crappies prefer clear water and somewhat colder temperatures, whereas white crappies are more likely to be found in warmer, turbid water. Although the two species coexist in some southern Minnesota lakes, northern lakes are

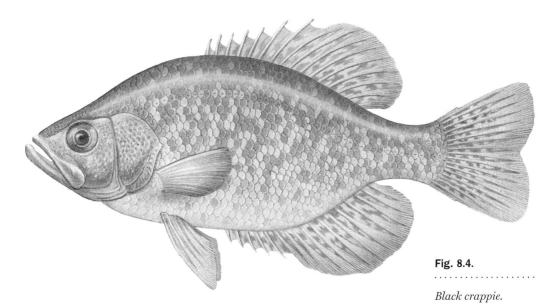

**Fig. 8.4.**

*Black crappie.*

populated almost entirely by black crappies. More than any other game fish, crappies are characterized by boom-and-bust cycles. A lake can be seemingly crappie-less for years, when suddenly for a couple of years everyone catches crappies. These cycles are usually based upon spawning success, much of which may be determined by water temperatures, but competition with other species is also a major factor. Nowhere has this been better demonstrated than in Minnesota's huge Upper and Lower Red Lakes. Once, these lakes were noted for their immense numbers of walleyes, but thanks to overfishing, the walleye populations completely crashed in the late 1990s. This huge ecological void was soon filled by crappies. For several years the crappie population exploded, and anglers regularly caught limits comprised of huge crappies. As of this writing, the walleye population is coming back, and the quality of crappie fishing is already dropping off a bit. Even still, anglers are coming off the lake with some mighty impressive catches of large crappies. Ten Mile Lake is not noted as a major crappie lake, but for those who target them, some nice fish can be caught from the areas that constitute good crappie habitat. I rarely fish specifically for crappies on Ten Mile, but I do catch them incidentally while night fishing for walleyes. These nighttime crappies are usually large; my last one was almost 17 inches long.

Although they share many similarities with other members of the sunfish family, crappies also exhibit some markedly different patterns of behavior. They are much more likely to be found in tight schools than are sunfish. They relate very strongly to cover, and one of the best places to find them is near a submerged tree or among the sticks near the underwater runways of beaver houses. They are also more likely, however, to suspend in midwater than any other member of the sunfish family. For the angler, finding crappies is often more of a challenge than catching them. Once they have been located, still-fishing with minnows or tiny jigs is the standard fishing method.

Although black crappies are not always easy to distinguish from white crappies, no other fish in northern lakes looks like a crappie. They are bigger than sunfish, although in heavily fished lakes large ones are becoming a rarity. A 10- to 12-inch crappie is quite respectable, but in some lakes with stunted populations, it may be rare to see one larger than 9 inches. They are slab sided and very silvery in color, with scattered black and dark green scales that give them a speckled appearance. In some lakes they are very darkly pigmented and can look almost black. They typically have an almost iridescent hue when first taken from the water. Crappies have relatively large eyes that are oriented upward. People who watch crappies' behavior in an aquarium find that they rarely go after food that is placed below them.

Crappies are active shortly after the ice goes out. They move into very shallow water and relate most strongly to the dead stems of bulrushes or other emergent vegetation. They are often found within a few feet from shore. At this time they can be readily taken with flies or with ultralight lures fished at a moderate speed. Crappies are known to have soft mouths, so care must be exercised when bringing them up to and into the boat. When the water temperature approaches the mid-60s, they prepare to spawn.

Crappies are more likely than either bass or sunfish to spawn on soft bottoms and near significant beds of vegetation. Their nests are somewhat smaller than those of sunfish and much smaller than bass nests—often not much more than 10 inches in diameter. Spawning crappies are much less communal than are sunfish, and the nests tend to be spaced 4 to 5 feet apart. Like all members of the sunfish family, the male makes the nest and tends it after the eggs have been laid. Crappie eggs are much more likely to be laid on bits of vegetation than those of the other sunfish.

Once spawning is finished, crappies quickly move into their summer mode of behavior and feeding. More than sunfish or bass, crappies have pronounced feeding periods around sunrise and especially at sunset, as well as after dark. In the evening they sometimes move toward the surface and feed on insects floating on the water. During this time they can be readily caught with dry flies—white being a very good color—but small spinners and ultralight baits also work well for crappies feeding near the surface.

During the day crappies move into deep water, but instead of hugging the bottom, they often suspend midway between the bottom and the surface. In shallower water they relate strongly to dense cover (fig. 8.5). One of the best places to find crappies is beneath floating bogs,

**Fig. 8.5.**
. . . . . . . . . . . . . . . . . . . .
*Crappie swimming in dense cover.*

which can be found on some northern lakes, but they also like dense weed beds, submerged logs, and trees. In reservoirs almost all crappie fishing is done alongside standing submerged timber. In such locations the standard way of fishing for them is to still-fish with small minnows or to fish vertically with tiny jigs, which crappies have a hard time resisting. In many lakes crappies have regular pathways that take them from their deepwater daytime haunts to the shallower feeding grounds. Schools of crappies have a much greater tendency to move from place to place than do most other members of the sunfish family, so finding them in the open water can be something of a challenge. A good fish finder is important for locating crappie schools.

Crappies are very catholic in their choice of food. Because of their long and fine gill rakers, even large crappies can effectively scoop up water fleas *(Daphnia)* and other large zooplankton, but their normal food consists of insects and, as they grow larger, small fish. The larger the crappie, the more fish constitute a major part of its diet. Although small crappies fall prey to a variety of predators, large individuals are relatively safe thanks to their round bodies and prominent spiny fins. Crappies feed readily during the winter, and in many lakes they constitute the bulk of the fish caught through the ice. They are very good eating, so relatively few anglers practice catch-and-release when fishing for crappies.

nimals beneath a lake's surface live in a world very different from our own. The most obvious difference is that they are surrounded by a liquid and not a gas. What goes along with this basic fact? First of all, underwater animals are subject to incredible pressures the deeper they go. Water is 800 times denser than air, and at 30 feet the water pressure is approximately 13 pounds per square inch. When people dive into a lake or the ocean, the water pressure compresses dissolved gas in their blood and tissues, and if they've gone deep enough and they come up too fast, they get the bends—a very painful and dangerous condition caused by the expansion of dissolved gasses in their blood. Fish run into the same thing, but instead of the gas in their blood, their swim bladder expands. Thus, a fish caught from deep water often floats belly up when released after being caught. This phenomenon is especially apparent in northern pike, whose distended swim bladder, which causes a bulge in their belly, is easy to see.

There is a lot more to water than pressure, however. Because water is so dense, sound travels five times faster in water (about 5,000 feet per second) than it does in air (about 1,000 feet per second). In addition to sound, water, because of its higher density, is also a much more efficient medium for transmitting vibrations, which play a large role in the daily life of a fish. Water also does important things with light. The intensity of light is much more strongly attenuated through a given distance in water than it is in air, so that in a typical clear water lake in Minnesota, such as Lake Itasca, the intensity of light 5 feet below the surface may be only $\frac{1}{1,000}$ of what it is at the surface. In addition, when water is stained or turbid, it absorbs specific wavelengths of light so that what one sees underwater takes on totally different hues from what is seen on land (see fig. 2.2). Then there is the matter of smell and taste. It is very hard for us land dwellers to relate how we detect odors in the air to what happens in the water. Think, though, about our sensitivity to even the slightest contamination or additive in a glass of water or to the subtle differences between bottles of red wine, and you can get some idea of what it may be like underwater. Some fish even have taste buds outside their mouth and must be constantly tasting different things throughout the course of their day.

Another sense difficult to imagine but shared by more species of fish than most people realize is an electromagnetic sense. Water, especially salt water, is an effective medium for conducting electric currents, and some fish have exquisitely sensitive organs for sensing (and sometimes producing) minute electrical currents. Two common senses that we take for granted are temperature and pain. To get some idea how important temperature is for an aquatic animal, just think about how long you could keep your hand in a refrigerator where the air temperature is set at 35 degrees, and then think about how long you could keep your hand in a bucket of water at the same temperature. They don't even compare. How fish handle and respond to different temperatures is a long story in itself. Finally, there is the issue of pain, which is principally relevant to the angler. Many of us know what it feels like to have a hook buried in our hand or arm, but do we have any idea what a hook feels like to a fish?

For all of these senses, fish have special adaptations, some of which are like ours and some of which are completely different. The most important thing to keep in mind is that fish have many more ways of sensing their immediate and distant environment than we do. When one sensory system fails, they have several back-up mechanisms that allow them to remain functional despite individual sensory deficits. Knowledge of this is highly relevant to the angler, but for those who do not fish, it should provide a greater appreciation of how the senses affect the pace and various rhythms of life in any body of water.

## Vision
. . . . . . . . . . . . . . . . . . .

With rare exceptions, such as blind cave fish, all fish have functional eyes; but what do they see and how important is it to them? In clear water vision is an important sense for most fish. Any trout angler can tell you that at times these fish can pick up the slightest movement from a person on a bank 30 feet away. If the water is turbid, however, the best eyes in the world won't be of much use, because no fish—or angler— could see more than a few inches in such water. In order to survive under such conditions, a fish has to compensate for its lack of vision by utilizing its other senses.

A fish's eye is in most major respects constructed much like ours (fig. 9.1). Light enters though a transparent cornea and then passes through

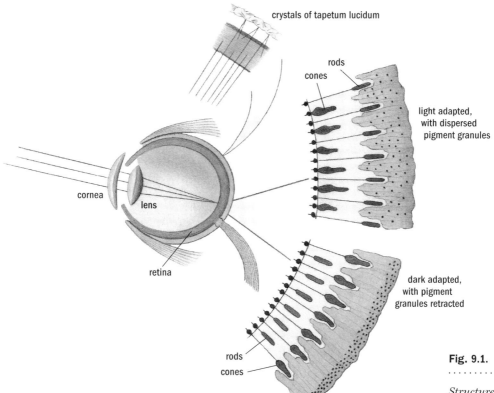

crystals of tapetum lucidum

rods

cones

light adapted, with dispersed pigment granules

dark adapted, with pigment granules retracted

cornea

lens

retina

rods

cones

**Fig. 9.1.**

. . . . . . . . . . . . . . . . . . .

*Structure of a wall-eye's eye.* **Top right**, *blowup of part of the retinal complex, showing the location of the light-reflecting tapetum lucidum.* **Middle and lower right**, *blowup of retina, showing the relationship of pigment granules (black spots) within the pigment epithelium to light levels. In bright light they expand to partially enclose the rod cells. In the dark they retreat, giving the rods maximal access to incident light. Rod and cone cells themselves shift positions under different lighting conditions.*

a lens, which helps to focus the light. The beam of light then hits the retina, which contains the actual light-sensing cells, the rods and cones. When the rods and cones are stimulated, they send messages to the brain, which processes them to produce the image seen. The cones in the retina are color sensors, and in most fish there are three kinds of cone cells, each with a sensitivity to specific wavelengths of light. Usually, these cells are most sensitive to blue, green, or red, giving fish the ability to sense almost all of the color spectrum that we can see. In addition, some fish, such as trout, minnows, suckers, and goldfish, have cones that are sensitive to ultraviolet light. Most species of freshwater fish have not been tested for ultraviolet sensitivity. Ultraviolet sensitivity, which is a relatively recent discovery in fish, is particularly useful to minnows and other fish that feed upon plankton, which reflect ultraviolet rays.

Even though the fundamental organization of a fish's eye is very similar to ours, there are, nevertheless, some notable differences. The first has nothing to do with eyes but, rather, concerns necks. In order to survive in the wild, an individual, whether a fish or a mammal, needs to have good peripheral vision in order to spot either danger or food. Humans have good binocular vision because our eyes both face forward. We then increase our peripheral vision by moving our neck from side to side. Fish, notably, do not have a neck. Having their eyes located on the sides of their head, however, to some extent compensates for their lack of a neck. Because predators often attack their prey from below, their eyes are often oriented slightly upward.

When humans or other mammals want to focus on far or near objects, they do so by contracting special muscles that change the shape of the lens, thus allowing the image to be in focus on the retina. This ability to adjust to different distances is called accommodation, and the increasing stiffness of our lens as we get older is why we can't read a newspaper without glasses any more. Fish don't have the ability to change the shape of their spherical lens. Instead, they have evolved several different mechanisms that can move the lens closer to or farther from the retina. To make things even more complicated, the shape and location of the retina often put certain areas of the retina different distances from the lens. Because of that, some directions of fish vision may be near sighted while others are far sighted, even within the same eye.

Fish eyes also differ from ours in how they deal with different intensities of light. During the course of a normal day, a fish may be exposed to an enormous range of light intensity, from very bright to very dark. Fish eyes cannot constrict the pupils, like those of mammals, so they need to find ways of protecting the retina from excessive light. In addition, many species are very active at night, when the level of light is negligible, and they need to make the most efficient use of the available light.

One way of their dealing with bright light is simply behavioral. Often on bright, calm days fish will move into deeper water or seek shade under a log or in dense vegetation. Another more physiological way involves pigmented cells located behind the retina. These heavily pigmented cells have long projections full of protective pigment granules that protrude among the rods and cones (fig. 9.1). During the day the highly light-sensitive rod cells actually embed themselves in the layer of pigmented cells, and within the pigmented cells themselves, the pigment granules move out into the cellular processes. All of this results in a shield of dark-colored pigment that keeps too much light from impinging upon the rod cells, whereas the cones, which are less sensitive and pick up actual colors, are exposed to the daytime light.

During the night fish face the opposite problem—how to see when light is extremely limited. Some fish simply have larger eyes that allow more light to enter. There is no better example than the walleye, whose huge eyes are wonderfully adapted for night vision. Aside from their large size, which lets in more light, the eyes of walleyes have an even better adaptation. This structure, called the *tapetum lucidum,* is located behind the retina and is a layer of reflecting crystals that acts like a mirror (fig. 9.1). Many animals that are active at night have this structure, as well, so that when you shine a light at a raccoon, a cat, or a deer at night, you see a pronounced bluish reflection. With walleyes, however, the reflection is orange. If you shine a flashlight at a walleye hooked at night, you will see a bright orange spot moving around underwater. This spot is the reflection coming back from its tapetum lucidum. When light first enters the eye it hits the retina, stimulating rods and cones, but the light that isn't picked up by these cells passes through the retina and is effectively lost in ordinary eyes. With animals that have a tapetum lucidum, the light that passes through the retina is not lost but reflected back onto the retina for a second time, resulting in the rod and cone cells' being stimulated a second time from the same source of light (fig. 9.1). One disadvantage of this mechanism, though, is a reduction in the acuity of the visual image. Nevertheless, the fact that so many animals have a tapetum lucidum suggests that it is more advantageous to see a somewhat fuzzy nighttime image than not to see it at all.

Regarding night vision, conventional wisdom has it that in very dim light the cones are not sensitive enough to respond to the small amount of light and that light reception is taken over completely by the rods, which are much more light sensitive but only see things in shades of gray. Certainly, in our human experience this is the case, and it has been assumed that this is the case with all animals. Recent research suggests, however, that the situation may not be this simple. A few years ago a group of Swedish researchers challenged the current dogma when they showed that a species of hawkmoth could distinguish blue and yellow from all shades of gray in light conditions corresponding to dim starlight. Later, they showed that nocturnal gekkos can distinguish blue from gray in moonlight. Other researchers have shown that sunfish can see some colors in near darkness.

Over the years, I have begun to wonder if walleyes might also have some ability to distinguish certain colors at night because of the greater success of certain colored baits at night. According to one of the standard texts on fish biology, there is some evidence that retinas of some fish have a small population of highly light-sensitive cones that might allow them to discriminate among certain colors even in very low levels of light. Interestingly, walleyes have about the biggest cones that have been found in any animal, and the light that gets to some of the rod cells has to travel through cones before reaching the rods. This sets up an anatomical situation that would place cone cells directly in the pathway of night vision. In addition, there exists a phenomenon, called the *Purkinje shift,* in which, during the transition from daylight to nighttime vision, not only do the cells of the retina become more sensitive to light but sensitivity to light of different wavelengths shifts toward light at the blue end of the spectrum. Whether this means that the fish can actually see blue as a color or can just pick it out more effectively among a spectrum of gray shades is not known.

At a practical level, this scientific data may explain something I have noticed over many years of nighttime fishing on Ten Mile Lake. A few years ago I was looking at the group of baits that are my all-time best and most consistent producers for nighttime fishing, and almost 80 percent of them are partly or all blue. It may be years before the idea of some nighttime color vision in fish is investigated in a scientific research laboratory, but from a lifetime of experience as a research scientist, I have learned that it is never wise to say that something in nature is impossible.

Despite the amazing adaptations of the eyes of fish for life underwater, many species of fish can get along amazingly well without using their vision. Some species rely quite heavily on eyesight for capturing prey, whereas others, especially those living in turbid water, make use of other senses for their daily routines. One day the importance of sensory back-up systems was impressed on me when I caught a 5-pound largemouth bass that was blind in both eyes. Yet it was in amazingly good shape.

## Hearing and Vibration

It is hard for us as humans to appreciate what it must be like to hear underwater, largely because the media (water and air) are so different. Because water is in a different physical state from air—being much denser and far more incompressible—things that we could never pick up in air are a daily part of the existence of aquatic animals. The fact that sound travels 5 times as fast in water as it does in air has already been mentioned, but in addition, water is 14,000 times less compressible than is air. This means that vibration is a much more important sense for a fish than it is for humans. We can feel massive air displacements, like that which occurs when we pass a semitrailer going the opposite direction on the highway, but we often don't pick up much more subtle displacements of air. One interesting analogy comes from the world of music. It is often said that we feel almost as much as we hear the notes on the lowest register of a large pipe organ, and musicians are very aware of "bass groupies," who seem particularly attuned to that lower part of the ensemble. There seems to be a sympathetic vibration between parts of the body and low musical notes.

Such sensations are greatly magnified in water, so much so that fish have evolved a special system for picking up vibration. It involves the lateral line, a strip of specialized scales running from head to tail (fig.

9.2A). These scales, each marked by a tiny dark dot, are the external manifestation of a long canal that has specialized vibration receptors arrayed along its length. In water the detection of vibration and sound merges from one to the other without a break into what are known as near-field and far-field domains. As the name implies, near-field is a region close to the source of sound, and far-field is farther away. The near-field is where vibration sense dominates, and the far-field is the region where hearing comes into play.

What is near-field and what is far-field depends upon the wavelength of the sound. Specifically, the boundary between the near- and far-fields is one-sixth the wavelength of the sound. For example, at a frequency of 100 hertz (Hz), somewhat more than an octave below middle C, the wavelength in water is 15 meters (about 49 feet). Divided by 6, this comes out to be a bit over 8 feet, so that in this case the source of the sound must be within 8 feet of the fish in order for the vibration sense of the fish to come into play. For those who have taken the time to check this calculation, don't forget that, since sound in water travels 5 times faster than it does in air, the wavelength at a given hertz is correspondingly longer. At 1,000 Hz, the upper range of hearing of most freshwater game fish, the near-field boundary is less than a foot. Frequencies produced by swimming animals are typically in the range of 3 to 40 Hz, which means that the near-field sense is likely much more important than is hearing for detecting fish or other animals in the vicinity. The lateral line is most effective in picking up frequencies no greater than 200 Hz (fig. 9.2B).

Regardless of the source and amount, changes from sound or vibratory waves are picked up by specialized structures called *neuromasts* (fig. 9.2A). Neuromasts contain cells (called *hair cells*) with tiny hairlike structures (called *cilia*) protruding from their surfaces. When the fluid surrounding a neuromast is displaced by a sound or pressure wave, the cilia move in a certain direction. This causes a nerve fiber that is connected to each hair cell to send a signal to the brain that lets the brain know what has happened to that particular cell. When the signals from hundreds of hair cells are received by the brain, the brain integrates all of that information and is able to form a type of image that tells the fish what is happening in its external environment. For instance, it may signal the presence of a huge predator or a small prey in the area. Most neuromasts are situated in a system of canals that course through the head and along the lateral line, but in goldfish, for instance, there are also over 1,000 free neuromasts on the head and 6 to 9 on each scale. With this scientific background, let's now look specifically at how a fish detects both vibration and sound.

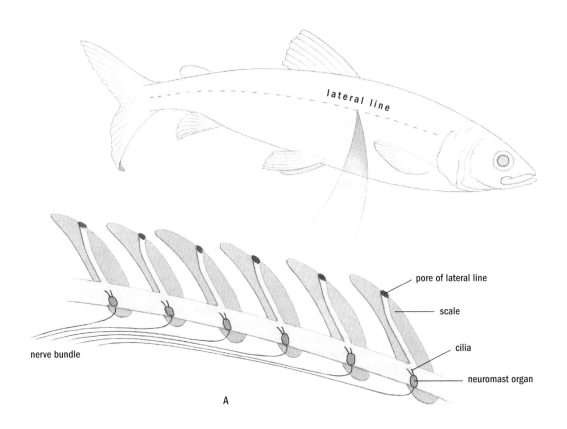

lateral line

pore of lateral line

scale

cilia

nerve bundle

neuromast organ

A

For near-field sense, essentially vibration, the fish utilizes its system of lateral-line canals, which is distributed over the head and body (fig. 9.2A). This system is spread over the length of the body in order to provide a long baseline for analyzing the location of the vibrations. The very fine lateral-line canals are filled with liquid, and when a fish is exposed to a source of vibration within the near-field, hair cells in the neuromasts along the lateral-line system become activated and signal to the brain not only that a vibration is taking place somewhere nearby but also approximately where the source is located. This information is independent of vision and could alert the fish to be on the lookout for whatever was the source of the vibration. During the day the eyes may then take over, but at night vibration sense may be the major way in which a hungry walleye begins to narrow in on a trolled crankbait. Some fish utilize their vibratory sense to detect insects struggling on the surface of the water, and schooling fish use it to orient themselves to the other members of the school.

If the source of sound is beyond the near-field, then the more conventional sense of hearing comes into play. One important question is, What can a fish really hear? This depends upon the species, but generally, fish operate in the lower ranges of conventional hearing. The range of human hearing is from about 20 Hz at the lower end to about 18,000

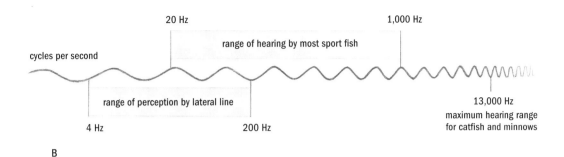

20 Hz                                    1,000 Hz

range of hearing by most sport fish

cycles per second

range of perception by lateral line

4 Hz                        200 Hz

13,000 Hz
maximum hearing range
for catfish and minnows

B

Hz at the upper. The older we get, the lower our upper range becomes. Women, in general, seem to have better upper ranges than do men (my wife hears things that I am totally oblivious to). Dogs have a much higher upper range of hearing than do humans, which is why we can't hear dog whistles. As for game fish, walleyes and perch may not hear much above 600 Hz, whereas bass may be able to pick up sounds at 1,000 Hz. One group of fish, however, has very acute hearing. This group includes members of the minnow (carp and goldfish belong in this family) and catfish families. These fish have evolved a special series of bones, called *Weberian ossicles,* that connect their swim bladder to their middle ear and greatly magnify their sensitivity to sound. These fish can detect sound frequencies as high as 13,000 Hz.

When a human is exposed to a sound, the sound waves enter the ear canal and cause the eardrum to vibrate. The eardrum is connected to a string of three middle ear bones, which are connected to another membrane that lines part of the inner ear. The vibrations of this membrane set in motion the inner-ear fluid, which stimulates hair cells that are tuned specifically for the wavelength of the sound. The hair cells then send off a message to the auditory centers in the brain, which interpret it as a specific note.

Hearing works quite differently for a fish. Without external ears or ear canals, the sound first has to get to the inner ear. This can occur because the body of a fish is acoustically transparent, and sound waves pass right through it, with the body vibrating much like the water as the sound waves pass by. One major structure in the fish that isn't acoustically transparent is the otolith, or inner ear bone. The otolith is actually a crystal, composed mainly of calcium carbonate embedded in a proteinaceous matrix, that rests on top of a bed of hair cells within the inner ear (fig. 9.3). The hair cells are oriented in different directions and are attuned to different frequencies. When sound waves passing through the fish's body strike the denser otoliths, they vibrate and stimulate the underlying hair cells, thus initiating the signal that will go to the auditory centers of the brain. In the species that contain Weberian ossicles, these

**Fig. 9.2.**

*Structure of the lateral line.* **A,** *Changes in water pressure owing to vibration are transmitted through the pores in the lateral line system and cause the cilia on the neuromasts to bend. This sets off a neural signal that is transmitted to the brain.* **B,** *This scale shows the range of fish hearing and that of vibration detection by the lateral line, as measured in hertz (Hz).*

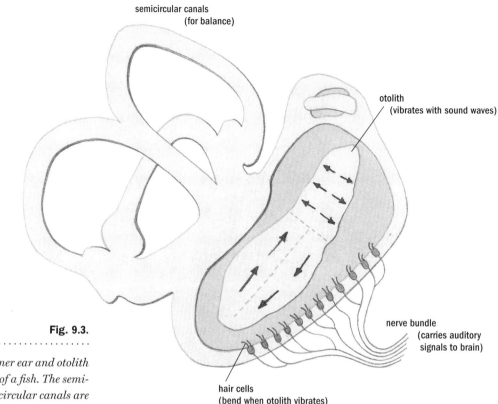

semicircular canals
(for balance)

otolith
(vibrates with sound waves)

nerve bundle
(carries auditory
signals to brain)

hair cells
(bend when otolith vibrates)

**Fig. 9.3.**

. . . . . . . . . . . . . . . . . . .

*Inner ear and otolith of a fish. The semicircular canals are used for balance, just as they are in humans. The otolith rests upon a mat of well-ordered hair cells. When sound vibrations get to a fish, the otolith vibrates, stimulating the hair cells to send signals along the auditory nerve to hearing centers in the brain.*

bones magnify the sound waves hitting the swim bladder and provide a much richer spectrum of sound to the inner ear than occurs in species lacking this adaptation. Like that of the human, the inner ear of a fish also contains semicircular canals and associated structures that act as gravity receptors for balance and also detect acceleration or deceleration.

How does a fish make use of its hearing? We know that a number of fish and other animals in lakes make noise, often monosyllabic grunts or clicks, and fish are able to detect them. In some cases sounds are used for communication, especially during mating season. Sound is also used to locate prey, and for almost two decades many fishing lures have been equipped with sound chambers designed to attract fish. These range from subtle clicks to loud buzzing noises, and fish react differently to them depending upon their mood. Sound is especially important in turbid water or after dark, when the effectiveness of vision is greatly reduced. Many times sound will attract a fish's attention and generally localize the bait, but when the fish gets close enough, vision or vibration sense take over as it makes its strike at its target.

One unexpected recent finding, in view of the generally low range of hearing in most fish, is that several members of the herring family, such as shad, alewives, and herring, are able to detect ultrasound in ranges from 50 to 180 kHz. How they do this is not known, but they are particularly sensitive to wavelengths of 90 to 100 kHz, which is also the frequency of the ultrasonic signals emitted by porpoises for echolocation of prey.

## Seal Whiskers and Wake-Tracking Fish Trails

One of the more unusual adaptations for life underwater came from studies in Germany on how seals are able to find herring, one of their favorite snacks, in often dirty harbor waters. Some oceanic mammals, like certain species of whales and dolphins, have evolved a sense of echolocation, much like bats use in the air to find insects. Seals, however, are not equipped with this sense. Instead, they have long whiskers that are exquisitely sensitive to any displacement. In addition to helping them figure out the nature of the physical objects that they may contact in the water, their whiskers are very sensitive detectors of water turbulence. When a fish or any aquatic animal swims, it leaves behind a trail of turbulent water. This is just a miniature version of the large swirls of water created by oars or a canoe paddle. The swirling water behind a swimming goldfish lasts for about 30 seconds, whereas that of a herring can persist as far as 400 feet behind the fish. Once a seal happens upon the turbulence left behind by a fish, it uses its whiskers to trail its quarry (called *wake-tracking*) until it catches up to it. In experiments on seals, when their whiskers were taped down, they lost their ability to trail swimming fish.

Wake-tracking is not just confined to seals. Studies on catfish have shown that they can locate a swimming prey as far as 50 body lengths away—probably by a combination of wake-tracking and smelling or tasting the chemical secretions of the fish. It may also have some relevance to nighttime trolling for walleyes. In my experience, when I use pure crankbaits for trolling at night, walleyes normally hook themselves on the front hooks. If the crankbait is tipped with a leech or piece of a worm, however, then the fish are almost invariably caught by the back hook. This observation can be related, on one hand, to laboratory studies in which visually based attacks are commonly made from the side or toward the front of the prey. When a predator follows a wake or an olfactory trail, on the other hand, it gradually approaches the prey from behind and ultimately engulfs it. One of the recent hot baits for walleyes is called a *thumper tail*—a plastic minnow with a flat tail that moves from side to side or up and down with a pronounced thumping action. One wonders if the success of these baits is due to their setting up a trail that larger fish follow.

## Taste and Smell

Like hearing and vibration sense, taste and smell are much more closely connected in water than they are on land. Although fish have olfactory pits (their equivalent of a nose) and taste buds, their senses of taste and smell both depend upon detecting small molecules dissolved in water. Some species of fish (e.g., bullheads) have over 4,000 taste buds scattered all over the surface of their body. Even within their mouth, taste buds are not as a rule located on the tongue but, instead, are scattered throughout the inner lining of the mouth.

Taste and odor affect fish in a variety of ways. One important function is to alert them to the presence of food. A number of fish physiologists feel that detection of specific chemicals, such as amino acids, by the olfactory organ or external taste buds acts as a general alert to a fish, and then other senses, like vibration or sight, take over for more accurate discrimination and localization. But when potential food is very close by, odor may be the final trigger that stimulates the fish to bite. Once a fish has grabbed an object, the taste buds in the lining of its mouth allow the fish to quickly decide whether the morsel is edible or not. If the decision is negative, the object is quickly expelled.

There has been tremendous interest among fishing tackle companies in the potential of taste and odor for enhancing the effectiveness of fishing baits of various sorts. It is possible to impregnate plastic baits with tasty or odoriferous substances, and all sorts of concoctions, ranging from salts to fish extracts to mostly secret formulas, have been integrated into plastic baits. Other kinds of odorants are available in spray-on or dropper-type packages, and these can be applied to any type of lure. With respect to fishing, the slower a bait is retrieved, the greater the chance that an associated odor may be an effective attractant. With rapid retrieves of casts or high trolling speeds, the time required for an odorant to diffuse through water is not likely to be fast enough to make much difference to the fish.

Fish vary considerably in the importance of taste and odor to their everyday lives. Members of the catfish family are legendary in their attraction to odors. Their eyesight tends to be very poor, so other senses pick up the slack. Catfish have a well-developed ability to home in on odors, especially in rivers, and that accounts for their susceptibility to the horrendously smelly stinkbaits that serious catfish anglers concoct. The gustatory sense of channel catfish is also particularly well developed, ranging from 100 to 10,000 times greater than that of most other freshwater fish. Trout and salmon also have highly developed senses of smell, about which more will be said later. Sight feeders like northern pike and muskies don't seem to react much to odors. Walleyes are also toward the low end of the scale. Bass are in the middle, although by far the vast majority of scents and scented baits are marketed to bass anglers.

Odors not only alert fish to the presence of food but also warn the fish of danger. Some trout fishing guides in New Zealand are convinced that a person wading bare-legged through a stream will spook the trout for as much as a quarter mile downstream. A well-documented protective mechanism among minnows and some smaller fish is the release of a warning chemical from the damaged skin, called *Schreckstoff* ("alarm substance" in German), when one of them is grabbed by a predator. When the other members of the school detect this odor, they immediately go into protective modes of behavior to avoid becoming meals themselves. There is increasing evidence that odors given off by certain species of female fish play a role in reproduction by either attracting or arousing the males. For fish like bass and sunfish, in which the male tends the young in the nest for a few days after hatching, the fry may emit an odor that allows the parent to recognize that these are young of the same species and not food to be eaten.

One of the fascinating uses of the sense of smell in members of the trout family is in homing. Salmon and trout lay their eggs in streams, and the young live in their natal stream for some time before going downriver to mature in the ocean or one of the Great Lakes. They spend several years in the large body of water before they are ready to reproduce. There is considerable evidence that they return to the stream in which they were born for spawning and that olfactory cues are important in guiding them to their home streams. There have been several experiments in which young salmon in the Great Lakes region were experimentally conditioned to specific chemicals. When these chemicals were released into a stream, the adult fish in the lakes were attracted to that stream.

## Electromagnetic Sense

One important, but poorly understood, sense is the bioelectromagnetic sense. All living beings are surrounded by very low-level electric fields, but most animals, as well as humans, are oblivious to them. The production or sensation of electricity is very important, however, for some species of fish. In addition to the static electric fields, some fish, like the electric eel or torpedo ray, have the ability to produce whopping doses of electricity—enough to stun a large animal—by electric organs, which are modified muscles. Other fish, mainly species that live in very muddy tropical rivers, produce weak electrical signals that are used in ordinary communication among members of the species.

Sharks and rays, in particular, have an extremely highly developed electromagnetic sense, which is used for both navigation and for locating prey. In fact, some rays use their bioelectric sense to find small flounders that normally live buried in the sand. Researchers have placed very weak sources of electric fields beneath the sand of aquariums and have found that rays will dive at the source of the electric field, thinking that it is something to eat.

Even in northern freshwaters, there are fish with a well-developed bioelectric sense. Lampreys in the Great Lakes use their electric sense for locating prey from intermediate distances. The long paddle of paddlefish, those primitive ungainly creatures that live in large rivers like the Missouri, is a highly specialized electroreceptive organ that is used for navigation and localization of the plankton upon which they feed. The lake sturgeon, another primitive fish found in some northern lakes, also has a functional electrical sense. Of the species that are found in typical north country lakes, such as Ten Mile, bullheads are the most commonly encountered electric fish. Dutch researchers have recently shown that in brown bullheads the head is electronegative and the tail electropositive, with a field strength in the range of 200 μv. The strength of their electric field peaks at 4:00 AM and reaches a low point at 2:00 PM. When these fish were stressed in the laboratory merely by the presence of people, the electric fields increased as much as fivefold. Since catfish have highly sensitive electroreceptors, it may be that they use their electric sense for some forms of communication.

Salmon anglers in the Pacific Northwest have used electricity to improve their catches. They initially noticed that some boats made better catches than others and found a correlation between the electric fields surrounding their boats and bait and the number of salmon caught. They found that salmon are attracted to a weakly positive charge and are repelled by a negative charge. There are now commercially available riggings that will provide a proper electrical field for a boat in salt water. Because freshwater isn't as good a conductor of electricity as salt water, it is not known if there are any reasonable applications of this method to freshwater trolling.

## Pain
. . . . . . . . . . . . . . . . . . .

One of the highly controversial issues in fishing and animal rights circles these days is whether or not fish feel pain. Articles of varying scientific quality have supported viewpoints on either side of this question. To provide a conclusion before presenting the evidence, I would have to say that we still don't know.

There are two major elements to feeling pain. One, called *nociception,* is the detection of a noxious stimulus by the body. The other is the sensation of feeling pain. Nociception is a primitive response that is seen even in animals without a brain, and it is often followed by an avoidance response. The sensation of pain, however, requires some mental processing, and different individuals may register different degrees of pain to a stimulus of the same intensity. The problem of what is pain and how much pain there is occurs in medical clinics every day. If you have gone to a doctor with a painful body part, the doctor will likely ask you to rate the pain on a scale of 1 to 10. The problem is that people's ranking of pain varies all over the map, so that all the doctor knows is how much you seem to be bothered by the pain.

Most vertebrates and many invertebrates can detect noxious stimuli through sets of nociceptors. Interestingly, nociceptors have not been found in a number of sharks and rays that have been tested, and these species do not seem to feel pain. I remember as a kid talking to an angler on Long Island Sound who said that earlier in the day he had caught a dogfish shark and had slit its belly open with a knife and thrown it back into the water. Within a few minutes he had caught the same shark, which had again gone after his bait.

For years physiologists have been uncertain whether or not bony fish possess nociceptors or feel pain. One recent study on rainbow trout reported finding five different types of sensory receptors in the face and lips. Some responded to touch or pressure; others, to temperature extremes or mechanical or chemical stimuli. When bee venom or acetic acid was injected into the lips with a small hypodermic syringe, which was about the same size as a small hook, the fish that were injected with venom rubbed their lips against gravel and the sides of the tank. This behavior was interpreted as indicating that fish do feel pain. Of relevance to the angler, fish that were injected with physiological saline responded no differently from fish that were merely handled in the same way, indicating that they weren't greatly bothered by the pinprick of the needle. Can we conclude that the fish that were injected with venom experienced discomfort and those that were injected with saline did not? It's hard to say. One could tentatively conclude that these trout had the ability to detect a noxious chemical stimulus but did not respond to mechanically induced pain. Further testing will have to be done before any firm conclusions can be drawn.

My own observations of many thousands of hooked fish lead me to suspect that fish hooked deeply in the throat region below the gill covers (which is where the heart is located) feel a deep type of pain, called *visceral pain,* because they often stop struggling when they get hooked in this region. Nonetheless, I would frankly be surprised if a fish either feels or at least is greatly bothered by a simple puncture wound in the mouth region, because I suspect that such trauma almost always occurs when a fish swallows a spiny-rayed fish like a perch or sunfish. Just look at what kinds of spiny plants some herbivorous animals eat, and you will quickly realize that what would be tremendously uncomfortable to humans is not necessarily bothersome to a sheep or goat.

Another element of the pain story that has hardly been touched on for fish is the extent to which opioids (naturally occurring painkillers), which are produced by the brains of many higher animals, may or may not play a role in the physiology of a fish. It is sobering how much we still don't know about what would seem to be a rather straightforward question concerning how fish function and respond to various stimuli. Before the question of pain is settled, a lot more scientific research will have to be done.

## Putting It All Together
. . . . . . . . . . . . . . . . . . .

Where does all this leave us? Probably the most important point is that aquatic creatures, in general, and fish, in particular, are endowed with a far greater variety of sensory systems than we are, but some individual sensory systems, such as vision and hearing, may not be as acute as ours. Fish also are able to integrate the input from several sensory systems as the basis for their actions. When the effectiveness of one system is compromised, others pick up the slack and make up for the missing function. For example, at night or when the water in a river becomes silty after a storm, the effectiveness of vision is considerably reduced, but under these circumstances the senses of hearing, vibration, taste, and smell compensate for the lack of vision, allowing the fish to remain almost fully functional. How all of these sensory inputs get processed and integrated into a coordinated behavioral response by a fish with a, literally, pea-sized brain is a real mystery.

Most fish have one or two dominant senses, but the others still act to modulate behavior. Understanding this concept is critical for the angler because, once you locate where a fish is likely to be, it is necessary first to attract it and then trigger it to strike at your bait. The most successful anglers either consciously or unconsciously build several sensory stimuli into their presentations, whether by the color of a lure, the type of retrieve, or the addition of sound, vibration, or odor.

With all that scientists have learned about fish senses, some major mysteries remain. Probably the biggest are how weather or lunar cycles affect fish behavior. I remember a radio interview of a restaurant owner from Gary, Indiana, who kept an aquarium containing Lake Michigan perch in his restaurant. Even though these fish were in a windowless room, he said that he could always tell that a storm was approaching by the way the fish lined up in the aquarium. We have no idea if periods of intense activity or periods of almost inert inactivity in fish are mediated by a known sensory system or if there are ways that a fish senses elements of its environment that we haven't even yet imagined. Even though we don't understand many aspects of fish behavior, the success of any angler is improved if he or she learns to think like a fish or at least gain some familiarity with how they react to different aspects of their environment. This can't all be learned from books. Just as important is keeping your eyes and brain open to tiny clues that you run across when you are on the water.

Nothing better characterizes a north country lake than the haunting call of a loon penetrating the late evening dusk. As long as loons and humans have interacted, loons have held a special place in the psyche and mythology of the people who share the northern lakes with them. That connection continues to this day. For many vacationers the high point of their stay at the lake is listening to the conversations of loons or watching a loon diving for its dinner and guessing where it will come up. The Canadians have honored the loon by placing its imprint on their dollar coin (called the *loonie*), and after much acrimonious discussion taking several more weeks than it did to pass the state budget, the Minnesota legislature in 1961 designated the loon as the state bird.

Ten Mile Lake is blessed with large numbers of loons. On almost any summer evening one can see groups of one or two dozen socializing in the middle of the lake. This is due in large part to the presence of the dwarf ciscoes in the lake (see chapter 4). These small silvery fish are the perfect meal size for loons, and because of the huge numbers of ciscoes in Ten Mile, loons fly in from neighboring lakes to fish and then just hang out together. Despite the large numbers of loons that visit the lake, the number of permanent residents on Ten Mile is much smaller. Many smaller lakes in the 50- to 200-acre range typically host only a single family of loons.

## Something about Loons

Loons are among the most primitive birds on earth, with close ancestors going back tens of millions of years. Loons are found in the northern regions all around the earth, but the loon family consists of only five species. The one that summers in our northern states and southern Canada is the common loon,

*Gavia immer.* Gaviidae in Minneapolis is the only shopping center I know of which is named for the Latin family name of a bird.

A full-grown loon is a large bird, almost a yard long from the tip of its bill to the ends of its feet when stretched out. Its wingspan is slightly over 50 inches, and adults weigh between 6 and 12 pounds. Their summertime color pattern is unmistakable. With a jet-black head and beak and a white-ribbed collar on its black neck, there is a sharp line where the black neck gives way to a stark white breast. The back and wings are black punctuated with prominent small white squares or dots all over. In contrast to most birds, it is almost impossible even for experts to distinguish males from females by their coloration. Another distinctive up-close feature of loons is their striking red eyes. Like most larger birds, loons are long lived. Although it has been hard to follow individual birds over the course of a lifetime, most ornithologists estimate the lifespan of a wild loon to be up to 30 years.

Loons are purely aquatic creatures, and with the exception of nesting, they very rarely are on the land. In keeping with this, their body is exquisitely designed for swimming and diving. Their large paddle-shaped feet are positioned far back on their body, and they cannot walk like most birds. If they do have to travel on land, they must run; if they walk, their chest brushes against the ground. They are visual feeders and use their eyes almost exclusively when chasing fish. For this reason loons are normally found only on lakes with clear water. In contrast to most birds, their skeleton is quite dense. Typical flying birds have pneumatic air spaces in their long bones to reduce their weight for flying, but these spaces are absent in the bones of loons. Such a dense skeleton is a very effective adaptation for diving, but it requires loons to adapt their flying style to conform to their unusually configured bodies.

Loons have sharp and powerful beaks, which are used both in fishing and in defending their territories. A major component of the head is a pair of very large salt glands, one running alongside each side of the skull. These glands are of crucial importance when they are in salt water. Loons, like many sea birds, are able to drink salt water. The salt glands are designed to tremendously concentrate the salt and then secrete it as a prominent stream that runs along their face, thus removing the excess salt from their bodies.

Anyone who has seen a loon fly from the surface of a lake knows that getting into the air is not easy for them. With a lot of wing flapping and running over the surface of the water, they finally clear the water after a several-hundred-yard take-off run. In fact, if a loon lands on too small of a pond, it might not have sufficient clearance to get into the air and can get stuck there. Like airplanes, they head into the wind when taking flight. Once in the air, loons fly very rapidly—typically around 75 MPH air speed and at times up to 100 MPH. They reach these speeds by flapping their wings very rapidly—about 260 beats per minute. Such rapid wing beats are necessary to compensate for both their dense bones and their small wing-to-body weight ratio—the smallest of any flying bird. Yet, loons can migrate over long distances. If you are fortunate to have a loon fly directly overhead, you can easily hear the whistling sound of the air caused by its rapidly flapping wings.

One of the constant activities of a loon is preening. This consists of stroking each feather on its body with its bill and, in doing so, straightening the individual barbs or veins of the feathers. Before doing so, the loon will either wet its beak in the water or reach back with its bill to an oil gland (uropygial gland) located at the base of its tail. This oily substance sticks to the bill and is then transferred to the feathers when the loon preens. To oil its head feathers, the loon deposits some of the oil on its back and then bends its head and neck backward and rubs the deposited oil onto the head feathers. All of this activity preserves the integrity of its feathery coating, which serves as both insulation and streamlining when the loon swims or dives. When a loon has finished a preening session, lasting perhaps 10 to 15 minutes, it commonly rises out of the water and flaps its wings a couple of times along with wagging its tail, signifying the end of the preening session. The net result is a loon that is prepared to dive after fish or crayfish.

When a loon is in its fishing mode, you may see it slowly swimming with its beak and the bottom part of its head underwater. When doing this, the loon is scouting about for fish or some other aquatic prey. When it sees a fish, the loon quickly submerges and begins chasing its prey. As it dives, its feathers are compressed, and its wings are held tightly to its body. In contrast to penguins, loons do not use their wings to assist them in diving. Rather, the propulsion and much of the steering is done by their large paddle-shaped feet. While diving after a fish, it maintains constant visual contact with its prey, and to do so, it must often move its head and neck to keep the fish in focus. If the fish makes a turn, the loon will follow, using mainly its feet, but if the turn is a very sharp one, it may use its wings as a brief stabilizer and rudder. The motions of the feet in both propulsion and turning are not unlike the moves one makes with a paddle to steer a canoe. Although loons may dive as far as 100 feet deep—they have been caught in fish nets placed 75 feet deep—most of their dives are less than 15 to 20 feet from the surface. A typical feeding dive lasts a bit less than 45 seconds. As protection from the high water pressure when diving, loons have flaps that close over their nostrils, keeping water from forcing its way into their nostrils. They also have interlocking bony processes joining their ribs, an adaptation that keeps their ribs from collapsing under the high water pressure of a deep dive.

Loons can eat up to a hundred small fish per day. A diving loon typically grabs a fish crossways just behind the gills. Firm pressure in that area temporarily paralyzes a fish (you can do the same thing with a fish that you are trying to unhook) and allows the loon to rearrange the fish so that it can be swallowed headfirst. Loons will eat most kinds of fish, but common quarries are yellow perch or small members of the whitefish family. In the Great Lakes alewives are favorites. Ciscoes and alewives are particularly desirable because of both their high nutritional content and the fact that, with their soft fin rays, they can be swallowed more easily. Most of the fish that a loon eats are less than 10 inches long, but they have been known to stuff themselves with fish as long as 18 inches. Loons swallow small fish when they are underwater, but with larger fish, since they cannot hold their breath long enough, they come to the surface and rearrange the fish so that it can be swallowed. Especially in the early morning during breeding season, loons are partial to crayfish and will often begin the day with a crayfishing expedition in the shallow waters before heading out to the main lake basin. It appears that loons do not have taste buds, so they savor their food by touch rather than by taste. One wonders if this same arrangement is how seagulls and vultures can stand to eat the rotten food that provides the bulk of their diet. Because loons hunt almost entirely with their eyes, they stop feeding at sunset.

One of the things that loons or any other swimming or diving bird must have is insulation from cold water temperatures. For most of their body, the close covering of oiled feathers provides a dead air space serving as wonderful insulation against the coldest water. They are left with one physiological problem—how to keep from losing excessive body heat through their large fanlike feet, much as elephants lose excessive heat by radiation from their big ears. In the case of loons and other aquatic birds, heat loss is dealt with by a striking anatomical and physiological adaptation called *countercurrent flow*. In order for such a system to work properly, the arteries leading to the feet must run parallel and close to the veins carrying blood away from the feet. With this arrangement the warm arterial blood heading toward the feet gives up its heat to the venous blood going the opposite direction back into the body. As a result the temperature of the feet is much lower than that of the rest of the body, which allows birds to swim in open icy water without going into severe overall hypothermia.

## Loon Calls

. . . . . . . . . . . . . . . . . . . . .

Nothing about loons is more memorable than their calls, which have a truly visceral impact on many people. Once you know what a loon sounds like, you realize how many times brief, almost subliminal segments of loon calls are used in movies or even advertisements on radio or television to elicit moods of fear, tension, or otherworldliness. Yet, to hear loons calling in their natural habitat is to unconsciously be drawn into their conversation, almost as an aural participant.

Those who have studied loon calls have subdivided them into four main types with several variations within each. These are the hoot, the wail, the tremolo, and the yodel. These have been wonderfully captured and dissected in the record *Voices of the Loon,* which I recommend picking up since the pages of a book cannot do justice to this topic.

The hoot is a short, single note that loons most commonly use among family members or in social gatherings. It has been described as a contact call or means of checking in, essentially saying, "I'm here. Are you OK?" Wintering loons are surprisingly nonvocal, and the hoot is about the only noise that they utter.

The wail is, in its simplest form, a single, long note, but a wail can progress up the scale to a second, higher note and sometimes a third, even higher note. This simple vocalization, often sounding almost mournful, is to many people the quintessential loon call. This is the call of loons making contact with one another at a distance. For years we had a small bichon frisé who spent most of his life on a soft pillow or in someone's lap. Mopsy was totally oblivious to any sound emanating from a radio or television set, with two exceptions. If he ever heard the sound of a loon's wail coming from the set, his ears instantly pricked up, and he was brought to full attention. Parenthetically, the other exception was the theme music from the TV show *M\*A\*S\*H,* which caused him to sway his head in time with the music. The wail often has the same effect on people, instantly transporting them to a different state of consciousness. Loons use the wail in certain types of family situations, like signaling for relief during nesting, but the wail is often the opening vocal salvo of an evening loon chorus. It is then followed by more complex vocalizations. When the chorus is finished, it is likely to wind down with a few more wails.

The tremolo, or laugh, is a more complex call, which has been subdivided into three basic types, which are much better listened to than described on paper. The tremolo comes in many shapes and may be used for many different purposes. At one level it is emitted when a loon is disturbed or frightened. If I am trolling at night and approach a sleeping loon, it will sometimes utter a very short and soft tremolo before it begins swimming slowly away from the approaching boat. The tremolo is used when something or someone encroaches upon a loon's territory, especially during the nesting season or when the young are still small. For those who don't have access to a recording of loon sounds, the tremolo is the only call made by flying loons. The tremolo is often the voice used by a pair of loons in nocturnal duets.

The last loon call is the yodel, which is an aggressive call emitted only by males, especially during confrontations over territorial borders. Their yodel is sufficiently distinctive to identify individual males. The yodel does not change appreciably over the years, and it is sometimes used to identify returning birds in a lake. The yodel is typically accompanied by an aggressive posture, which more effectively gets the message across. To begin, the yodeling male lies flat on the water with its neck outstretched and its open beak pointing at the intruder. Then, when the territorial male has had enough of the intruder, it may rise up in the water with wings outstretched and head pointed toward the intruder in what has been called the *vulture posture* (fig. 10.1). This can be viewed as the last straw before actual combat begins.

**Fig. 10.1.**
. . . . . . . . . . . . . . . . . . . .

*Loon in an aggressive posture, also known as the vulture posture.*

## Arrival in the Spring, Courtship, and Nesting

. . . . . . . . . . . . . . . . . .

As if by magic, loons begin to arrive at our northern lakes within days after ice-out. Their springtime migration to their summer home is not a nonstop trip from their wintering grounds; it may be interrupted with intermediate stops on their way up north. The males arrive at the lake, often the same one that they occupied the previous year, and begin to stake out their respective territories, which can range from 20 to 200 acres. A good territory consists of a nesting site: protected shallow water that is shielded from the largest waves but which also has good fishing and some emergent plant cover for the protection of the young chicks. A couple days later, the females arrive on the scene.

Territorial defense among male loons is serious business, and by both their posture and calls, a territorial male signals to an intruder, often an unattached male, that it has gotten too close. The intensity of territorial defense is strictly a matter of hormones, and it peaks when hatching occurs. Defense involves lots of yodels and posturing, the most aggressive being the aforementioned vulture position. By far the majority of territorial confrontations end with a lot of puffery, with the intruder slinking away and the resident male feeling justified and quickly settling down to his normal routine. If things get to the point where conflict is inevitable, however, the combatants go after each other with their sharp beaks. The loser is often impaled and may well die from the wound.

Establishing both territorial lines and courtship involves increased vocalization, and during the breeding season the lake is alive with loon calls both day and night. Courtship for loons is a rather quiet affair when compared with that of other birds. One of the major activities is nest site selection and building the nest. Loon nests are built either on or right next to the water. A prime criterion for a good nesting site is an area where there is a steep underwater slope leading to the nest, because loons like to approach or leave the nest underwater as much as possible. The nests are made at ground level on masses of floating vegetation, old muskrat houses, or even bare sand or rock. The nest, which is about two feet in diameter, is not an elaborate affair. Both the male and female loons participate in nest building by throwing small masses of vegetation over the nesting site. The nests are built in sheltered areas, with protection from terrestrial egg predators, mainly raccoons and skunks, being a desirable characteristic. Ravens are major aerial predators of loon eggs, and the presence of nearby ravens' nests usually means bad luck for the nesting loons. If the lake has islands, these are favorite nesting areas. Frequently, the nest is in the same location as the previous year's nest.

Shortly after copulation, which almost always occurs on land, the female lays her eggs, usually two, but occasionally one or three. The second egg is normally laid a day after the first one. The eggs are large, measuring about 3½ by over 2 inches, and range from deep olive to a grayish brown color. Their incubation period is roughly four weeks, during which time both the male and the female take, roughly, two-hour turns sitting on the nest. In order to keep the eggs warm, the parents develop an increased blood supply to their superficial chest and abdominal tissues, but they don't lose breast feathers as the legendary pelican is supposed to do. While sitting on the nest, a loon keeps a low profile, usually with head facing the water, while the other parent is out fishing and preening. The nest sitter usually turns the eggs over about once per hour.

Sitting on the nest is no piece of cake for the parent on duty. One of the plagues of nesting loons is a species of black fly that seems to be attracted only to loons. These pests continuously buzz around the head of the nesting loon, which has no realistic way of warding them off. What there is about loons that makes them so attractive to black flies is not known, but one option is the oil from their uropygial glands that the loons spread over all their feathers. In one experiment museum specimens of skins from loons and ducks were laid out near the water. The black flies left the duck skins alone but swarmed about the loon skin.

## The Life of a Young Loon

By the end of the incubation period, usually about 70 percent of the eggs hatch, typically in late June or early July. If for some reason all the eggs are destroyed or fail to hatch, the parents are likely to re-nest later in the summer. Within the egg the loon embryos have developed a special adaptation, called an *egg tooth,* which facilitates their exit from the egg. This tooth, which is located on the outside tip of the upper beak, is used to cut through the membranes that surround the embryo and then to help the loon embryo break through the eggshell. The newly hatched loon chick, which weighs a bit more than 3 ounces, is covered with a blackish fuzz and has only a short beak. The first laid egg hatches a day before the second egg. Within 10 to 14 days, the black feathers are replaced by steel-gray down feathers.

Within a day after hatching, the loon chick makes its way to the water, and once off the nest it rarely returns. If the other egg has not hatched, one parent stays with the egg, and the other deals with the chick. Once in the water, the loon chick is quite a capable swimmer, and within a day or two, it can even dive for 2 to 3 seconds, although serious mimicking of the diving behavior of the adults begins at about two weeks. The dive of a very young loon has been described as something like trying to keep a ping-pong ball submerged, because their bodies aren't yet adapted for real diving. Initially, the young loons are totally dependent upon the adults for food, and they eat at hourly intervals all day. One loon chick was seen to have eaten 73 meals in one day. If food is scarce, the first hatched loon exerts its dominance, often to the detriment of the younger sibling, which may even starve to death. By a certain type of submissive posture and call, the young loons beg for food from the adults.

For the first few weeks the loon chicks are highly dependent upon their parents, who keep them in shallow, protected nursery areas away from the wind. The young are very vulnerable to predators—large fish, such as northern pike and muskies, below the water and herring gulls and eagles above. Young loons ride on the backs of their parents (about two-thirds of the time during their first week), who actively protect their young by both posturing and emitting tremolo calls (fig. 10.2).

**Fig. 10.2.**
. . . . . . . . . . . . . . . . . . . .
*Mother loon carrying a newborn chick on her back.*

They may also swim under a wing of the parent. Back riding may also serve to keep the young loons warm, as they have to deal with very cool springtime water temperatures.

Toward the end of their first month, the young loons begin to take a more active role in obtaining food. One is imposed on them by their parents, who are likely to drop the fish that they bring back into the water for the young to retrieve. In addition, the shallow nursery waters are usually rich in fish, crayfish, and insect life, and the young loons can try their hand at independent fishing. By about eight weeks, the juveniles can get much of their food by themselves, and the adults leave them alone about half of the time. Nevertheless, they remain under some level of parental care for their first three months, by which time they are pretty much full grown. They are able to fly by their eleventh or twelfth week. As the summer wears on, the two young loons begin to establish their own feeding territories, but they have often been observed to sleep together in a neutral location between their territories at night. Loons sleep on the water with their head turned toward the tail and resting on its back. Loon biologists have not seen evidence that young loons exhibit any behavior patterns that could be interpreted as play. Loon families spend most of the summer together, but as early fall approaches, they begin to settle into a pattern of premigratory behavior.

## Getting Ready for Fall

With the shortening of the late summer days, the loons' hormonal balance changes, and they are less likely to feel the need to defend territories. They have also begun their fall molt, which begins at the end of the breeding season. This molt is not as complete as the spring molt, and it doesn't impair their ability to fly. With the reduction in territoriality, they begin to exhibit patterns of social behavior and collect together into loose aggregates, at first perhaps 15 to 30 birds, especially in the early morning or late afternoon. The earliest groups probably consist of single birds and unsuccessful breeders, but as the summer progresses, the nesters join the ever-larger groups. Starting in September in Minnesota, staging groups of over one hundred are not uncommonly seen on larger lakes. This behavior is called *rafting*. As fall progresses, the family units break up, and the loons prepare to migrate. The specific signal to begin their migration is unknown, but usually, just days before the lake freezes over, the loons take off and head for their wintering grounds.

## Wintertime

Common loons, which spend their summers over most of Canada and the northern parts of just a few states (fig. 10.3), winter on the ocean along the Pacific, the Atlantic, and the Gulf Coast. Most of the loons from Minnesota seem to head for the Gulf Coast of Florida, whereas those slightly to the north and east in Ontario fly to the coasts of the middle and southern Atlantic states. Once at the ocean, loons stay close to shore, preferably in protected bays. They rarely vocalize in the winter, except for occasional quiet hoots. This, plus their gray winter

summer range

winter range

**Fig. 10.3.**
· · · · · · · · · · · · · · · · · ·

*Summer and winter ranges of common loons.*

plumage, makes them relatively inconspicuous members of the oceanic bird community. The family units have totally broken up by winter, but wintertime loons still may aggregate in small numbers in saltwater bays. Individual loons seem to stake out small territories when in salt water, but they are not defended by loud vocalization. In the evening they may flock together around sunset for social gatherings.

Oceanic loons continue to feed upon fish, with herring, sea trout, and small flounders being favorite foods, although they will also eat small crabs and other invertebrates. It is during this period that the salt glands on their heads get put to full use in removing excess salt from their bodies. The young loons also migrate to the ocean, where they remain for the first two to three years of their lives before they return to the freshwater lakes of their birth.

From late January through early March, loons undergo a complete spring molt, which includes losing their flight feathers, making them unable to fly. By early spring, however, they are able to fly again and also ready to undertake their migration back to the northern lakes, often the same lake they resided on the previous year. Then the many-thousand-year-old cycle of reproduction and growth repeats itself.

## Loons and Humans and Other Issues

Like any wild animals, loons are beset by a host of problems, many of them directly or indirectly related to their coexistence with humans. Of the direct human-related problems, hunting, which was prevalent a century ago, is no longer an issue except for relatively small harvests by Native American groups in Canada.

Of greater contemporary relevance is loss of habitat and shared use of lake space. With the increased development of closely spaced cabins and the attendant "improvement" of the beaches by removing marsh vegetation, potential nesting areas for loons have been significantly reduced in many lakes. In recent years, however, many progressive lake associations, including that of Ten Mile Lake, have been putting out artificial floating loon islands in good nesting areas and have then put up warning signs to keep boat traffic away from the nests. Well-constructed and well-positioned artificial nesting islands are often safer from predators than are natural ones, and when the nesting territories are respected by those living on the lake, success rates of reproduction can be quite high.

Loons also adapt very well to boat traffic, as long as they are not chased. It is not uncommon for loons to allow a slow-paced boat to pass within 50 feet of them without their exhibiting overt signs of nervousness or escape behavior by diving. During the nesting season, when the males' territorial instincts are the strongest, they require greater distances from humans.

In a few localities entrapment of diving loons in commercial gill nets has caused significant loon mortality. One well-known example was on Great Slave Lake in Canada in the early 1960s, where over a two-year period at least 5,000 loons drowned after being entangled in nets.

Acidification of lakes (discussed in greater detail in chapter 13) does not directly affect the reproductive success of loons, but it does indirectly affect reproduction through the reduction of sensitive fish populations—often the favorite food of loons. This is particularly hard on young loons that have just begun foraging for themselves. Apparently, the adults do not have the instinct to realize that their young are not getting enough nourishment at this stage in their development, and the fledglings either become malnourished or starve.

Loons are also highly susceptible to heavy metal contamination. Like other animals at the top of the food chain (including humans), loons can get mercury poisoning from eating fish that contain mercury. Some major winter loon die-offs off the Florida coast may have been initiated by a weakening of the loons from mercury contamination, which made them more susceptible to other deleterious influences, such as certain parasites, that would normally not have affected them so adversely. Other chemical contaminants, such as DDT, which thins eggshells and interferes with reproduction, affected loons relatively less than they did other birds when they were a major environmental problem. Now, the impact of DDT on loons is almost insignificant.

More recently, botulism has been on the rise among loons of the Great Lakes. Botulinum is a deadly toxin (and the active ingredient of Botox) produced by a bacterium. Periodically, outbreaks of this disease have killed thousands of loons by paralyzing their neuromuscular systems. Whether or not there is even an indirect relationship between humans and these die-offs has yet to be determined.

Overall, the future of American loons looks guardedly bright, mainly because of the great public interest in their collective welfare. Recently, loons have begun to nest on certain New England lakes and reservoirs where they had been absent for decades. Yet in other areas their numbers continue to decline. I remain optimistic, however, that the public will not allow the symbol of north country lakes to disappear.

## *11*  BEAVERS, MUSKRATS, AND OTTERS

On a late July day a couple of years ago, I noticed several freshly cut alder branches at the foot of our dock and wondered how far they must have drifted in order to get there. The branches bore the distinctive marks of beaver teeth. When this happened a couple more times with the wind blowing away from our shore, I realized that something strange was going on. With a little looking around, I found that these alder branches came from our property, which is at least 1½ miles from the nearest beaver house. This was confirmed that evening when I was going out walleye fishing around 11:00 PM. I heard a noise in the bushes and the noise of some animal slithering into the water. When I shined a flashlight in that direction, the beaver rewarded me with the characteristic sharp slap of its tail, as it submerged to get me off its back. The same thing happened the next night, and by then I was getting more than a little worried about the fate of a few large nearby poplar trees. So far, the poplars have remained safe, but I can't for the life of me figure out why the beavers had singled out our yard so far from their homes for the location of their evening snack.

At the other end of the lake, the small outlet stream goes out under a bridge, and almost every year beavers build a dam there that not only obstructs the little boat traffic that exists on the stream but also raises the lake level. Periodically, members of the lake association destroy the dam, but invariably it is rebuilt within a day or two.

Several years ago, beavers almost provoked a diplomatic crisis in Washington, D.C. One morning several valuable cherry trees, gifts from the Japanese government, were found cut down along the Potomac River. After several days of more tree cutting, people realized that it was the work of beavers rather than George Washington's ghost, and the U.S. Fish and Wildlife Service was called into action. They finally trapped the culprits and moved them to a location where they could munch upon less valuable trees.

Hunted and trapped to near extinction for their pelts almost two centuries ago, beavers have made a major comeback because of strong governmental protective measures. They are now very common in our northern states to the extent that they are often regarded as pests by those sharing land with them. Nevertheless, like loons, beavers are symbolic of the north and have many supporters.

Muskrats are accorded much less status than beavers. Living in shallow bays or in marshes, they are mainly evident by their low grassy houses that protrude above the winter ice. Muskrats, like beavers, have also been the quarry of trappers for as long as anybody can remember. Muskrat pelts make wonderful hats, and a lot of Russian ears would be much colder without their characteristic muskrat hats with prominent ear flaps.

**Fig. 11.1.**

*Distribution of North American beavers.*

## Beavers

. . . . . . . . . . . . . . . . . . . .

*A Bit about Beavers*

Beavers, which were originally distributed over almost all of North America (fig. 11.1), have played a remarkable role in the history of our continent. With the beaver craze in Europe during the 1600s and 1700s, fur traders spread out throughout North America to exchange cloth, knives, and trinkets for beaver pelts with a variety of Indian tribes. With the founding of the English Hudson Bay Company in 1670 and its French counterpart, the Compagnie du Nord, in 1682, the economics of beaver trading and trapping reached a high political level, resulting in several major wars between the English and the French. Intense competition continued until the time of the American revolution. After the United States became a fledgling country, the beaver politics continued, and excess trapping of beavers was actually used as a political tool to make the American westward migration less attractive.

The reason for a lot of this was beaver hats. Beaver hats were not made of beaver skins but rather from a beaver felt, which came from the soft down-like hairs of the beavers' undercoat. The hairs, roughly 9 ounces of which were required for a beaver hat, were shaved from beaver skins and rolled into damp sheets so that the fine barbs on the hair would link the cut hairs together. The felt-like sheet of beaver hair was then soaked in a hot liquid containing sulfuric acid. Earlier versions of this solution also contained mercury, resulting in mercury poisoning for many of the hat makers (mad hatters' disease). After this treatment, which compressed the felt, the wet material was placed upon a mold, which began the process of turning hair into hat.

Beavers are rodents, like rats, mice, and squirrels. A standard adult beaver is about 3½ to 4 feet from the nose to the tip of its tail, and it weighs 30 to 40 pounds (fig. 11.2). Beavers live to be about 12 years old in the wild. Both ends of a beaver exhibit its most pronounced specializations. The head is dominated by its massive cutting teeth (incisors), which are embedded in an equally massive skull that both supports the cutting teeth and buffers the head while the beaver is chewing on wood. The eyes and ears are very small, and neither sight nor hearing is very acute. Interestingly, the eyes, ears, and nose are laid out in a straight line, which keeps them all above the surface of the water while the beaver is swimming.

At the other end is its large flattened tail, a scaly appendage measuring 16 to 17 inches by 6 to 7 inches by ¾ inch. A beaver uses its tail for many things. On land the tail is used as a balance when cutting down trees. In the water the tail is used as a rudder when diving, and the sharp

**Fig. 11.2.**

*Swimming beaver.*

slap of the tail on the surface of the water is a powerful alarm signal. Less obvious functions of the tail are physiological. In the late summer and fall, fat stores build up in the tail to help the beaver get through the winter. The tail is also an important factor in controlling body temperature. Just like the feet of a loon, the tail can radiate heat away from the body when it gets too warm. In the summertime 25 percent of a beaver's heat loss occurs from its tail. In the winter heat loss through the tail is reduced to 2 percent of the total. Temperature control by the tail is accomplished through a countercurrent mechanism at the base of the tail, which, like that described for the loon's foot (see p. 162), removes much of the heat from the blood before the blood enters the tail. According to frontier legend, beaver tail is supposed to be one of the true delicacies of the wild. I ate beaver tail once and found it to be most unmemorable.

Although beavers don't dive deeply, they have nevertheless evolved a number of adaptations for diving. These include flaps of tissue that close off the nose and ears while underwater. A transparent membrane, called a *nictitating membrane,* protects the eyes when the beaver is swimming underwater. One of their most unusual adaptations for underwater work is lips that close behind the cutting teeth. This allows the beaver to chew sticks and peel bark while submerged without filling its mouth with water.

To protect and insulate it while underwater, the beaver has a heavy coat of fur with two types of hair—long (2 to 2½ inches) guard hairs and short (1 inch) underfur, which is what beaver hats were made of. But heavy fur isn't enough. In order to provide effective insulation, the beaver preens itself, like diving birds, with the oily secretions of anal glands. This serves to keep water out of the fur and preserves the air spaces, which serve as insulation, in the fur. The oily product of the anal glands contains dozens of chemical compounds and smells like rancid fat. This secretion may also serve as a major recognition mechanism for members of a beaver family. Like birds, beavers molt in the late summer so that they can start the winter with a fresh coat of fur.

Unseen, but vitally important, are physiological adaptations that allow beavers to undertake, on average, 5- to 6-minute dives, with a 15-minute maximum. When a beaver dives, its heart slows from about 120 to 60 beats per minute, saving oxygen consumption. When a beaver's nose first hits the water, blood preferentially flows to its heart and brain, the two organs that need the most oxygen. A diving beaver has a large degree of tolerance for high levels of carbon dioxide in its tissues. This is very important because, when we hold our breath, it is not so much the lack of oxygen as a buildup of carbon dioxide that drives us to take a new breath.

For swimming, beavers use mainly their large webbed hind feet as paddles. The front paws are pressed against the body when swimming. The second toe on each hind foot has a split nail. The beaver uses this like a comb when preening. The front feet are much more coordinated and are used for grasping, grooming, handling food, and digging into mud.

## Lodges and Dams

There is no question that beavers are nature's ultimate construction engineers. The level of engineering that goes into both their lodges and their dams would equal or exceed that of any human construction project that had to work with the same materials.

In lakes the lodge (beaver house) is the most visible evidence of the presence of beavers. Ten Mile Lake has several beaver lodges, mainly in western bays. What the person passing by in a boat or canoe sees is a mound of sticks, sometimes with plants growing out of the mud covering them, that may be 20 feet in diameter and 4 to 6 feet above the surface of the lake (fig. 11.3). Like an iceberg, however, most of the house is below the water.

If you approach a beaver's house, which is usually close to shore in a protected bay, you are likely to see a pile of sticks, mostly below the surface, seemingly scattered at random near one side of the lodge. This is the food cache, which is essentially the pantry of the beaver family and provides food that will help the beavers get through the long northern winter. Closer examination of the area just around the lodge typically reveals well-defined canals that lead from the lodge toward deeper water. If you look carefully into the deeper water alongside the sticks of the food cache, you may see a few large crappies suspended in the shadows. In heavily fished lakes canny anglers probably know this pattern and have fished the crappies out of this area. As a default one can almost always find some small sunfish or rock bass. A beaver lodge typically has several underwater entrances, each with a channel leading to it for better access.

Inside the lodge the most prominent structure is a dry platform, which has an opening that allows access from the water below. This is, in effect, the living quarters of the beaver family. In the lower level, below the platform, there may be a feeding ledge, where the beavers can gnaw upon sticks without messing up the living platform. The lodge is designed to be cool in the summer and to protect the beavers from the icy winter winds. Insulation is provided by a layer of mud plastered around the outer sides of the lodge. At the top is an unplastered vent area that allows air exchange. During much of the winter the air temperature within the lodge remains at about the freezing point, which is a tolerable temperature for the beavers.

Most lake-dwelling beavers don't need to build dams, the main function of which is to provide deep enough water in streams to allow underwater entrances to the main lodge. For years the Ten Mile Lake beavers have built a low dam across the small outlet stream about one-third mile downstream from the lake. This can make a difference of several inches in the lake level. Most beaver dams are built across narrow, slow-moving streams, causing a pond to form upstream of the dam (fig. 11.3).

**Fig. 11.3.**

. . . . . . . . . . . . . . . . . . . .

*Beaver dam built across a stream, with a lodge in the pond.*

water leaking through dam          dam

The dam is started by the beavers' placing long sticks at each edge of the stream. Dam building normally takes place at night. The sticks are weighed down by stones, and a packing of grass and mud is placed in the spaces between the sticks. The downstream side of the dam is fairly steep walled, with the sticks exposed. The upstream side of the dam has a much more gentle slope, and it is covered with a layer of mud, as well as silt and debris carried to the dam by the current. Water often seeps through the dam rather than flowing over the top. There are many varieties and configurations of beaver dams and ponds, but since these are not highly relevant to lakes, they will not be discussed further here. Male beavers seem to be the main tenders of the dams, whereas females see to the lodge.

## The Beaver Family

The fundamental social unit of beavers is the extended family, comprising two parents, three to four young-of-the-year kits, and a couple of yearlings from the previous summer. The female beaver seems to run the family. Early in the summer, just before the birth of the new litter of beavers, the two-year-olds are expelled from the family unit and have to find and establish new territories of their own. It may be that the solitary beavers that are seen in odd locations of lakes in the summertime are

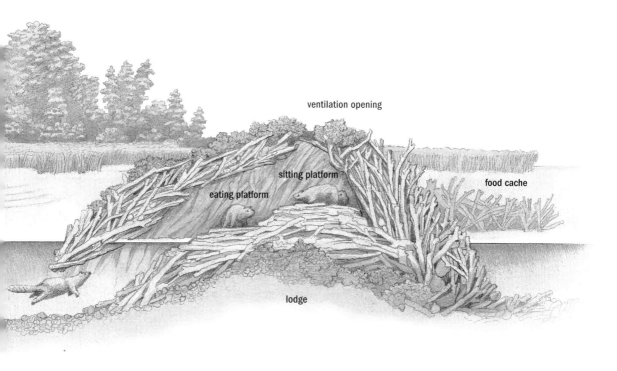

deportees who are looking for a new territory in which to settle down.

The monogamous beaver breeds during the late winter, and after a gestation period of around 110 days, three to four kits are born in late May or June. The newborn young, which weigh about a pound at birth, have a full set of teeth and fur, and their eyes open within minutes. They nurse for 2 to 3 weeks, during which time the mother begins to supplement their diet with tender twigs and leaves. The young are totally weaned by about 10 weeks. The kits stay in the lodge for about 1 month, but then the mother urges the less-than-enthusiastic young to start swimming by pushing them into the water. The kits' anal gland begins to function at about 3 to 4 weeks, and before that, their fur is not water-repellent. By 2 months the young beavers can dive and remain submerged for a while. Food is delivered to the kits in the lodge for 2 to 3 months, often by the yearlings of the family. By late summer the young will leave the lodge for swimming and feeding expeditions.

Beavers are highly scent oriented, and olfactory cues play a large role in staking out territories and recognizing members of family units. Castoreum, the yellowish product of a set of large (about 2 ounces) castor sacs that open into the urethra, is a legendary substance, with human applications going back centuries. The Romans burned it in lamps, and it was used by beekeepers to increase honey production in medieval times. Among its various medical uses, up to the 1700s its fumes were thought to induce abortion. Castoreum contains a variety of plant derivatives from the beavers' diet, and how it is made is poorly understood.

Like the secretion of the anal glands, castoreum gives off a distinctive odor that allows members of a beaver family to recognize one another. It is also used to mark the boundaries of the territory of a family. One of the ways this is done is to build foot-high scent mounds of mud and deposit either castoreum or the secretions of the anal glands upon the mud. The dampness of the mud keeps the distinctive odor in the air, warning interlopers that they are encroaching upon other beavers' territory.

*Feeding and Tree Cutting*

Beavers are crepuscular and nocturnal creatures, meaning that they are most active during periods of dim light and at night. In the summertime they remain in their lodge during the daylight hours, coming out in the late evening to begin feeding and construction work. Beavers spend on average 4 to 5 hours per day foraging for food.

Beavers are vegetarians, but within that general category of feeding, they need a highly varied diet. Although an adult beaver eats between 2 and 4 pounds of bark, twigs, and leaves per day, beavers in the summer also eat a variety of soft aquatic plants or grasses and roots. They are particularly fond of water lily roots and the roots of certain marsh plants and ferns. Aquatic plants, in particular, concentrate iodine, and eating them is one way that beavers in the iodine-poor central part of the country avoid developing goiters.

It is their consumption of tree bark and branches that attracts the most attention and creates the greatest environmental impact. Beavers have definite preferences for certain types of trees. Aspens, poplars, and yellow birch are by far the most highly preferred, with willows and alders next in order. If necessary, they will feed on certain maples, white birch, or even some pine and spruce, but only if nothing else is available. Like many herbivorous animals, beavers don't produce intrinsic cellulases, enzymes that digest cellulose from plants. Instead, they host in their stomach large numbers of bacteria that produce these enzymes.

In streams the ideal foraging territory is within 200 feet of the pond, but if food is sharply limited, they have been known to cut trees as far as 500 feet from the water's edge. In lakes they have a wider range of available water, and they don't normally forage so far from shore. Extensive excursions on land make them much more susceptible to predation by their main natural enemies—wolves, coyotes, and mountain lions. It is not uncommon for a beaver to sample the bark of a tree before cutting it down. A beaver's teeth are ideally designed for cutting wood. The cutting teeth have hard enamel in front and softer dentine in back. This produces a wear pattern that results in a chisel-shaped cutting surface in these teeth. Like all rodents, the cutting teeth grow constantly, and if a tooth is broken or somehow misaligned, its counterpart on the other jaw continues to grow until sometimes it forms a complete circle, thus rendering the beaver incapable of real chewing.

Once a beaver decides to fell a tree, it does so with great dispatch, taking less than an hour for a tree 6 inches in diameter and up to 4 hours for larger trees. They have been known to cut down hardwood trees up to 18 inches in diameter and softer cottonwood trees well over 2 feet in diameter. Large trees are often not cut at one time, but sometimes the process is carried on intermittently, even over a couple of years. According to some naturalists, a couple members of a beaver family may cooperate in cutting down large trees, but in most cases the cutting is done by only one beaver. Tree cutting intensifies in the fall, when the beavers are stocking up food for the winter, or during periods when they are building or repairing dams and lodges. Beavers leave an obvious trail between their feeding grounds and the water. It may be something as simple as a short, muddy pathway with flattened grasses and other plants leading from the shore. On the other hand, the pathway in a marshy area can be excavated to form a shallow canal leading to the trees, which the beaver uses for transporting the cut wood to the pond or lake. In longstanding beaver ponds, the canals can be elaborate affairs up to 400 feet long, with mini dams or other devices to maintain a functional amount of water in them.

In most cases the cut trunks or branches (beaver sticks) are 2 to 3 feet long, but there is considerable variation. The general rule is that the thinner the stick, the longer the segment, with large-diameter branches being only 1 foot or so long and branches less than 2 inches in diameter being cut into segments up to 8 feet long. Often when they are found along the shore of a lake, beaver sticks are completely denuded of bark, indicating that they were a past meal. In the fall, however, the sticks, covered with bark, are brought to the food cache for consumption in future winter meals. As the sticks soak in the water, unpalatable defense compounds, often produced by plants and trees to protect themselves from predation by herbivores, are leached out of them. Tree cutting intensifies in the late summer and fall as beavers build up stores for the winter months. There are also periods of greater activity during the summer, when the beavers need materials for building or repairing their lodges and dams. When the beavers are in a tree-cutting mode, their activity is reflected in their feces, which look like balls of sawdust and are dropped into the water.

*Beavers in the Winter*

Despite their thick fur coats and buildup of body fat, beavers are not totally well-adapted for life in ice-cold water. Their thick pelt accounts for about one-quarter of their total body insulation, and body fat, for the remaining three-quarters. Still, beavers lose considerable body heat while swimming in icy water. After a 40-minute immersion in winter water, an adult beaver loses 3 degrees of body temperature, and a young beaver, up to 12 degrees.

Beavers spend much of their time in the lodge during the winter, with a reduced body temperature and overall metabolism. They live off their stored fat and sticks in the food cache. The supply of sticks in the food cache is not sufficient to get the beavers through the winter, so stored body fat is of critical importance. Body fat is built up during the summer and autumn. There is also considerable fat buildup in the tail, to the extent that the volume of the tail doubles from spring to fall. Despite all this, it is common for adult beavers to lose about 5 pounds during the winter.

A wintertime beaver lodge is a busy place, but the goings-on within were largely a mystery to biologists until cameras were inserted into some lodges. One of the surprises was that, occasionally, muskrats, mice, and voles were seen inside beaver lodges. The beavers make occasional forays to the wood cache for wood to eat, and this activity causes a mess on the platform within the lodge. Even inside the lodge, the beavers are busy, pushing out decaying wood and other leftovers from meals. The yearlings of the family seem assigned to do much of the cleaning, which takes place every 2 to 3 days.

## Muskrats

In many respects, muskrats would seem to be the beavers' little cousins, trying to emulate their larger, more accomplished relatives. Both of these rodents lead an almost totally aquatic existence; both are largely vegetarians; and both build houses in and above the water. They share some unusual adaptations, as well, such as lips that close behind their incisors that allow them to chew under water. Like beavers, muskrats have long guard hairs that overlie a soft undercoat of shorter hairs which are resistant to water and allow a layer of air, estimated to average more than 20 percent of their body's volume, to insulate and provide buoyancy when they are swimming.

Although their color is quite similar to that of a beaver, muskrats are much smaller, measuring about 20 inches from their nose to the tip of their tail and weighing 2 to 3 pounds (fig. 11.4). In contrast to a beaver's 12 to 15 years, muskrats typically live only about 3 years. They have a long, scaly tail that is flattened along the sides. Their legs are short, with unwebbed front feet and partially webbed hind feet that are used as paddles. Muskrats swim along the surface using sculling motions of

**Fig. 11.4.**

*Muskrat, with its house in the background.*

their tail and paddling actions of their hind feet. In calm water a swimming muskrat is often first noticed by the gentle wake left by its almost submerged head as it slowly makes its way across a pond. Normally, a muskrat swims at about human walking speed. If disturbed, it makes a quick porpoise-like dive and continues the rest of its way underwater, with forefeet pressed against its body like those of a beaver. Muskrats can remain submerged for a long time, commonly 10 minutes and as much as 20 minutes. They share the physiological characteristic with many aquatic mammals of being able to tolerate much higher levels of carbon dioxide in their tissues, which accounts in large part for their impressive diving prowess.

Muskrats are creatures of swamps, and in the shallow marshy bays of most lakes, their presence is advertised by their domed houses made of aquatic vegetation (fig. 11.4). The domes of muskrat houses protrude 2 to 3 feet above the surface of the water and are 5 to 8 feet in diameter. In lakes with less-shallow water and muddy banks, muskrats forgo building houses for burrows in the banks. They are particularly partial to the root systems of willow trees, where they construct complex burrows, with several underwater entrances and aboveground ventilation holes. In both their houses and burrows in banks, they construct above-water living quarters, which may be occupied by as many as a dozen muskrats within an extended family. A muskrat house has an above-water platform of cattails, reeds, or grasses on which the family members spend most of their time; burrows also have an expanded above-water chamber that is lined with grasses. Muskrats also construct smaller feeding shelters that protrude slightly above the water. These hold only one animal at a time.

The bulk of a muskrat's diet is vegetarian, with cattails, rushes, and other emergent aquatic plants being favorite foods. Occasionally, they include crayfish, clams, or even fish in their diet. Late in the fall they greatly increase their food intake, and on warm fall nights I have seen them make repeated trips to beds of pondweed and swim toward their shoreline burrows with bunches of these plants in their mouths. In a region rich in vegetation, their feeding territory may have a radius of only 50 to 100 feet from their house, but they are not averse to swimming several hundred yards to obtain food. Although they may store some food in advance for the winter, they certainly do not make the enormous food caches that characterize the water around beaver lodges.

Muskrats are polygamous and are much more prolific than beavers. After a 25- to 30-day gestation period, the first litter of five to six young is born in late April or early May. This is likely to be followed by a couple more litters before the close of the summer. Newborn muskrats are much more rodent-like than are newborn beavers. Much like newborn mice and rats, they are born blind, have only a fine coating of hair, and have no incisor teeth for the first week. Their eyes open at about two weeks, about when they are first able to swim. Within a month they have been weaned, so that the mother can prepare for the next litter. By fall the members of the first litter are fully independent, but they are likely to remain with the family unit until early in the next spring.

Muskrats are also like beavers in having weak eyes, good hearing, and an excellent sense of smell. They get their name from a pair of glands that secrete a yellowish, musky-smelling substance in the urine. Like the castoreum of beavers, this secretion, which is deposited on the house, travel routes, and defecation areas, is used to mark territories and is also probably a main means of identifying members of the family unit.

Because of their small size, muskrats are subject to predation by a variety of natural enemies, such as large hawks and owls, foxes, and raccoons. One of the most dangerous predators is the mink, which goes after them in their houses. The other significant predator is human trappers. Muskrat fur is highly valued, although not in the same league as beaver pelts. Nevertheless, millions of muskrats are trapped every year. With their high reproductive potential, however, muskrats are not endangered. Because of their proclivities for burrowing, muskrats have the potential to cause damage to earthen dams and dikes. Other than that, their impact on humans is minimal.

## Otters

Although we frequently see otters on canoe trips on small rivers, late last summer was the first time my wife and I had seen otters on Ten Mile Lake. Just inside the point at the entrance of Kenfield Bay, we saw a lot of commotion near shore and graceful dark backs undulating on and under the surface of the water. When one of them stuck its long neck out of the water to try to figure out where we were, there was no doubt that what we were seeing was a family of otters. Otters are incredibly graceful swimmers that seem to have a zest for life like no other mammal. Although not all biologists agree, it seems that they really enjoy playing. Perhaps their efficiency at catching food and their relative lack of natural enemies allows them more leisure time than most other animals.

Otters, members of the weasel family, are large animals, about 3 to 4 feet long and weighing from 12 to 20 pounds. In contrast to beavers and muskrats, their body is designed for serious swimming, since their main food is fish (fig. 11.5). They can dive to considerable depths (at least 50 feet) and can swim underwater at speeds of up to 7 MPH. They are fast enough and agile enough to catch trout, although most of their diet consists of more-slowly-moving fish like suckers, minnows, and sunfish. In addition to fish, they eat crayfish, clams, frogs, and even some insects. Otters have long whiskers (vibrissae), which are apparently used to sense the presence of fish and other moving animals in the water in much the same way that seals use their whiskers to catch herring in ocean bays.

Otters keep a low profile on lakes, but signs of their presence are much more prominent along the banks of streams and rivers, especially early in the summer when the young are still small. Otter dens are usually quite inconspicuous, sometimes consisting of another animal's abandoned burrow or lodge, a space in the hollow of a stump, or a space among roots or piles of timber. The most characteristic sign of otters is their slides on steep banks, especially in the winter. Otters use slides heavily, and the extent to which this is play versus a utilitarian activity is debated. In contrast to beavers and muskrats, otters are very active during the winter months, and they may troop as much as a couple of miles overland in the snow to reach another body of water. They swim actively under the ice and make use of air bubbles under the ice for breathing.

**Fig. 11.5.**

. . . . . . . . . . . . . . . . . . . .

*River otter.*

After the female has established a birth den, two to four young otters are born in late winter or early spring. The newborn otters, weighing a bit over a half pound, are fully furred, but they have no teeth and their eyes and ears are still closed. After a month their eyes open, and the playful young otters set out to explore their world. They remain with their mother much of the first summer, but by fall they must set out on their own so that the mother can prepare for the next litter. The reproductive cycle of the otter has a few interesting twists. Shortly after the birth of her young in the early spring, the mother goes into estrous (heat) for a month or so. If mating is successful, the embryos begin to develop, but in contrast to most mammals, the very early embryo goes into a stage of suspended animation before it attaches to the lining of the mother's uterus. This stage, called *delayed implantation*, can last from 8 to 9 months and is considered an adaptation that serves as a buffer against adverse environmental conditions.

Otters have few enemies except humans, and because of their pelt, they are prime targets of trappers. Presently, the trapping of otters is closely regulated, but in the nineteenth century excessive trapping resulted in their extinction from many parts of the continent. Currently, there are an estimated 12,000 otters in Minnesota.

## *12*  THE LAKE THROUGHOUT THE SEASONS

A lake is never static. Instead, it is constantly changing according to cycles of varying lengths. The longest cycle, measured in hundreds or thousands of years, takes a lake from its birth—after the melting of the last glacier—through maturation and ends with the lake's filling in with silt and becoming a marsh. Other cycles, usually measured in decades, relate to climate, with periods of higher or lower temperatures or greater or lesser amounts of rainfall. There are also irregular short-term cycles based on the passage of warm and cold fronts, and of course, there is the day-night cycle. The most regular cycle is, however, the annual cycle of the seasons.

## Spring

The lake in late March is still completely covered with ice, but the ice is now gray and softened by the increasingly strong rays of the springtime sun. As the weather warms, the ice begins to thin and disappear along the shore or in areas where an inlet stream or springs enter the lake. Even before the ice has melted, some of the animals in the lake are already preparing for spring. This is particularly noticeable in some of the fish that are early spawners. Large northern pike move toward shallow dark-bottomed bays, and walleyes and suckers begin to aggregate near the mouths of the streams in which they will spawn.

With rising temperatures and increasing daylight, the ice becomes honeycombed as the edges of the ice pack recede from the shorelines. Smaller bays are likely to be completely ice free, whereas the main lake basin is still covered with ice. This is a wonderful time to do some exploring by canoe in the narrow channel between ice and shore. But you have to be careful because if the wind picks up or changes direction, the ice pack can shift until it hits the shoreline, and you might find yourself stuck on the wrong side of the lake. On one such springtime trip on Ten Mile, I was treated to a fascinating sight. An osprey was flying away from the lake with about a two-pound fish in its claws, when it was dive-bombed by a passing eagle. The outgunned osprey dropped the fish, which was then picked off by the eagle while it was falling through the air.

After more melting, there usually comes a time when the remaining ice breaks up very quickly. Breakup often happens on a warm, windy day. This drives the remaining needle-like ice crystals into piles along the windward shore, and the ice crystals hitting against one another sometimes create an almost ethereal sound of pure high-pitched chimes.

Almost as soon as the lake becomes ice free, major things happen both on and below the surface. On the surface groups of northern ducks, such as scaups, ring-necked ducks, buffleheads, canvasbacks, and hooded mergansers, that are migrating from their wintering grounds spend a few days on the lake before continuing their northward journey. They are likely to be joined by various gulls, terns, geese, and possibly even a pair of trumpeter swans. Below the surface the large female northern pike have already moved into the marshy bays, where they begin to spawn in the flooded grass. In the right light you can see clouds of midges humming in the air after emerging from the cold lake bottom in their first hatch of the year. On the lake bottom the first green sprouts of newly emerging aquatic vegetation are seen among the decaying remains of the last year's crop.

The temperature of the water determines much of what happens in a lake just after ice-out, and there is surprising variability among different parts of the lake. The water in the main basin of the lake will remain in the mid- to high 30s for some time, depending upon the air temperature and the depth of the lake. In Ten Mile Lake the main basin, with its 100- to 200-foot depths, often remains frigid for weeks, and much of the early biological action takes place in the shallow bays, like Lundstrom's Bay or Long Bay (see fig. 1.4). Fish are very sensitive to small variations in water temperature, and water only a few degrees warmer than that of the main body of the lake will attract actively feeding fish. The surface water in Lundstrom's Bay can be in the 50s, whereas that in the middle of the lake is barely above 40 degrees.

One of the best times for fishing in the early spring is a sunny afternoon when the sun has warmed the shallow waters from the previous night's dip in temperature. Both sunfish and crappies patrol the shallows, especially around the remains of the previous year's reeds and grass hummocks, as they pick off insects or minnows that have been similarly activated by the warming water. Surprisingly, early in the spring largemouth bass also move into the shallow flats of bays, looking for schools of small fish and minnows. When they first arrive, they may suspend almost at the surface as the sun warms a thin layer of calm water. It is almost as if they are soaking up the heat after being nearly inert from cold all winter. This early in the season, smallmouth bass, in contrast, are nowhere to be seen. In most Minnesota lakes by the beginning of fishing season, the large northern pike have already left the shallow bays in favor of the cold deeper waters of the main lake. For a while, though, they may remain near the entrance to the bay in which they spawned. Walleyes are moving toward their spawning areas, as well, and before the water has warmed to a temperature appropriate for spawning, they congregate around the mouths of inlet streams or the rubble reefs where they sometimes spawn in the lake.

In a clear-water lake one of the most interesting forms of springtime nature watching is to canoe or slowly motor a boat through an extensive bed of bulrushes. You often won't see any traces of the bulrushes protruding above the water because the tops have been encased in the ice and are then broken off as the ice shifts. The remainder of the bulrushes consists of the dark brown stems that typically stop a few inches below the surface. In such habitat you can see a variety of fish, like large crappies, sunfish, northern pike, and even an occasional whitefish, suspended in the water among the reed stems. The reeds must give them a sense of security, because the fish don't dart away from the boat as readily as they typically do in open water.

Within a week or two of ice-out, activity in the lake picks up tremendously, with most of the action still in the warmer bays. By this time the water in the bays is likely to be in the mid-50s. The panfish and largemouth bass are feeding actively among the pondweeds and other plants that are now rapidly emerging from the bottom. They share their shallow-water feeding sites with the great blue herons that have returned to the lake. In the trees along the edge of the lake, newly arrived kingfishers, flying with their characteristic rat-a-tat sound, are also on the lookout for a meal of an unwary fish. Warm days see the emergence of painted turtles, which can be seen basking on protruding logs or rocks warmed by the sun. With dragonflies zooming around capturing midges and mosquitoes, the bays are a beehive of activity.

This burst of springtime energy does not cease with the oncoming night. At dusk muskrats and beavers begin their evening forays for fresh plant food, and the air is filled with the deafening chorus of spring peepers and other frogs that are participating in their annual mating rituals in the nearby swamps. The air along the shore is filled with clouds of nonbiting midges (chironomids) that are so dense it is hard to avoid inhaling them. When they are present in this density, a constant high-pitched hum, which can sometimes be heard 50 feet in from the shore, greets anyone who ventures out on a dock. Later in the evening walleyes begin to feed heavily as they recover their energy from the rigors of spawning a couple of weeks earlier. Throughout the night the loons are engaged in their most active conversations of the year, while they are staking out territory and preparing to nest.

The main basin of Ten Mile Lake is still very cold at this time. The ciscoes remain in the deep waters, but sometimes they are densely concentrated at one end of the lake. The whitefish can be anywhere in the main lake at this time from very deep to very shallow water. It is quite common to find large schools of whitefish in water 20 to 30 feet deep, where they are probably feeding on small fish and emerging insect larvae. This is the one time of the year when whitefish feed actively on the surface, on floating insects that are spent after their own mating activities. In the weedy flats the perch have congregated in their spawning activities, which leave the plants covered with gelatinous accordion-like sheets of eggs. Both walleyes and northern pike are patrolling these areas looking for an easy meal of an unwary perch or whitefish.

At this time trees have a major temporary impact on the lake. In late May the poplars send out enormous quantities of fluffy white seeds, which can thickly cover the entire surface of the lake. These are a pain in the neck to anglers because they bunch up in little white balls around their fishing line. Shortly after the rain of poplar seeds subsides, much of the lake again gets covered—this time with pine pollen. On windy days the water on the windward shore turns an unappetizing yellow-green color as the pollen grains collect there. This rapidly subsides, and the water regains its springtime clarity.

If there is a stretch of hot and calm weather, a temporary but pronounced temperature stratification can occur. A thin band of warm water forms on top of the still icy-cold water of the lake basin. This provides a pathway for walleyes to spread out over the main lake, where they go on a cisco-eating binge in the evening. This warm layer is very fragile, and it can disappear quickly on cold, windy days.

Late spring is dominated by the spawning activities of the members of the sunfish family. Sunfish construct their groups of closely spaced nests in all of the bays, and largemouth bass follow suit with their own larger nests. The crappies are more likely to be nesting among the remains of last year's reeds. When the water in the main lake reaches the mid- to upper 50s, smallmouth bass appear in the shallow rubble flats or rocky bars. They often swim in aggregates of ten to twenty fish, feeding together after the long, inactive winter. The males then begin to make their nests, which are quite obvious in the shallow water.

Late spring to early summer is also the time of the major insect hatches, and of these the mayfly hatch is the most prominent. Responding to some poorly understood signal, the distinctive mayfly larvae emerge from the bottom silt in great numbers and swim toward the surface, where they transform into winged mayflies. This trip to the surface is fraught with danger because fish just love these large, juicy insects. Fish, ranging from panfish to walleyes and even whitefish, go on a mayfly-feeding binge at this time of the year, often to the extent that they feed on nothing else. This can be a very challenging time for the angler who uses conventional lake techniques. Surprisingly, few lake anglers have done what is second nature to trout anglers, match the hatch and use flies or baits resembling larval mayflies.

## Summary

Things settle down in the summer for a relatively long period of well-defined behavior by most of the lake's inhabitants. The thermocline, which had begun to take shape by late spring, is now fully formed, dividing the lake into warm-water and cold-water compartments. Even in the deeper waters above the thermocline, the aquatic vegetation constitutes a prominent part of the underwater landscape. Recently hatched fish fry are for the most part concentrated in the shallow waters or just beneath the surface over the deeper water. The young loons and ducks are being taught by their mothers how to forage for food and protect themselves from enemies. Most inhabitants of the lake have settled into a pattern of eating and avoiding being eaten by something bigger. Adding to all the activity is a greatly increased amount of boating activity, with its attendant noise and disturbance of the water.

The steady rhythm of summertime daily activity is strongly modulated, however, by the influence of the weather systems that cycle through the north country. Typically, every week or so a series of weather fronts rolls through, and these exert a significant influence on both the appearance of the lake and what goes on beneath the surface. The two major players are warm fronts and cold fronts.

After a series of a few nice summer days, the weather becomes warmer, with the wind blowing from the south. The folks on vacation notice an increase in humidity, and the kids are likely to be spending more time in the water. Sometimes, when the kids (or adults) come out of the water, they develop an intense itching of the skin. This is likely to be a classic case of swimmer's itch (see sidebar). When you look across the lake, the atmosphere is hazy, and the sunsets are redder. At night the moon is not so distinct. These conditions herald the coming of a warm-weather system, which is sometimes punctuated by the entrance of a full-fledged warm front. Warm fronts are relatively narrow bands of warm, moist air that are propelled from the subtropical regions by strong southerly winds, which with a strong front can blow up to 30 MPH.

# SWIMMER'S ITCH

Swimmer's itch, which I liken to a case of aquatic chiggers, is actually a parasitic condition in which people act as accidental and inappropriate hosts. You know that you have it if, within a few minutes after coming out of the water, your skin tingles, burns, or itches and then develops a reddish rash. Within twelve hours you may develop small, reddish pimples, which can develop into small blisters on your skin. The itching may last from several days to a week or two before it subsides.

## WHAT IS SWIMMER'S ITCH?

Understanding how people get swimmer's itch and how to control it requires a knowledge of the life cycle of the parasite. Swimmer's itch, more officially called *schistosome cercarial dermatitis,* results from the infestation of the skin by a larval stage of a schistosome parasite (actually a blood fluke). There is no single parasitic species. As many as fifteen species of schistosomes may be able to cause swimmer's itch in our northern states.

The adult form of the schistosome is a tiny flatworm about the size of a hair on a watercolor brush that lives in the blood vessels (mainly veins) around the intestines of ducks or some mammals, such as muskrats. Ducks are by far the most common host, and common mergansers are typically more heavily infected than any other species. In lakes where swimmer's itch is a problem, almost all of the mergansers are likely to be infected. The flatworms lay eggs that make their way into the intestinal cavity of the duck and are excreted with the feces. The feces of mer-

gansers may contain over a hundred times more eggs than those of other species of ducks or geese.

Once exposed to water, the eggs hatch within an hour and develop into free-swimming but nonfeeding larvae called *miracidia.* In order to survive, the miracidia must then find their way into the body of an intermediate host—a species of snail that is different for each species of the parasite. Within the snail a miracidium forms a reproductive sac called a *sporocyst.* Usually, only one species of snail can serve as a host for a specific species of parasite. In a month or so, the sporocyst begins to produce a second generation of larvae called *cercariae.* As many as 2,000 to 4,000 cercariae burrow their way out of the host snail each day. Most cercariae are released during the midday hours (12:00 PM to 2:00 PM) as the lake waters warm from late May through July. Depending upon the snail population and their percentage of infestation, tens of millions of cercariae per day can be released on a 100-foot beach. The cercariae are weak swimmers and tend to congregate near the surface, where they are more likely to encounter a duck. Because they are present near the surface, they can be blown long distances by the waves and can become concentrated near the shore on the windward side of a lake. An individual cercaria lives less than a day.

Of all these free-swimming cercariae, a few lucky ones attach themselves to the body of a duck, where they penetrate the skin or the wall of the mouth. From there they make their way into the blood, where they turn into mature flatworms and then repeat their complex life cycle by laying more eggs. Unluckily for both

the cercariae and infected humans, some of the cercariae, being indiscriminate in what they attach to, latch onto swimmers. If able to burrow into the skin, they set off a local immune reaction characterized by histamine release, which is the main cause of the itching and redness. Perhaps 30 to 40 percent of humans are sensitive to the presence of these schistosomes in their skin, and for these unfortunate folks subsequent reactions are likely to be increasingly severe. The cercariae are killed by the human's immune system and never develop into adult worms.

## WHAT CAN YOU DO ABOUT SWIMMER'S ITCH?

At an individual level the best thing is not to get it in the first place. This means avoiding swimming in areas known to be contaminated. This may not be practical, however, for cabin owners, who are often tied to one swimming area. Most important is not to let yourself air-dry after swimming. This is tough for small children, who spend lots of time playing in the shallow water near shore. Immediately after leaving the water, dry yourself with a towel or take a shower. Both of these can remove any cercariae that have not yet penetrated your skin. If you have contracted swimmer's itch, you are stuck with it. The less you scratch it, the better, but if the itching becomes intense, the application of calamine lotion or a hydrocortisone cream may alleviate the itching. Too much scratching may open skin sores that can become infected by bacteria. Swimmer's itch cannot be spread from one person to another, nor will the lesions spread like poison ivy. As the immune reac-

tion dies down, over several days or a week, the symptoms will gradually disappear. According to some anecdotal reports, lathering yourself with a waterproof sunscreen may ward off the cercariae. It is also advisable not to spend time near the shoreline water on a windy day, since the cercariae can be concentrated in this area.

The best recipe for reducing the likelihood of contracting swimmer's itch is to discourage the presence of ducks, especially mergansers, in a swimming area. The amount of infestation is directly proportional to the number of infected ducks and the amount of time that they spend in a given area. Sometimes the snails are infected by the droppings of migratory birds in the spring or fall. There is not much one can do about this. One of the best pieces of advice is not to feed the ducks. Once the ducks are gone, the infected snails will decrease because the parasite cannot be transmitted from one snail to another. Thus, you will have to wait until all infected snails die (often several months) before a contaminated beach is parasite free. There is no sure way to get rid of swimmer's itch, any more than one can eliminate all mosquitoes or wood ticks, but you can make it less likely to get infected. Ongoing experiments involve trying to treat infected ducks by feeding them with bread infused with veterinary medications to kill the worms. Attempts to control it chemically by killing snails are often imprecise and result in killing many other plants and animals, as well. Most of these treatments would require the approval of your state's department of natural resources.

Warm fronts have been described as conveyor belts that are several thousand miles long and often less than 200 miles wide (fig. 12.1). According to classical descriptions, as the warm air travels north and encounters cooler air, it gradually rises over the cold air. This results in an expansion and subsequent cooling of the warm air, resulting in the condensation of the water vapor in the air and the formation of clouds.

Strong warm fronts have a profound effect on the life of a lake. Above the water the heat and humidity can get intense, and it brings out the worst in flies, which seem to multiply in numbers and bite voraciously. Beneath the water feeding activity of the major predatory fish intensifies dramatically. This is clearly evidenced by the increased aggressiveness of game fish. Canny anglers long for the appearance of warm fronts because these brief periods are typically the times when fish seem to jump into the boat. This is the time to be using faster retrieves and larger baits. When the fish are really aggressive, a person fishing a clear-water lake can sometimes see another fish or two following a hooked fish to the boat. This behavior is most common with bass, but on Ten Mile Lake I have also seen it with walleyes. Radio-tagging studies on some Ten Mile walleyes show that warm fronts often stimulate the walleyes to swim across the lake—often within a few hours at night. Why they do this is anybody's guess.

Typically, when fishing under these conditions, a glance at the western horizon will pick up large white clouds building up into thunderheads. The increased activity among the fish builds up as the thunder-

**Fig. 12.1.**

. . . . . . . . . . . . . . . . . . .

*Conditions leading to the formation of thunderstorms. A column of warm, moist air moving up from the southwest is met by a wave of cool, dry air coming in from the northwest.*

warm air "conveyor belt"

storms form until they sometimes go into a true feeding frenzy just before the storm hits. Northern pike and muskies are particularly affected by these conditions, and this is often the prime time to catch a true whopper. I still remember one day when I was just pulling in my line before heading home to beat an oncoming thunderstorm. An 8-pound walleye hit my bait, which was connected to a fly rod. By the time the fish was in the boat and I was steaming home as fast as my 3-horsepower outboard would take me, conditions were getting downright dangerous. Speaking of danger, one day my parents and sister were out fishing when they noticed that their hair was standing on end. Fortunately, they decided to get off the lake, because this indicates a major buildup of static electricity, and those in a boat (or on a golf course) are in imminent danger of being struck by lightning. The best rule still is to take cover when the interval between seeing lightning and hearing the corresponding thunderclap is less than 20 seconds. Then wait a half hour after the storm is over before going out.

When a major thunderstorm approaches, events are usually measured in minutes rather than hours, and it is important to recognize the signs. Typically, on the day before the storm, the wind shifts from the southeast to southwest, and the barometric pressure begins to fall rapidly. As the storm approaches, the often brisk southwest wind may die down, leaving the lake almost calm. By this point you should be heading off the lake if you are in a small boat, because the thunderstorm is likely to be preceded by a short period of intense west to northwest wind, often blowing from 40 to 60 MPH. The wind may persist, or it may calm down a bit as the actual thunderstorm hits.

A thunderstorm is the product of a collision between the cold, dry air of a cold front that has run into the warm, moist air of a warm front. Cold fronts typically roll in from the northwest, and they ram into the side of the warm front, which is advancing from southwest to northeast (fig. 12.1). The denser cold air slides beneath the warm air, pushing it up into high columns, as evidenced by the towering cumulonimbus clouds that spawn thunderstorms (fig. 12.2). As the warm, humid air rises, it expands and cools, resulting in the condensation of its humidity into droplets of rain. These droplets rise and fall in the upper reaches of the cloud. With repeated cycles in the cold upper atmosphere, the droplets can freeze around a nucleus of dust or other particles and turn into hailstones, which along with the raindrops are dumped onto the surface of the lake. Both the air and the rain from a thunderstorm are cold, and the air temperature can rapidly drop by 10 to 20 degrees during a thunderstorm. The rain and cool air also cool the surface water of the lake, and the surface water temperature is likely to decrease by a few degrees after such a storm.

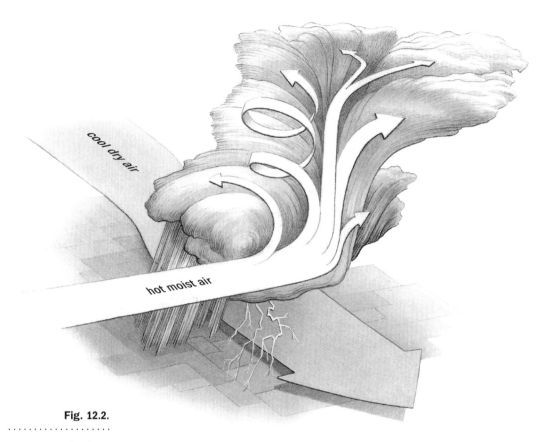

cool dry air

hot moist air

**Fig. 12.2.**
...................

*Anatomy of a thunderstorm. A mass of warm, moist air rises above the cool, dry air of an incoming cold front, forming an anvil-shaped cumulonimbus cloud. As the air rises, it cools and releases water as raindrops.*

The aftermath of a severe summer storm is very distinctive. Often, early the next morning the lake is as still as glass, with a bright sun in a cloudless sky. The haze of the previous day is gone, and it seems like you can reach out and touch the other side of the lake. If the wind before and during the storm was severe, the shore that was windward will be strewn with an odd collection of plastic beach toys, sticks, water plants, and an occasional floating minnow bucket. On Ten Mile Lake, at least, this is absolutely the worst period for fishing. In over fifty years of fishing that lake, I don't remember ever having caught a walleye the morning after a severe thunderstorm.

The period of the early morning post-storm calm is typically followed by a drop in temperature that accompanies the appearance of a strong northwest wind in the range of 15 to 30 MPH. The skies above are punctuated with white, puffy cumulus clouds that form and are torn apart by the winds. The barometric pressure has risen considerably since the storm. These conditions usually last for two to three days, during which time fishing is lousy, the water is cold for swimming, and indoor cabin games are popular. One of the side benefits of a cold front is the near disappearance of the flies and mosquitoes.

We have almost no understanding of how the passage of weather systems—both warm fronts and cold fronts—influences fish behavior. Theories abound, but most of them fail to pass close scrutiny. One involves changes in air pressure, which are certainly correlated with fish behavior. The absolute change in air pressure is so minute compared with the pressure of the water, however, that it is hard to imagine that a fish could detect it, when just swimming a few inches higher or lower in the water column would more than equal that effect. Another common theory, especially used to explain the subdued behavior of fish after the passage of a cold front, is that the increased light intensity from the clear, sunny sky puts them down. This could likely have some effect, but for fish in deep water, the amount of light penetrating to those levels is so small that again it would have a lesser absolute effect than just swimming higher or lower in the water. Another idea that has never really been tested is that strong storm systems have an electromagnetic effect on fish. The bottom line is that we really just don't know. Nevertheless, the effect is there.

Whatever the reason, the fishing for most species usually slows to a crawl after the passage of a cold front. Unfortunately, these beautiful blue days are those favored by many inexperienced anglers, and the combination of inexperience plus difficult fishing conditions almost guarantees a poor catch of the larger game fish. Not all fish are equally affected by cold fronts. Panfish often continue to bite, whereas their cousins, the bass, develop a severe case of lockjaw that can make it difficult even for professionals to make a decent catch. Similarly, walleyes are strongly affected by cold fronts. Northern pike are also affected by cold fronts, but not so severely as bass or walleyes. These effects are most pronounced in clear lakes but are often little felt in rivers. The rule of thumb for fishing during a cold front is to go deep, use small baits, and use a slow retrieve, but sometimes breaking all the rules by retrieving or trolling large baits at a super-fast speed is most effective. Many anglers gravitate toward the use of live bait. Fishing for walleyes is often best at night after a cold front has passed through. I haven't done enough night fishing for bass under these conditions to make meaningful observations on these fish. Often in the summertime a cold front is followed by a lengthy period of nice, stable weather. Typically, the quality of fishing improves the longer the good weather continues.

As summer progresses, subtle changes take place in the lake. If the weather is cold, there may be little change from early to late summer. Regardless of the weather, the plants continue to grow; the fish, from young-of-the-years to adults, get larger; and the thermocline becomes more pronounced (fig. 12.3). In a hot summer the water in the epilimnion layer above the thermocline takes on a uniform temperature

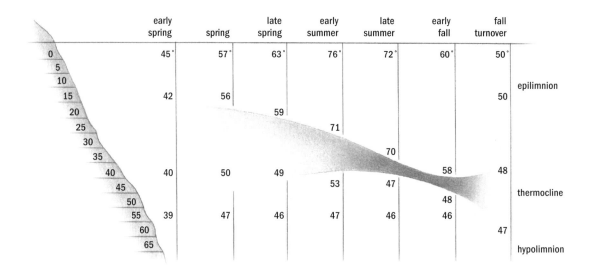

**Fig. 12.3.**

*Formation and dissolution of the thermocline during the course of a single open-water period in a northern lake.*

from the surface to the top of the thermocline layer. The warm water is also conducive to algae blooms. If the water gets very warm, it forces many of the larger fish into or below the waters of the thermocline, which late in a hot summer may be very sharp—sometimes only a few feet thick. Scuba divers have told me that at such times they can suspend in the warm upper water and drop an arm into the thermocline and have it feel uncomfortably cold. One August on Ten Mile Lake, the water temperature dropped from 70.1 degrees at 35 feet to 54.6 degrees at 40 feet.

Ten Mile Lake has sufficient oxygen for fish life in the hypolimnion layer below the thermocline, but in some shallow, more eutrophic lakes the water below the thermocline becomes depleted of oxygen. This places cold-water fish like whitefish and ciscoes in a real bind because they have to choose between living in poorly oxygenated water of a reasonable temperature or better-oxygenated water that is above their temperature tolerance. This can result in massive fish kills of such cold-water fish and could possibly wipe them out from a shallow lake. Fortunately, very young fish have a higher temperature tolerance than do larger members of the same species. Survival of more temperature-tolerant young individuals may be why populations of ciscoes or whitefish can persist over the years in shallow lakes at the southern end of their range. It is not unlikely that large northern pike in shallow hot lakes become similarly stressed and die at the end of a hot summer.

In many lakes fishing, especially for walleyes and northern pike, becomes quite poor in August. It has been traditional to blame this on their shedding their teeth during the late summer; however, there is no scientific evidence for this. It is most likely that the big pike have gone deep where most anglers don't think to fish for them. Because of the abundance of increasingly larger young perch and minnows, the angler is having trouble convincing an already stuffed walleye that it should go after his bait.

By late July one can already see the first traces of the coming change of seasons. Bonaparte gulls, which nested in northern Canada, have already begun their fall migration toward their wintering sites in the south and appear in significant numbers on Ten Mile Lake. The loons have also finished the critical period of raising their young and have begun to engage in greater social group activity, including forming rafts of many dozens of birds. This is accompanied by a reduction in their nighttime calling.

In northern Minnesota the end of the first to second week of August has been the traditional time when the back of summer begins to break. The evenings are getting noticeably shorter, and the cold fronts seem longer and more severe. This by no means signifies the end of hot weather, but prolonged stretches of heat are much less likely to occur. A pronounced decrease in the number of mosquitoes and, to a lesser extent, flies is a welcome change. On the land around the lake, late summer flowers, like asters and goldenrod, dominate the shoulders of the roads. The incidence of thunderstorms is diminished, and the frequency of cold windy stretches is correspondingly increased.

Within the lake subtle changes are also occurring. Hatches of mayflies are a thing of the past, and the number of caddis flies that swarm around boat lights at night is markedly diminished. The aquatic vegetation has matured, and the weed beds are not likely to get any denser. On many lakes fishing is not very exciting for the average angler. In fact, it is likely to be worse than it was earlier in the summer. Experienced anglers, however, notice subtle changes. Night fishing is likely to be better than it was earlier in the summer, and the fish are now attracted to somewhat larger baits than they were in July. Although the numbers may be less, the average size of the fish is larger. Because of the warm water throughout the epilimnion, shallow-water fishing is often not very productive, but for those who probe the boundaries of the thermocline, the fish are still biting. Late at night on Ten Mile Lake, some unusual behavior of small fish takes place. Large schools of an as yet unidentified fish (minnows or young ciscoes?) aggregate about 10 to 12 feet below the surface in the hours after midnight. Some schools that I have mapped out are close to a quarter of a mile long but are much narrower. They slowly move from one place to another, and when they intersect with good walleye habitat, it is a good place to try some late-night fishing.

By late August the nights become noticeably colder, and the shallower bays become foggy as the cool night air hits the warm surface waters. Labor Day, the traditional end of summer on most lakes, is a period of contrasts. Some years there is no doubt that fall is arriving, and the weekend is cold, gray, windy, and often damp, as well. Other years the temperature is still in the 90s. The water has often cooled enough so that only the kids still go in swimming. Regardless of the weather, the kids have to go back to school, the pace of work in the office increases from its summer slump, and folks in cabins pull in their docks and close up for the winter. On the drive home from the lake, bright crimson maples are seen in the northern swamps. It is unfortunate that for so many families their lake experience ends on Labor Day, because fall can be a magical time on a north country lake.

## Fall

Both above and below the water, fall is a period of preparation. The rafting activity of the loons increases, and by late September groups of ducks and geese, as well as gulls and terns, begin to stop at the lake on their way south. In the bays the muskrats are very active building their houses and generally preparing for winter. The beavers have taken renewed interest in cutting down trees, as they gather branches for their food caches to take them through the long northern winter.

Hot days are a thing of the past, but cool nights with occasional frosts alternate with beautiful warm days. On the other hand, cold fronts are more frequent and more severe. As early as mid-September, strong northwest winds bringing in snow flurries are not unheard of. By late September the maple leaves have begun to turn bright yellow or orange, starting at the top of the tree, and the sumac and poison ivy leaves turn an equally brilliant shade of red. A couple weeks later the birch trees are covered with yellow leaves, and the poplars have also joined the fall color parade in a more subdued fashion.

Many mornings in the early fall, the bays are blanketed in fog as the sun rises. This signifies the cooling of the water, as well. In a reversal of what happens in the springtime, the shallow bays, with less water to act as a buffer, cool more rapidly than the main lake, but in general the water temperature falls steadily from its early August highs. As the cooling continues, the lake water reaches a point where the water temperature on the surface is lower than that at the bottom. Because the density of water increases as its temperature approaches 39 degrees, the cool surface water begins to sink and displace the warmer, less dense deeper water. A point is reached when these waters mix and things in the lake get all confused. This is called the *fall turnover*, and it can often be recognized by seeing gunk from the lake bottom floating on the surface of the water. Depending upon the weather conditions, a lake can have more than one turnover event if significant periods of warm weather follow cold stretches. The time of the fall turnover varies considerably in lakes depending upon their depths. A lake that has a maximum depth of 15 to 20 feet can turn over weeks sooner than a lake that is deeper than 100 feet. Because of its extreme depth, the main fall turnover in Ten Mile Lake is one of the last in the region. By the time the main lake basin has cooled to the point of turning over, shore ice has begun to form in the shallow bays on cold nights.

These changes have a profound effect on the plant and animal life below the surface of the lake. Although the preparations for winter are not as obvious as on land, they are equally intense. Starting in September, the fish begin feeding in earnest. Part of the reason for this is an unexplained instinct that they should take in as much food as they can to prepare them for the long, cold winter, when their metabolism is greatly reduced. For females there is the additional need to take in nourishment to support the growth of the thousands of eggs in their ovaries. Each egg must itself store sufficient nutritional reserves to get the future fish embryos to the hatching stage and also support them for the first days to weeks of life until they get large enough to catch their own food. Most of this advance preparation is best done before the water gets so cold that the fish's reduced metabolism can't handle the needs of the maturing eggs.

For the serious angler fall is the time to go after trophies. For almost all species of game fish, the largest specimens, which seemed nonexistent in the summer, move into feeding grounds and are accessible to the angler. It is no accident that most professional anglers, who need photos of themselves holding big fish for publicity purposes, reserve the fall for trophy fishing. For the inexperienced angler, however, fall fishing can be both a bit intimidating and unfamiliar because many of the rules that work for summertime fishing have to be modified in the fall. Most important is where to find them, and next is what to use for baits and how to present the baits.

Let's start with a few generalities. The first involves the aquatic vegetation. As fall progresses, patches of the summer growth of aquatic vegetation begin to get brown and die off. A general rule of thumb is that the fish tend to abandon such areas and seek areas where the vegetation is still green. This is particularly true for largemouth bass. Another generalization involves water temperature. When the water first begins to cool from the summer high temperatures, many of the larger game fish leave the depths and move into shallower water. Then, as the water cools further, they move back into deeper water, but not exclusively. The time of the fall turnover is probably the worst time of the year for fishing, because of the general disruption of the lake, but fortunately, this usually doesn't last more than a week. Over the years I have experienced the best fall fishing during the time when the maple and birch leaves have turned to their brightest color.

By October the fish can be at almost any depth, and it is necessary to experiment. Walleyes, for instance, can be caught at depths as great as 60 to 80 feet during the day, or they may be in shoreline waters at night, depending upon weather conditions. Biologists conducting lake surveys in September regularly find 8-pound walleyes in trap nets that are set in bays in water less then 3 feet deep. Bass also move into deeper water, but not so much as walleyes. Smallmouth bass begin to seek deepwater wintering sites, where they are literally stacked side by side. They become quite inactive in cold water. When they are in deeper

**Fig. 12.4.**
. . . . . . . . . . . . . . . . . . . .

*Ice formations at the edge of the lake during early winter. These form on very cold, windy days before the lake has frozen over. The spray from waves freezes upon contact with grass and horsetail stems, forming sta-lagmites of ice.*

water, both walleyes and largemouth bass show a strong preference for steeply sloping banks and are often concentrated near the bottom of the slope. Many of the larger pike move into shallow bays or off points or in saddle regions between islands. Night fishing for walleyes can be excellent in the fall, especially around the full moons of September or October. In many lakes the walleyes move into very shallow water at night, and some of the best catches of large ones are made by those who cast for them with long minnow-shaped baits from shore.

A very important generalization is that in the fall, especially, the game fish will be associated with concentrations of smaller fish on which they feed. In some lakes minnows congregate into large, dense schools, and that's where you will find the walleyes, regardless of depth. In lakes where there is still a large fall frog migration, walleyes will also be concentrated in the areas where the frogs enter the water. Fall fish are really looking for calories, and this is one time of the year when it is almost impossible to use a crankbait that is too large. Six- to seven-inch minnowbaits are just fine for fall walleyes, and the same holds true for bass, although they can still be caught on small baits, as well. Large pike and muskies will go after the largest baits in your tackle box in the fall. Remember that a favored size of prey is one-quarter the length of the fish.

When the water cools further, a major event in Ten Mile Lake is the spawning of ciscoes and whitefish. Like several other members of the trout family, these are fall spawners. In late October and November, when the water temperatures are in the 40s, these fish move to their spawning grounds. This is the time when netting for whitefish is legal and popular in some lakes. Much of the spawning activity of both whitefish and ciscoes takes place at night, and their activities are also attended by numbers of hungry walleyes and pike, which are looking to pick off an easy meal.

By late fall the shallow bays have frozen over, but the deep main basin of Ten Mile Lake takes a long time to cool and does not freeze until all the other lakes in the vicinity have a complete ice cover. Ten Mile often doesn't freeze over until early December. In 2004 cold, windy weather late in the fall caused large waves to crash on the eastern shore, and for over a mile the freezing water droplets formed vertical ice formations resembling stalactites and stalagmites (fig. 12.4).

## Winter

Winters in the north country are long and severe, and the lakes are encased in thick ice for four to five months. Yet life goes on below the ice, although at a reduced pace. The water has settled into a stable winter pattern, with the water temperature just beneath the ice close to freezing.

The warmest water, 39 degrees, is at the bottom of the lake because, at that temperature, water density is at its maximum. This small difference in water temperature means that there are no thermal barriers for fish and that they can be found at almost any depth. Even in the winter finding food is still the number one priority for fish, so regardless of the water temperature, the larger fish will gravitate toward the shallower water, where many of the smaller fish are concentrated. Unless there is no snow on the ice, the inhabitants of the lake live in dim twilight during the day and virtually complete darkness at night. Nevertheless, life goes on. Neither beavers nor muskrats hibernate in the winter, but their overall activity is reduced. Most of the time beavers remain in their lodge on the living platform above the water. When they do venture out to gather branches from their food cache, even their heavy coat is not sufficient to keep them from losing body heat to the cold water. Within a well-made lodge the air temperature is much warmer than that outside owing to both the mud insulation on the outside of the lodge and the combined body heat of the several-generation beaver family.

Fish show varying degrees of activity during the winter. At one extreme are the smallmouth bass, which spend most of the winter tightly huddled and for the most part inactive in deepwater refuges. At the other extreme is the eelpout, or burbot (see fig. 2.10), which is almost invisible in the summer but feeds actively during the winter. These deepwater relatives of codfish are sometimes caught incidentally by ice fishers who are targeting walleyes.

Most game fish are active during the winter, and thousands of anglers haul out their fish houses and set them on likely sites, which sometimes resemble small villages situated on the ice. Walleyes, crappies, sunfish, and perch are the most popular species sought by ice fishers. Another subset of ice fishers is the group of spearers, who set their houses on shallow bays and wait for northern pike to glide under the long hole that they have made in the ice. Without a doubt, more large pike are seen in the winter than at any other time of the year. This is largely because, in the summer months, the large pike stay in much deeper water than most anglers suspect. Pike spearers dangle fish decoys below their holes in order to attract their quarry. Some of the best-made pike decoys are very artistic and are now collected as works of folk art. They can be worth quite a bit of money.

In the early winter walleyes remain in the same type of habitat that they occupied in the late fall, and their feeding habits can be just as finicky as they are during the open-water period. They usually bite better during periods of changing light. Rather than drilling one hole and waiting for the walleyes to come to the bait, many ice fishers will drill multiple holes and move around until they find the fish. Such folks have a different mind-set from those who occupy traditional fish houses, and they must be more willing to deal with the weather. In recent years ice fishing technology has boomed, however, and in addition to new models of fishing tackle, fish finders, underwater cameras, and a variety of mobile shelters that can protect the angler from the worst of the elements are now readily available.

Panfish—sunfish, crappies, and perch—all bite readily in the winter for those using the proper tackle. One of the trickiest parts of fishing for panfish under the ice is knowing how deep to fish. Crappies, in particular, commonly suspend at various levels within the water column. If bait is presented below the school, the crappies are not likely to bite, because they almost never go after food that is below them.

As winter drags on, some lakes get into trouble with oxygen deprivation. These are typically shallow lakes with lots of decaying weeds and muddy bottoms. Especially if the ice is covered with snow, the balance between oxygen production by plant life and the utilization of oxygen by decaying vegetation and organisms in the silt is tipped toward the latter, and the oxygen levels can drop to levels that will not sustain fish life. This results in winter kills. Each kind of fish has different tolerance levels for low oxygen, but unfortunately, game fish tend to be more susceptible to low oxygen than are many of the rough fish. Conservation crews use a variety of methods to try to prevent fish kills, but in certain lakes wintertime fish kills are almost predictable. In some of these lakes, netting operations are carried out to rescue fish, like northern pike, and stock them in other lakes.

The winter ice is an amazingly dynamic system. Anyone who has lived by a northern lake in the wintertime is familiar with the groanings and the sometimes sharp cracking noises made by the ice on very cold nights. As winter comes to a close and temperatures get warmer, the ice expands. On larger lakes the expansion is sufficient to cause large ridges of buckled ice to form alongside the shore, and the expanded ice often pushes the soft materials of the beach itself into the ice ridges that are familiar to many cabin owners when they first arrive at their cabins in the spring.

By the end of winter, fishing seasons for all but panfish have closed in most states, and the ice begins to get gray. This is the period when most of the fish in the lake are anticipating the upcoming spawning season. They feed less as winter progresses, and they begin to stage in areas close to where they will spawn. Then, with the melting of the ice, the annual cycle of reproduction begins again.

## 13 THE FUTURE OF NORTH COUNTRY LAKES

A lake is very much like a living organism. It is born, grows up, gets old, and then dies. Most north country lakes were born after the last glacier receded, although the circumstances surrounding their births were not always identical. For thousands of years these lakes went through their childhood and adolescence pretty much uninfluenced by anything but the local climatic cycles. Only in the last couple hundred years, since the American settlers first burst onto the scene, has there been a significant human influence on our northern lakes. As a result, some lakes have sped through certain parts of their life cycle, whereas others have remained relatively untouched by direct human intervention. Yet even many of the lakes in that latter category have been profoundly affected by human activity through significant changes in the air, the surface water flowing into them, or the groundwater that contributes to many lakes.

For better or worse, lakes are in constant equilibrium with their environment. When their environment is polluted, they can go downhill extremely rapidly, but a few hopeful examples have shown that they can also recover to a surprising extent when the sources of pollution are removed. I still remember a seminar that I attended at the University of Michigan in the late 1960s. One of the foremost experts on lake pollution was discussing the sorry state of Lake Erie. (At the time some of its feeder streams were so polluted by industrial waste that they regularly caught fire.) This expert declared that Lake Erie would be dead for at least a hundred years, if it would ever recover. Yet ten to fifteen years later, after a massive effort to stem the flow of pollutants moving into the lake, the fishing had already recovered, and the water looked better than it had in decades. It is important to note, however, that this apparent recovery didn't mean that the lake was completely healthy. It turned out that many of the pollutants, such as mercury, had gotten trapped beneath a fresh layer of silt and organic matter on the bottom but were still in the lake. Nevertheless, Lake Erie's water quality had improved enormously over a remarkably short period of time. Let's look at some of the ways that a typical north country lake can be affected by human activity and what can be done about it.

## A Pristine Lake

In its pristine condition a north country lake has clear water, although the color of the lake water may be brown because of tannins fed into it by effluent from bogs or swamp water. Unless the lake has a rocky shoreline, like those in the region of the Canadian Shield, much of the shoreline is lined by beds of bulrushes, patches of arrowhead, occasional clumps of wild irises, and a scattering of other emergent plants. The skeletons of fallen trees extend from the shoreline into deeper water, providing cover for a variety of fish and insects below the water, resting spots for turtles and frogs, and hunting stations for raccoons above the water. Beds of aquatic vegetation are scattered along the shallower waters, especially in the bays, but there is likely to be a clear area between the inside edge of the weed beds and the shore where the plants have been uprooted by the scouring action of the waves and ice. In sandy areas freshwater clams leave their irregular trails, like lines drawn by a stick.

The fish populations are dominated by large specimens. These bruisers of the fish world pick out the most desirable habitat, like large rocks or fallen trees, for their resting spaces or ambush points. This forces those farther down the pecking order into slightly less favorable locations, although a typical pristine lake has an abundance of good underwater habitat. This is one situation where large predators, like pike and walleyes, can die of old age, because nothing in the water poses any danger to them.

## The Impact of Humans on a Lake

Conditions like those described above went on for centuries before the first humans visited the lakes. Until the first habitations were built at the edge of a lake, humans had little impact on its ecology. Water could be drunk safely directly from the lake. With the appearance of the first settlement, a small area of beach was cleared for access and for storing boats or canoes. Local pollution of the beach area occurred when women washed clothes at the water's edge or if the remains of cleaned fish or other garbage were tossed into the lake. When additional homes were built, the same scenario was repeated. Over time, simple wooden docks were built for the leaky flat-bottomed boats that were rowed around the lake.

The first settlement on many lakes often coincided with the invasion of the lumberjacks, who a century ago roamed through the north country, cutting down the virgin forests. Even though their presence at a given site was only temporary—usually just a few years at most—the lumberjacks often made the first major human impact on the lake. Water was used for moving timber, and both lakes and rivers were impacted. Logs were floated from one place to the next, and not all logs made it to their destination. Some became waterlogged and sank to the bottom, creating new habitat for fish and insects. In rivers these often persisted as deadheads, with just the tip of one end protruding from the surface. These mostly submerged logs provided excellent ambush points and current shelters for fish and sunning spots for turtles, but they made the waterways more hazardous for boat traffic.

The Great Lakes were the site of transport of much cut timber, and because of the nasty weather, often entire shipments of logs were lost and sank to the bottom. Even today the Great Lakes contain huge piles of waterlogged virgin pine logs that are proving to be extremely valuable because of the way the water has preserved them. Such logs, which are often many feet in diameter, are worth up to a thousand dollars each. At least one Japanese piano company has made arrangements with the new generation of underwater loggers to provide it with wood for their best-quality pianos. Certain inland lakes also have large piles of logs on the bottom, but considerable controversy exists as to whether or not these long-standing features of the lake bottom should be removed.

Logging had less salutary effects, as well. After the trees had been cleared alongside the banks of rivers and streams, the water was exposed to more sunlight, and it became much warmer in the summer than it used to be. This made some of the streams unsuitable for the native brook trout that once lived in them. In addition, scarred riverbanks began to erode after heavy rains. The eroded sediment was carried down the inlet streams and eventually settled into the lakes, depositing a thin layer of silt over the bottom.

Other activities of the loggers also impacted the lake. Sometimes sawmills were built at the edge of the lake, and huge piles of sawdust settled to the bottom. The sawdust effectively choked off most insect life and drastically reduced the area's suitability as habitat for other invertebrates and small fish. Sometimes large docks or structures for retaining log booms were built into the lake and were subsequently abandoned when the logging camps moved on. Of course, there was the occasional axe head or snoose jug that managed to find its way to the lake bottom. These days one has to look very carefully for even a trace of the lumber camps. Often the most visible remnant is a hard-packed former road or trail whose compressed soil is still a hostile substrate for tree growth.

Very often, trappers moved in parallel with the lumberjacks if they weren't already working in the area. The turn of the nineteenth century saw trapping activity reduce the population of beavers almost to extinction and make major inroads on the numbers of other fur-bearing mammals as well. Fortunately, strong restrictions placed on trapping and hunting at the time prevented the extinction of several valuable species.

After the lumberjack era some folks found themselves with sufficient leisure time and financial means to come to the lake for their summer vacations. Groups of friends built small clusters of simple cabins, usually along the high pine-forested banks of the lake because there weren't so many mosquitoes and other biting insects in these areas. On Ten Mile Lake the low areas with gorgeous sand beaches were considered to be totally unsatisfactory for human habitation by the early settlers. If only these pioneer vacationers could have known how many thousands of dollars per front foot these beach lots now command!

By this time not all of the lake residents felt comfortable in drinking water straight out of the lake, and shallow wells with hand pumps were installed. The standard sanitation was the outhouse or biffy tucked away in the woods behind the cabin. When an outhouse filled up, another was built, and the first one was abandoned, after being liberally treated with lime. In that era it wasn't appreciated that much of the organic matter, as well as the soapy water that was thrown away after each washing or cleaning episode, percolated into the ground and ultimately entered the lake, enriching the water with phosphorus and nitrogen compounds. In some of the smaller shallow lakes, longtime residents began to notice an occasional algae bloom in hot summer weather or the appearance of small patches of aquatic plants in the shoreline water below the cabin where previously there had been none.

Starting in the 1930s and 1940s, an occasional lake resident would buy a very heavy and usually unreliable outboard motor that, when it worked, propelled the old flat-bottomed boat across the lake at what seemed to be an amazing speed. For several decades these motors were fueled by pouring gasoline into a built-in gas tank. When done on the water, it was usual to spill some gas into the water during each fueling episode, especially when it was wavy.

By the 1950s and 1960s, many of the north country lakes followed the pattern of their counterparts near cities and became pretty much ringed with cabins—bigger than the first-generation cabins on the lake and equipped with electricity (see appendix 6). Along with electricity came running water, indoor plumbing, and the construction of septic systems. This helped to contain lots of waste for each cabin, but there were now many more cabins. The increased density of cabins had a significant effect on the lake front because many cabin owners cleared fallen trees and what they thought of as weeds both above and below the water to make better beaches, and often the rocks were removed from the beaches, as well. With these so-called improvements, the beds of bulrushes were typically the first plants to go.

Many cabin owners decided that they wanted lawns around their cabins, so they cleared the trees and brush and planted grass. One of the unexpected side effects of the lawns and groomed beaches was the invasion of Canada geese onto the lawns, along with the one-third pound of poop that each goose contributes each day to the premises. In order to get the grass to grow better, the lawns were fertilized regularly. As a result, more phosphates and other nutrients ran into the lake when it rained, and the water became fertilized as well. Fertilizer in water acts just like it does on land; it lets plants grow luxuriously. In water the first plants to take advantage of increased nutrients were the algae. The algae multiplied, and water clarity correspondingly decreased. In some lakes water clarity was reduced to a couple of feet, and for the first time in old timers' memories, summer fish kills occurred. Usually, the dead fish were ciscoes or suckers, but sometimes a large, bloated pike would also be seen floating on the surface. Although not always recognized at first, there were signs of oxygen depletion below the thermocline, which was due to the increased amount of decaying organic matter in the lake.

Another activity that has significantly changed the complexion of many lakes is fish stocking. In the early days of fisheries biology, starting in the late 1800s, the mind-set was to improve lakes and streams by stocking them with nonnative fish. In 1877 some ill-guided fishery managers, who considered carp to be nature's perfect fish, undertook a major initiative and introduced European carp into eastern and western bodies of water. Another more successful experiment from the same era was the introduction of brown trout from Europe into many of our streams. The brown trout adapted very well to their new surroundings and have become a major sport fish, but in doing so they displaced many of our native brook trout from their original habitat. In retrospect, this may have been a good move since, over succeeding decades, the concurrent logging activity resulted in the warming of many formerly pristine streams, thus transforming them into an environment that was far more favorable for brown trout than it would have been for brook trout. Wherever the railroads went, too, enthusiastic anglers succumbed to the temptation to carry a few buckets of their favorite fish in order to stock the lakes that they fished. Many northern trout lakes were stocked with smallmouth bass in this manner, sometimes resulting in the disappearance of the trout, which were ultimately replaced by large populations of stunted bass. The natural tendency of anglers to dump their remaining minnows into the lake at the end of their fishing trips also led to some major shifts in the minnow populations of some lakes.

By the time lakes had become ringed with cabins and motorboats had given people more ready access to all parts of the lake, anglers began to complain that fishing wasn't what it used to be. Stories of huge northern pike as long as an oar became the subject of local legend, the veracity of which depended greatly upon the teller. Walleyes weren't as readily caught as they were a decade previously. Similarly, although it was still possible to catch good messes of sunfish and crappies, one-pound sunfish and two-pound crappies were largely a thing of the past. One would occasionally hear grumbling that the lake was fished out. To a certain extent this was true, especially for the large pike and panfish, but what was more true was that the cream of the crop and the easy pickings had been removed. The real problem was that few anglers really understood the basics of fish biology, and they didn't know how to find locations where game fish spent the bulk of their time.

A real revolution in fishing began with a few pioneers in the 1950s and 1960s. Some were anglers who understood that a lake was more than a big bathtub with fish randomly swimming around the water. Others pioneered new equipment. Back in the 1950s and 1960s, a common sight on many lakes was a plastic bottle tied to a string and tethered to a "fishing hole" in the lake. These were usually placed by anglers who located bars or underwater islands by lowering heavy fishing sinkers on marked lines into the water. This same period brought to market the first generation of fish finders—whirring affairs, called *flashers*, that gave off various arrays of lighted bars on a circular screen. With these finders most users could determine bottom depth and, with practice, pick out clusters of lighted lines that signified weeds or possibly even fish. Those few anglers who caught on to the emerging new ways of fishing often came in with astounding catches, but by and large the average angler was still not getting much for his efforts. Another major technological development from the 1950s was the introduction of spinning tackle. This made bait casting far easier for the average angler, who was accustomed to devoting a good share of his casting time to untangling backlashes, which bedeviled users of the standard casting reels available at the time.

Since the 1970s, a regular flood of new information and new technology has opened up angling opportunities that were unimaginable to previous generations of anglers. The present-day angler, armed with a huge array of rods and tackle, can quickly reach any part of a lake with large boats powered by enormous motors. No longer is it necessary to use finely developed senses and instinct to find the best fishing areas, because built-in global positioning system (GPS) units in conjunction with highly sophisticated depth finders that operate at high speed allow the angler to quickly home in on fishing hot spots. Now one can even buy lake maps showing the GPS coordinates for the best fishing areas. Once at the fishing spot, new-generation trolling motors, some with foot-pedal controls, allow the angler not only to have precise boat control but to devote more time and attention to actual fishing. If there is any doubt about what the blips on the fish finder represent, underwater cameras are now available that allow one to see firsthand what the underwater terrain looks like and what kinds of fish are down there.

All of this knowledge and technology is a real boon to those who are both curious and serious anglers, but they come at a cost. It is now possible to seek out fish wherever they are and to fish with an efficiency that would have been unimaginable to our parents. Increased numbers of anglers, fishing with greatly increased efficiency, have the real potential to seriously alter the population structure of many species of game fish. The usual result is the cropping off of the large game fish and the relative expansion of the small- to medium-sized specimens (fig. 13.1). Such shifts are particularly noticeable in relatively easy-to-catch species like northern pike, sunfish, and crappies.

The 1960s brought high-powered motors and speedboats to our northern lakes. For many families this introduced an era of new recreational opportunities, but for others it made the lakes more crowded and more noisy. This trend has inexorably continued with greater varieties of more-powerful boats. The introduction of jet skis into the mix during the late 1990s is one of the latest manifestations of the evolution of recreational boating. In addition to noise, boats and motors in sufficient numbers also affect lakes in more substantial ways. The early generations of large motors were highly inefficient, and some lakes experienced considerable pollution from gasoline by-products. Another important effect of larger, faster boats has been shoreline erosion in narrow, low-lying areas due to their wakes. The collapsing of unstable shoreline areas introduces additional silt into the lake and degrades habitat.

A couple of decades after the introduction of indoor plumbing to cabins, septic systems began to fail if they were not properly maintained. In many lakes these unseen sources of pollution have contributed to further reductions in water quality. Many of the increased problems of lakes during the late twentieth century were due to more of the same thing, rather than to anything new.

The latest generation of challenges to north country lakes is just beginning. Foremost is the potential for an amazing variety of exotic

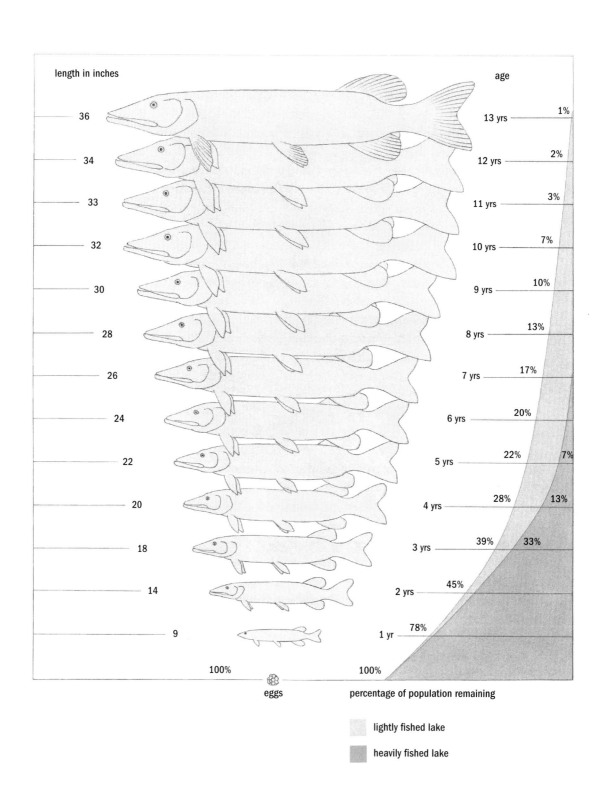

length in inches

age

36 — 13 yrs — 1%

34 — 12 yrs — 2%

33 — 11 yrs — 3%

32 — 10 yrs — 7%

30 — 9 yrs — 10%

28 — 8 yrs — 13%

26 — 7 yrs — 17%

24 — 6 yrs — 20%

22 — 5 yrs — 22% — 7%

20 — 4 yrs — 28% — 13%

18 — 3 yrs — 39% — 33%

14 — 2 yrs — 45%

9 — 1 yr — 78%

100% — 100%

eggs — percentage of population remaining

lightly fished lake

heavily fished lake

plants and animals to dominate our lakes. These invaders have been both accidentally and purposefully introduced into our lakes, and some have already exhibited the capacity to totally change a lake's ecology.

## Exotic Species
. . . . . . . . . . . . . . . . . .

Many of the invaders first found their way into the Great Lakes (fig. 13.2). These huge bodies of water have a sorry history of wave after wave of ecological disasters caused by foreign invaders. The first came with the opening of the Welland Canal in 1932. This canal was constructed between Lakes Erie and Ontario to allow ocean shipping to enter the Great Lakes by bypassing Niagara Falls. What was not foreseen was that it also allowed the entry of sea lampreys, which adapted beautifully to the freshwater and proceeded to decimate the native lake trout in the 1950s, before turning their attention to whitefish, ciscoes, and sometimes even swimmers.

A less catastrophic, but nevertheless massive, event was the explosion of the smelt population. Smelt, normally ocean fish, were stocked in the very deep waters of Crystal Lake in Michigan in 1912, but some of them found their way into Lake Michigan. By the early 1940s large numbers of smelt were already present in Lake Michigan. From there they spread to Lake Superior and Lake Huron and multiplied in such numbers that, during their annual early spring spawning runs in the 1950s and 1960s, people would drive up to Duluth and fill the backs of pick-up trucks with pails of these small, shiny fish. During my first summer, in 1956, as an aquatic biologist's aide in the Minnesota Conservation Department, one of my main jobs was analyzing the stomach contents of hundreds of Lake Superior smelt to see what they were eating. (At the time there was a theory that they ate lake trout eggs and may have been responsible for the precipitous decline in lake trout numbers.) The smelt arrived in five-gallon cream cans full of formaldehyde. In those unenlightened times, we stuck our hands directly into the formaldehyde to pull out smelt. As a result of this exposure to formaldehyde fumes, I burned out my sense of smell, most of which has yet to return.

During my studies on smelt stomachs, I once ran across a flat, silvery fish with a serrated belly. It turned out to be the second alewife (another ocean fish) identified in Lake Superior. Within a decade these fish had taken over Lake Michigan. Alewife die-offs often covered the beaches with deep windrows of smelly corpses.

This population imbalance led to one of the few really successful programs of fish introductions in the Great Lakes. Dr. Howard Tanner of the Michigan Department of Natural Resources (DNR) proposed the introduction of Pacific salmon into the Great Lakes to both control the

**Fig. 13.1.**
. . . . . . . . . . . . . . . . . .

*Population pyramids of northern pike in a nonfished and a heavily fished lake. The upper part of the pyramid, containing the largest fish, is sharply attenuated in a heavily fished lake, resulting in a population highly skewed toward smaller, hammerhandle pike.*

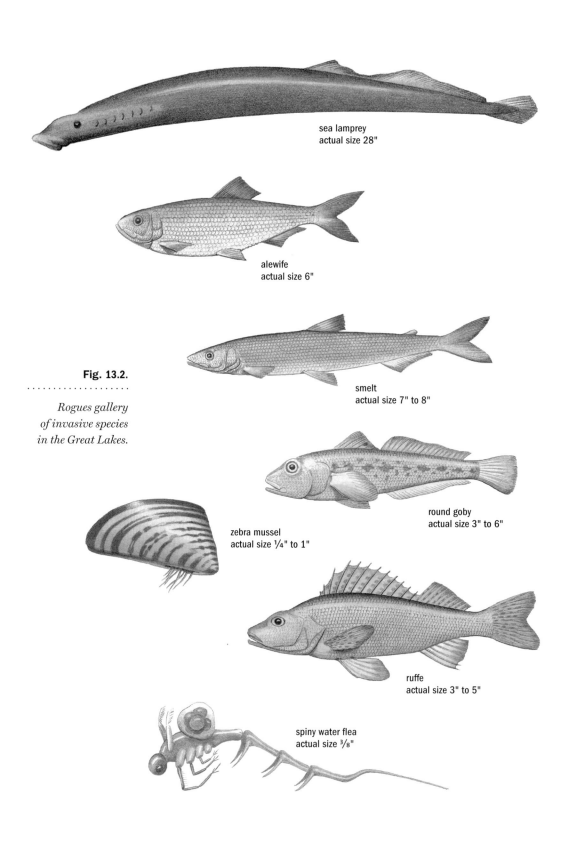

sea lamprey
actual size 28"

alewife
actual size 6"

smelt
actual size 7" to 8"

**Fig. 13.2.**

*Rogues gallery
of invasive species
in the Great Lakes.*

round goby
actual size 3" to 6"

zebra mussel
actual size ¼" to 1"

ruffe
actual size 3" to 5"

spiny water flea
actual size ⅜"

out-of-control alewife population and to provide a new sport fishery. The decimation of the lake trout and whitefish by lampreys had wiped out a thriving commercial fishery, which was also competing mightily with the lampreys in killing off these fish. The salmon stocking was a great success, and it generated a huge sport fishery industry in all of the Great Lakes.

None of the animals mentioned above pose a significant threat to our inland lakes, and for a decade or so, all seemed fine in the Great Lakes. Then, all sorts of things began to happen. In some of the international harbors, like Duluth and Cleveland, small, new fish began to appear. In addition, some of the drainage pipes and screens on water intake pipes in Lake Erie began to become encrusted with a new mollusk that nobody had seen before. These creatures had hitchhiked across the Atlantic in the ballast water of European freighters, and when the ballast water was emptied into the lakes, so were the animals living in it.

The mollusks were zebra mussels, and starting in Lake Erie, they have become a billion-dollar problem because of their blocking of pipes and screens. They literally cover the bottoms of the lakes in dense beds and are threatening many species of native mollusks. Like other mollusks, zebra mussels are filter feeders. They suck in water, strain out phytoplankton and zooplankton, and expel the water, minus its plankton. They are so efficient and so numerous that the water of Lake Erie has undergone a major change. It is now much clearer than it was twenty years ago. As a side effect, the increased water clarity has forced walleye anglers to dramatically change their fishing style, because the stronger light levels have caused walleyes to hold in deeper water during the day.

Other ballast tank escapees are fish—especially the ruffe and several species of goby. They reach only a few inches in length, but they are voracious feeders on small fish. We don't yet have an idea of the final impact that these still-expanding populations of fish will have on our native fish. The goby population in Lake Erie is already so large, however, that they have become a major food source for smallmouth bass and walleyes. As a testament to their prominence, goby-colored crankbaits are now commercially available at local sporting goods stores. What we don't know is how many small bass and walleyes are eaten by the gobies and ruffes. With the number of anglers and boaters who take their boats from one lake to another, zebra mussels in particular have already begun to spread to smaller northern lakes and streams in the Mississippi drainage that are not directly connected to the Great Lakes.

Another equally devastating invader is a plant—the Eurasian milfoil (fig. 13.3). Although it shares a name with our native northern milfoil, the Eurasian variety forms dense mats that can virtually choke off a lake. Most of the lakes in and around the Twin Cities are already infected with

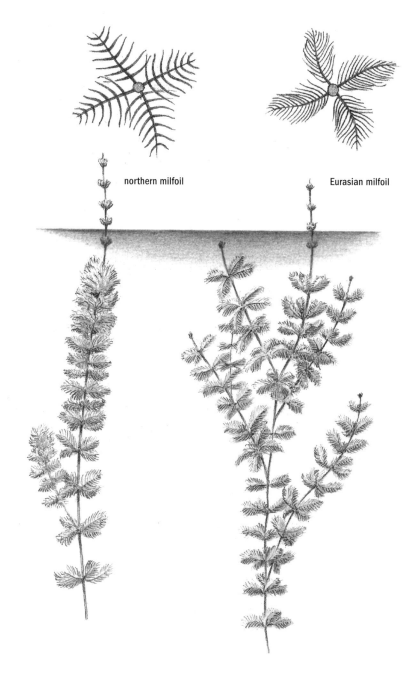

**Fig. 13.3.**

. . . . . . . . . . . . . . . . . . . .

*Northern and
Eurasian milfoil.
Note the more ex-
tensive branching
and more delicate
leaf structure
of the Eurasian mil-
foil. The leaves of
Eurasian milfoil
also have more pairs
of leaflets, usually
over 14, and they
are spaced closer
together than those
of northern milfoil.*

northern milfoil

Eurasian milfoil

Eurasian milfoil, and it is only a matter of time before it spreads to many of the northern lakes where Twin Citians fish or have cabins.

As if the above is not enough, the Mississippi River drainage and the Great Lakes now face a bizarre challenge—this time coming from Asia thanks to some incredibly short-sighted policies related to fish farms in some of our south-central states. Two huge Asian fish—grass carp and big-headed carp—were imported to serve as aquatic lawn mowers. Nat-urally, some of these fish, which can grow to be four feet long and weigh up to a hundred pounds, escaped into the local rivers and got into the Mississippi River. Then they began to reproduce and make their way upstream. They now pose a great threat of entering Lake Michigan through the Chicago shipping canal, which connects Lake Michigan to the Mississippi River drainage. The threat is so great that the Army Corps of Engineers has been allocated, but not yet given, millions of dollars to construct an electric fish barrier across the canal. By the time it is built, it is likely that some of these fish will already be on the Lake Michigan side of the barrier.

The big-headed carp, which have already been found in Lake Pepin, a Mississippi River lake between southern Minnesota and Wisconsin, poses another unique challenge. These fish bask on the surface of the water and, when startled, can leap several feet above the water. At least one boater has already been knocked out when a big-headed carp, frightened by an oncoming boat, jumped into the air and hit the person's head. The list of foreign invaders goes on, with one of the most recent entries being the snakehead fish from Southeast Asia. Some of these were apparently released into Maryland ponds, where they seem to have taken hold despite the complete draining of several suspect ponds. At least one of these fish has been discovered in a Wisconsin lake.

The story of human influences on lakes is a long and often sorry one. Nevertheless, the picture is not totally bleak. There have been some major success stories in the battle against lake degradation, and one of the major messages from these efforts is that the natural environment has a remarkable buffering and regenerative capacity if given half a chance.

## Maintaining and Improving North Country Lakes

Until the popular ecology movement began in the late 1960s, relatively little thought was given to improving lakes other than often ill-considered demands for stocking more fish. With the publication of Rachel Carson's *Silent Spring* in 1962, a public awareness of the devastating effects of pesticides on ecosystems developed, and some of the worst, such as DDT, were eliminated from general use. The passage of several decades since then has already seen a major turnaround, with the recovery of populations of high-end predators, such as eagles, whose eggs are no longer decimated by the eggshell-thinning effects of DDT. My wife and I still vividly remember the near absence of songbirds the year in the early 1970s when the land around Ten Mile Lake was sprayed for insects.

Deterioration of water quality can be a tougher nut to crack, depending upon the source of water supplying the lake. Ten Mile Lake is fortunate in being at the head of a watershed, with the input to the lake being springs, groundwater flow, swamp seepage, and rain. The drainage area is limited and consists mostly of forested land and swamps. Most lakes are fed by one or more input streams in addition to local sources, so their water quality is highly dependent upon what happens farther up in the watershed.

The most important element in improving water is a collective recognition that it is getting worse and a determination by the stakeholders—usually the cabin owners—to do something about it. An active and forward-looking lake association is often the best means of coordinating remedial action. For decades Ten Mile Lake has had such an association, and its Ecology Committee has for many years monitored the water quality through regular Secchi disk readings by volunteers and water chemistry determinations by private companies or the Minnesota Pollution Control Agency. By the 1970s the lake was well known locally for a beautiful turquoise green cast, but the Ecology Committee was becoming increasingly concerned about diminishing Secchi disk readings—which were still at a very healthy 17 feet. Through the leadership of that committee and the authority of the Ten Mile Lake Association, cabin owners were made aware of the situation. One of the first and most concrete steps taken was a campaign to maintain or upgrade septic systems around the lake. This included offering cabin owners testing kits that introduced a dye into the water of the septic tank. If the system was leaking and close to the lake, some of the dye found its way into the lake as an indicator that nutrients from the same system were entering the lake water. In 2005 the Ten Mile Lake Association retained a professional, using more sophisticated techniques, to check almost all septic systems around the lake. In addition, the association has coordinated an educational effort to warn cabin owners of the dangers of high-phosphate soap and fertilizers near the lake. These efforts have paid off over the years. Now Secchi disk readings are as high as 25 feet. Many old-timers miss the lovely turquoise color that characterized the lake in the 1970s, but we now know that it was due to algal growth, which has now largely disappeared.

Improving water quality has economic benefits, as well. According to a study quoted in the *Guide to Lake Protection and Management* (2004), produced jointly by the Freshwater Society and the Minnesota Pollution Control Agency (and available online at www.mpca.gov or www.freshwater.org), for every meter of increase in water clarity, land values increase by $423.00 per shoreline foot. For every meter of decrease in clarity, values decrease by $594.00 per shoreline foot.

A very dramatic change in water quality is well illustrated by a medium-sized lake fed by the upper Mississippi River a few miles south of Bemidji, Minnesota. Although the water in the river seemed quite clear, as soon as it entered the lake, it became pea soup green, and water clarity was reduced to inches, rather than feet. When the city upgraded its treatment of sewage, water quality in the lake improved dramatically over a remarkably short period of time. The same story has been written many times in rivers and streams throughout the world, once sources of pollution are capped. One of the most important sources of contaminants that lead to the deterioration of water quality in both streams and the lakes that they feed is agricultural fertilizers and live-stock waste. Another is land-use practices that allow nutrient-enriched soil to be washed off the land. Because of the widespread origins of these sources, as well as economic and political obstacles, dealing with this issue has proven to be very difficult.

Lake improvement is not limited to water quality alone. There is presently a much greater degree of awareness of habitat destruction than was the case not many years ago. Departments of natural resources, as well as some forward-looking lake associations, are encouraging cabin owners not to clear-cut all of the vegetation along a beach or underwater, because much of the life in a lake depends in some manner upon the rooted vegetation near the shoreline. Especially for those lakeshores with goose problems, leaving a zone of tall, mature grasses or other vegetation just above the beach discourages the geese from coming on land, because they feel nervous if they don't have direct visual access to the water. Experts from the DNR are even recommending leaving fallen trees in the water, if they don't directly impact swimming or boat access, because of the habitat that they provide for fish and other aquatic creatures.

Shoreline erosion is also something that can be effectively dealt with at a local level. Posting no-wake zones in narrows or small bays can help, but other ways of dealing with erosion include buttressing the shore with rocks and introducing vegetation with spreading root systems. One of the best ways to avoid erosion is not removing vegetation, both above or below the shoreline, in the first place.

Loons are favorites of almost all who enjoy the northern lakes. Two main measures have been employed to protect and sustain these symbols of the north. One is purely local in implementation. That is providing artificial nesting islands for loons and ensuring their privacy during nesting season so that breeding success will not be disrupted. Such efforts have proven to be remarkably successful on many lakes.

A less direct issue with loons and other diving birds is that of lead poisoning from fishing sinkers. Loons can ingest fishing sinkers resting on the lake bottom, and these remain in the bird's digestive system, much like the gravel in the crop of a chicken. This is still a controversial issue, with both strong proponents for and detractors against taking action. On some lakes lead seems to be a significant problem, whereas on others it has minimal impact. There are movements in a number of states to outlaw lead sinkers and replace them with other, less-toxic materials. The fishing tackle industry has been slow to respond to this issue, but recently, lead substitutes have begun to poke their way into the fishing tackle catalogs and onto store counters.

## Lake Surveys and Lake Management

For many anglers lake improvement means being able to catch more fish. To a great extent fisheries management is something that should be left to those professionals who do it for a living, but lake dwellers can often help them out in addition to doing some things individually. Early in the days of fisheries management, managing mainly meant keeping tabs on commercial fishing, if there was any, and stocking the lakes with either new species or more of what seemed to be in short supply. As the science of fisheries management matured, great efforts were made to conduct lake surveys, which charted the physical and biological characteristics of the lakes, as well as generating contour maps of the lake bottom. With the initial survey as a baseline, the same lake is typically resurveyed at regular intervals as a check on the progression of water quality, the fish populations, and the composition of the vegetation.

A typical lake survey, which can last from a couple days to several weeks, depending upon the size and complexity of the lake, consists of several fundamental components. One is conducting some baseline water chemistry determinations, including tests of water hardness and measures of dissolved oxygen at selected depths (see appendix 1). Secchi disk readings for water quality are routine, as well. Then the survey crew sets test nets—both gill nets with varying-sized mesh in the deeper water and trap nets in the shallows—to sample the fish populations. The fish are typically measured and weighed to get a general sense of their health, and from selected numbers of fish, scale samples are taken so that the age of the fish can be determined in the laboratory later in the winter. With the length and age information, fishery biologists can get a good idea of the condition of the fish and the structure of the population (see appendix 4). A final part of a typical survey is shoreline seining of small fish to check on reproduction for that summer (see appendix 3). This is often accompanied by a survey of the types and abundance of aquatic vegetation (see appendix 2), with special emphasis on the presence of Eurasian milfoil. Conversations with local anglers often constitute an informal part of the survey. For some important lakes biologists conduct a separate, often summer-long creel census to determine fishing success and sometimes to obtain biological samples (see appendix 5).

Although there are still debates in the scientific literature concerning the accuracy of the sampling by netting procedures, the data nevertheless provide information that can be useful in managing the fishery in a lake. One of the most important pieces of knowledge relates to spawning success. Some lakes are quite able to support healthy populations of trout, northern pike, or walleyes, but the appropriate habitat for spawning is not present. For such lakes stocking often makes a lot of sense. Other lakes may have good spawning habitat, but a succession of years of bad spring weather or other factors may have reduced the population of a particular species to the point where it needs a boost. Normally, this is not a problem, because the reproductive potential of fish is so great that a good year following a couple of bad ones will more than compensate for the poor spawning success of the previous years.

There are other lakes, Ten Mile being a good example, where spawning conditions for walleyes are questionable and stocking may be desirable. In these cases the DNR may choose to experiment in various ways to determine whether or not natural reproduction does occur. One method, presently used on Ten Mile, is to stock only every other year and then to check by analyzing the ages of scale samples whether any walleyes were born in the nonstocking years. At other times populations can be checked by tagging fish in various ways and asking local anglers to report on the fish that they have caught—both their length and whether the fish had a tag. The value of such surveys depends greatly upon cooperation by the local anglers.

In addition to monitoring reproduction, fisheries biologists also try to analyze the population structure of a lake. Along with statewide regulations (size and number), recommendations specific to a particular lake may be made. These are designed to protect certain age classes of fish, especially those that are likely to be most successful in reproduction—usually the largest females. A common method is to establish slot limits. As an example of a typical slot limit, one may not be allowed to keep any walleyes in a slot between 16 and 24 inches and only one larger than 24 inches. Because of their potential for growing big fish, some lakes may be managed to produce trophies—especially northern pike. Ten Mile Lake is one of several Minnesota lakes that are being managed to produce trophy northern pike. For a ten-year period nobody is allowed to keep any northern pike over 20 inches long in hopes that with the growth of the protected fish a more natural population structure will develop. Other lakes are plagued with large populations of small pike but have few large ones. In attempts to correct this size imbalance, catch limits on smaller pike may be expanded while greater restrictions are placed on keeping larger specimens. Sometimes these strategies work, and sometimes they don't. Sorting out the results will be a task for the future.

Another issue confronting fisheries managers is what kinds of fish should be stocked in a lake. Discussions can become very intense when it comes to trout. Generally, trout and spiny-rayed fish, like walleyes and bass, don't mix, and in many lakes stocked trout simply become food for the native bass and pike. In fact, in certain Southern California lakes that have been stocked with populations of giant Florida-strain largemouth bass, yearling rainbow trout are stocked with the overt purpose of providing food for the bass so that one day the world-record largemouth bass will be credited to California. Some very deep lakes, especially in Minnesota's Arrowhead region, are now being managed as *two-story* lakes, which means the warmer waters of the epilimnion are managed for bass, walleyes, and panfish while stocked trout are maintained in the cold waters of the hypolimnion. Like so many things in fisheries biology, this strategy may or may not be successful. Despite the availability of lots of information, these are still times when trial and error is the most practical management method.

Contemporary lake management is concerned not only with the fish in but also with the land surrounding the lake and with how all components of this complex ecosystem interact. There is increasing recognition that all parts of a lake are not the same, and future lake management may involve treating ecologically sensitive bays in a different manner from the main lake basin. As of this writing, various governmental agencies are actively discussing the most rational manner for wisely managing lakes.

## Acid Rain and Other Airborne Contaminants
. . . . . . . . . . . . . . . . . . .

### Acid Rain

One of the most insidious and widespread threats to north country lakes is airborne pollution, the classic case being the epidemic of acid rain that peaked during the 1990s. Acid rain was unseen and largely unfelt until people began to notice that the fish in some of our remotest lakes were looking thin and generally unhealthy. Things got to the point where some of the pristine, poorly buffered trout lakes in the Adirondacks were essentially devoid of fish. At the same time, mountaintop forests in equally remote areas, like the Great Smoky Mountains, were dying. When biologists checked the lake waters, they were shocked to find that the pH in some of them had dropped to levels even less than 5.0 pH. Below 4.0 pH, almost no fish can survive. One study reported in the early 1990s recorded almost 7,000 lakes and streams with a pH less than 5.0 to 5.5. Fortunately, Minnesota has not been as severely affected by acid rain as some other parts of the United States and Canada.

A neutral pH is 7.0, and most lakes' pH ranges from 6.5 to 7.5. Distilled water has a pH of 7.0. A number less than 7.0 means that a solution is on the acid side, and one over 7.0 signifies alkaline water. Each number in the pH scale is an increment or decrement of 10, so a pH of 6.0 is 10 times more acid than 7.0 and a pH of 5.0 is 100 times more acid. Normal rain is slightly acidic (about 5.6 pH) because the water combines with the carbon dioxide in the air to form a very weak acid.

Most natural lakes in Minnesota are slightly basic, with a pH in the range of 7.2 to 8.3. Dissolved materials that provide buffering power in lakes are referred to as total alkalinity. For example, the total alkalinity of Ten Mile Lake ranges from 87 to 105 milligrams per liter. Minnesota lakes show a rough gradient of alkalinity and buffering capacity from very low in northeastern lakes to very high in the southwest. The greater the buffering capacity of a lake, the less the likelihood of its becoming acidified.

The source of the acid in the air was a variety of types of industrial smoke stacks, which spewed sulfites ($SO_3$) into the air. When these ions combined with water ($H_2O$), they formed sulfuric acid ($H_2SO_4$), one of the strongest possible acids. When it rained, the rain pouring down from such a polluted atmosphere was literally acid, and as it hit the lake waters or ran into streams, it added acid to the lakes with each rainstorm. In the lakes not all fish were affected equally. Unfortunately, the most desirable game fish, like trout, were among the most sensitive to acid water.

Living in increasingly acid conditions has a generally debilitating effect on fish. Acid water damages the highly sensitive red gill filaments and results in ionic imbalances in the blood and tissue fluids. It also damages the skin, resulting in an increased susceptibility to a number of chronic infectious diseases. Overall, growth of fish in acid water is retarded. One of the most sensitive functions affected by acid water is reproduction. Egg production is reduced, and the mortality of developing eggs is increased.

In acid lakes, each year fewer young fish hatched, resulting in less food for the larger fish, which became increasingly weakened due to poor nutrition. With the reduction or disappearance of the fish, other animals that feed on fish were also affected. Loons regularly visited many of these lakes and nested on them. In some of the acid lakes, there was a sufficient fish population for the adults to eke out a sustainable diet, but very severely affected were the young-of-the-year, which were unable to obtain sufficient food to get them through the perilous first summer.

Governmental air-quality legislation has resulted in a notable reduction in industrial acid emissions, and the lakes in both the United States and Canada that are downwind of these plants are slowly beginning to recover. It will take years, however, for natural recovery processes to restore these formerly dead lakes to their original pristine condition.

*Mercury Pollution*

Another unseen threat from the air is mercury pollution. Cabin owners on Ten Mile Lake were shocked a couple of decades ago to learn that mercury warnings for fish consumption had been posted by the Minnesota DNR. Where did the mercury come from? Here is a spring-fed lake with no inlet stream and a tiny watershed that consists mostly of untouched forest! The same scenario of fish consumption warnings has been repeated for hundreds of northern lakes.

Potential sources of mercury are either from the ground or from the air. In some regions of the country, mercury in the ground can contribute significantly to the levels of mercury in fish. In fact, a couple studies on fish that were collected by museums well over a century ago have shown mercury contamination from areas that had no industry at the time. Nevertheless, there is now little doubt that much of the mercury in our lakes comes from the air. Mercury in the air is deposited in lakes through rain. A major source of emissions is coal-fired power plants and taconite processing plants. (Mercury is a trace element found in coal.) These two sources account for almost two-thirds of the airborne mercury in Minnesota. Solid-waste incineration and other miscellaneous sources contribute the rest. An estimated 90 percent of the mercury that enters Minnesota waters comes from out-of-state air driven by the wind.

Mercury enters the water directly from the wind or when combined with raindrops or snowflakes. After it has entered the lake water, it is converted to methylmercury through bacterial action. Methylmercury accumulates in all living beings and does not readily exit the system, which is bad news for predators because, as they eat plankton or smaller fish, the mercury contained in their prey becomes transferred to their own body. Top-of-the-line predators—such as large fish, loons, eagles, otters, and humans—accumulate the most mercury in their bodies. By the time a walleye reaches 8 pounds, for instance, it has spent many years eating mercury-contaminated fish, resulting in even-higher levels of mercury in its own flesh. Thus when we eat walleyes or other large fish, we are adding their accumulated mercury to our own bodies. Environmental toxicologists measure amounts of mercury in fish and, from these measurements, extrapolate the total accumulation in humans after consumption of given amounts of fish. This is how the recommendations for fish consumption are derived. According to 2001 Environmental Protection Agency standards, fish containing more than 0.3 mg/kg of mercury is unsafe to eat.

We are still far from solving the mercury problem, which requires technology, money, public pressure, and legislation. Only when mercury stops entering our lakes can the process of recovery really begin. It will take a lot longer to rid our lakes of mercury than it will for lakes to recover from acid rain, but over time it is possible.

## What Does the Future Hold?

There is no doubt that lakes will hold the same fascination for future generations as they do for us. Another certainty is that in succeeding years there will be more of us. Sad to say, the number of north country lakes will not multiply to keep pace with our burgeoning population, so we must care for them if we want our children and grandchildren to enjoy them, as well. A lake really is a living organism that can improve or go downhill depending upon how we treat it. Just like people, where taking care of our bodies when we are young or middle-aged can greatly enhance life in our later years, taking care of a lake in its middle age will slow its entry into old age or eutrophication. Even in old age, diet and exercise can result in significant improvement in the health of people who may have neglected their bodies earlier in life. So also, tired, old lakes can be brought to a more youthful condition by correcting the sources of their problems. With a little help, a natural regenerative mechanism kicks in and helps out those who are helping the lake.

The critical element for the future of lakes is people. And it starts with the individual. Each of us who appreciates what lakes have to offer our collective well-being must translate this appreciation into action. The actions can be purely personal, like checking your boat for Eurasian milfoil before putting it into a new lake or ensuring that your septic system is up-to-date and is functioning properly. And they can be collective. There is no better way to begin than to form or become active in a local lake association. A good association can be an important force in maintaining community standards and in initiating community action on matters that directly affect your own lake. One of the most effective ways of maintaining lake quality is for lake associations to work together with local units of government to ensure that the best lake management practices are applied and adhered to in both the lake and its watershed.

Then there are issues beyond the capacity of single lake associations to handle. Associations of lake associations are now forming in a number of states. These can be wonderful forums for education that attract top speakers for general education and for sharing experiences. For those issues that can be dealt with only at the political level, cabin owners and lake associations can also become one of the many competing special interest groups able to express its particular viewpoint about a given issue. These larger groups can exert powerful political pressure when their potential influence is used effectively. Never to be forgotten is the power of a single individual, however, to raise consciousness and effect change. With these elements in place, our north country lakes will be left in good hands so that they can work their magic upon future generations.

## Limnological Data on Ten Mile Lake

*(Representative data for the month of July)*

### Topographic Data

Surface area: 4,640 acres (18,750,000 square meters)
Maximum depth: 209 feet
Mean depth: 49 feet
Total water volume: 309,100,878 cubic meters
Water volume at 0 to 10 feet: 54,745,064 cubic meters
Water volume at 10 to 20 feet: 42,347,802 cubic meters
Catchment basin: 8,909 acres
Outflow (Boy River): 7,421 acre feet per year
Mean residence time for water entering the lake: 13.2 years

### Water Analysis Data

Typical Secchi disk reading in main lake basin: 22 feet
Typical early July temperatures
    Surface: 71°F (22°C)
    150 feet: 44°F (7°C)
pH: 7.7
Dissolved oxygen
    Surface: 8.4 PPM
    150 feet: 6.8 PPM
Alkalinity: 87 to 105 mg/L
Conductance: 212 μm
Total phosphorus: 0.02 mg/L
Total nitrogen: 0.212 mg/L
Chlorophyll: 0.7 μm/L

## Aquatic Plants of Ten Mile Lake

| Type | Common name | Scientific name |
|---|---|---|
| **Macroalgae** | Muskgrass | *Chara vulgaris* |
| | Stonewort | *Nitella* sp. |
| **Moss** | Watermoss group | N/A |
| **Submerged vascular** | Wild celery | *Vallisnaria americana* |
| | Water marigold | *Bidens beckii* |
| | Coontail | *Ceratophyllum demersum* |
| | Canada waterweed | *Elodea canadensis* |
| | Quillwort | *Isoetes* sp. |
| | Whorled milfoil | *Myriophyllum exalbescens* |
| | Northern water milfoil | *Myriophyllum sibiricum* |
| | Bushy pondweed | *Najas flexilis* |
| | Large-leaf pondweed | *Potemogeton amplifolius* |
| | Fries pondweed | *Potemogeton friesii* |
| | Variable pondweed | *Potemogeton gramineus* |
| | Illinois pondweed | *Potemogeton illinoensis* |
| | Narrow-leaf pondweed | *Potemogeton* sp. |
| | Whitestem pondweed | *Potemogeton praelongus* |
| | Clasping-leaf pondweed | *Potemogeton richardsonii* |
| | Robbins' pondweed | *Potemogeton robbinsii* |
| | Flatstem pondweed | *Potemogeton zosteriformis* |
| | Water buttercup | *Ranunculus* sp. |
| | Water bulrush | *Scirpus subterminalis* |
| | Sago pondweed | *Stukenia pectinata* |
| | Bladderwort | *Utricularia* sp. |
| | Flat-leaved bladderwort | *Utricularia intermedia* |
| | Water stargrass | *Zosterella dubia* |
| **Free floating** | Lesser duckweed | *Lemna minor* |
| | Greater duckweed | *Spirodela polyrhiza* |
| **Floating** | Watershield | *Brasenia schreberi* |
| | Yellow waterlily | *Nuphar variegata* |
| | White waterlily | *Nymphea odorata* |
| | Floating-leaf smartweed | *Polygonum amphibium* |
| | Floating-leaf pondweed | *Potemogeton natans* |
| | Floating-leaf burreed | *Sparganium* sp. |
| **Emergent** | Common cattail | *Typha latifolia* |
| | Spikerush | *Eleocharis* sp. |
| | Hardstem bulrush | *Scirpus acutus* |
| | Giant burreed | *Sparganium eurycarpum* |
| | Wild rice | *Zizania palustris* |

*Note: This table is based on an ongoing study by the Minnesota DNR.*
*Information courtesy of Donna Perleberg.*

## Fish of Ten Mile Lake

| Common Name | Scientific Name |
|---|---|
| Bowfin | *Amia calva* |
| Lake whitefish | *Coregonus clupeaformis* |
| Cisco | *Coregonus artedii* |
| Common sucker | *Catostomus commersonii* |
| Northern redhorse | *Moxostoma auroleum* |
| Longnose dace | *Rhinichthys cataractae* |
| Blackchin shiner | *Notropis heterodon* |
| Blacknose shiner | *Notropis heterolepis* |
| Common shiner | *Notropis cornutus* |
| Emerald shiner | *Notropis atherinoides* |
| Mimic shiner | *Notropis vollucellus* |
| Pugnose shiner | *Notropis anogenus* |
| Spottail shiner | *Notropis hudsonius* |
| Brassy minnow | *Hybognathus hankinsoni* |
| Fathead minnow | *Pimephales promelas* |
| Bluntnose minnow | *Pimephales notatus* |
| Black bullhead | *Ictalurus melas* |
| Brown bullhead | *Ictalurus nebulosus* |
| Yellow bullhead | *Ictalurus natalis* |
| Central mudminnow | *Umbra limi* |
| Northern pike | *Esox lucius* |
| Banded killifish | *Fundulus diaphanous* |
| Brook stickleback | *Culaea inconstans* |
| Burbot (eelpout) | *Lota lota* |
| Yellow perch | *Perca flavescens* |
| Walleye | *Stizostedion vitreum* |
| Iowa darter | *Etheostoma exile* |
| Johnny darter | *Etheostoma nigrum* |
| Least darter | *Etheostoma microperca* |
| Northern logperch | *Percina caprodes* |
| Largemouth bass | *Micropterus salmoides* |
| Smallmouth bass | *Micropterus dolomieui* |
| Bluegill | *Lepomis macrochirus* |
| Longear sunfish | *Lepomis megalotis* |
| Pumpkinseed | *Lepomis gibbosus* |
| Black crappie | *Poxomis nigromaculatus* |
| Rock bass | *Ambloplites rupestris* |
| Northern mottled sculpin | *Cottus bairdii* |

*Note: This list is derived from lake and non-game fish survey reports of Ten Mile Lake done by the Minnesota DNR. Courtesy of Paul Radomski.*

# APPENDIX 4

*Length in Inches of Common Ten Mile Lake Game Fish*

| Species \ Age | 1 | 2 | 3 | 4 | 5 | 6 | 7 | 8 | 9 | 10 | 11 | 12 | 13 |
|---|---|---|---|---|---|---|---|---|---|---|---|---|---|
| Walleye | 5.0 | 8.4 | 13.1 | 15.8 | 18.6 | 20.3 | 21.3 | 23.0 | 24.4 | 25.5 | 25.6 | 27.4 | N/A |
| Northern pike | 8.8 | 14.7 | 18.2 | 20.8 | 22.7 | 25.4 | 28.3 | 30.5 | N/A | N/A | N/A | N/A | N/A |
| Largemouth bass | 3.2 | 5.8 | 8.0 | 10.4 | 12.1 | 13.6 | 15.0 | 16.2 | 17.6 | N/A | N/A | N/A | N/A |
| Smallmouth bass* | 4.1 | 6.8 | 10.7 | 13.8 | N/A | N/A | N/A | N/A | N/A | N/A | N/A | N/A | N/A |
| Bluegill | 1.5 | 2.3 | 3.0 | 3.8 | 4.7 | 5.7 | 6.5 | 6.8 | 7.1 | 7.5 | 7.6 | 7.9 | 8.6 |

*Note: Data represent averages from various Minnesota DNR age and growth studies on fish from Ten Mile Lake.*

*\*Apparently, smallmouth bass have been only recently introduced into Ten Mile Lake, and therefore, the population, as of the only age and growth study conducted to date (2003), is a very young one.*

*Minnesota* DNR *Creel Census Data on Ten Mile Lake Fishing for 1995*

*Daytime fishing pressure: 50,877 angling hours (10.9 hours/acre)*

*Total fish kept of all species: 15,031 pounds (3.22 pounds/acre)*

### Angling Data by Species

| Species | Number caught | Number released | Number kept | Pounds kept |
|---|---|---|---|---|
| Sunfish | 29,036 | 21,469 | 7,567 | 1,969 |
| Rock bass | 23,612 | 18,889 | 4,723 | 2,363 |
| Crappie | 2,392 | 331 | 2,061 | N/A |
| Largemouth bass | 6,888 | 4,443 | 2,445 | N/A |
| Smallmouth bass | 254 | 223 | 31 | N/A |
| Northern pike | 3,435 | 2,777 | 658 | 1,644 |
| Walleye | 3,272 | 505 | 2,767 | 4,850 |
| Perch | 16,694 | 14,538 | 2,156 | 516 |

### Catch Rates

| Species | Number per hour | Hours per fish |
|---|---|---|
| Sunfish | 0.57 | 1.75 |
| Rock bass | 0.46 | 2.2 |
| Northern pike | 0.068 | 14.7 |
| Perch | 0.32 | 3.1 |
| Walleye (day) | 0.064 | 15.6 |
| Walleye (night) | 0.258 | 3.9 |

### Catches by Walleye Anglers

| Number of fish per outing | 0.0 | 0.1–0.9 | 1.0–1.9 | 2.0–2.9 | 3.0–3.9 | 4.0–4.9 |
|---|---|---|---|---|---|---|
| Percent of anglers | 79.5 | 5.1 | 5.1 | 7.7 | 0.0 | 2.6 |

## Changes in Lake Usage on Ten Mile Lake

| Year | Cabins | Resorts | Boats | Other |
|------|--------|---------|-------|-------|
| 1948 | 165 | 16 | 81 | 1 farm |
| 1958 | 310 | 17 | 379 | 1 farm, 1 camp |
| 1971 | 292 | 9 | 395 | 1 farm, 1 trailer camp |
| 1983 | 450 | 2 | 608 | 1 trailer camp |
| 1997 | 453 | 2 | * | 1 trailer camp |
| 2003 | 506 | 1 | * | 1 trailer camp |

*Following a 1993 protocol, DNR lake survey crews no longer made watercraft counts during lake surveys.*

**acid rain**  Rain droplets containing pollutants, such as sulfur and nitrogen oxides, that make them acidic.

**algae**  Primitive aquatic plants that thrive best in fertile water. The most common types of algae in freshwater are the slimy, hairlike blue-green and green varieties.

**anal fin**  A single fin located on the bottom side of a fish close to the tail (see fig. 5.3).

**annuli**  Thin rings on fish scales (see fig. 5.1).

**back-trolling**  Slow trolling with the motor in reverse. The blunt stern end of the boat faces forward, slowing the trolling speed and allowing for better boat control.

**blade bait**  A flat metal artificial bait that vibrates greatly when pulled through the water.

**bronzeback**  A colloquial name for smallmouth bass.

**buzzbait**  A bass bait with a propeller ahead of a rubber-skirted hook that is retrieved very rapidly over the surface of the water (see fig. 7.5).

**cabbage**  A name given by anglers to varieties of broadleaf pondweeds that provide excellent cover for game fish (see fig. 2.8).

**Carolina rig**  A plastic worm that is suspended several inches behind a sinker that is dragged over the bottom (see fig. 7.8B).

**castoreum**  An oily secretion from the anal glands of beavers that is used for social communication and marking territories.

**chironomid**  A member of the midge family (see fig. 3.3).

**circle hook**  A strangely shaped hook becoming popular with live-bait anglers because the fish tend to get hooked in the lips rather than swallow the bait and hook.

**cones**  Cells in the retina of the eye that perceive color (see fig. 9.1).

**countercurrent mechanism**  A heat-saving arrangement of blood vessels in which an artery supplying an extremity runs in parallel to a vein leading from it. The blood in the artery transfers heat to the blood in the vein before the arterial blood gets to the foot or hand.

**crankbait**  A contemporary term for a fishing plug, usually one with a lip (see fig. 7.2).

**crepuscular**  A term describing an animal that is most active at dusk and at dawn.

**ctenoid scale** Scales with a rough edge, seen in more advanced fish like walleyes and bass (see fig. 5.1).

**cycloid scale** Smooth-edged scales, seen in more primitive fish like whitefish and pike (see fig. 5.1).

**cyst** A stage in the life cycle of a parasite in which the parasite embeds itself into the flesh of a fish.

**deadhead** A mostly submerged waterlogged log that, usually, has only one end protruding above the surface of the water.

**delayed implantation** Arrested early embryonic development, seen in otters.

**detritus** Fine particulate organic matter at the bottom of a lake.

**diurnal** Twice-daily cycles of activity, usually at dawn and dusk.

**dorsal fin** The fin sticking up from the back of a fish (see fig. 5.3).

**drop-shot** An arrangement with a sinker at the bottom of a fishing line and the hook tied 1 or 2 feet above the sinker (see fig. 7.9).

**dun** A sexually immature mayfly with dull wings that is one molt away from its final reproductive stage of life. Also called a subimago (see fig. 3.1).

**echolocation** Finding prey or navigating by reflecting ultrasonic sounds off of objects and instantly calculating their location in sonar-like fashion.

**epilimnion** The upper warm layer of a lake (see fig. 2.1).

**eutrophic** A nutrient-rich lake that is in the last stages of its life cycle (see fig. 1.3C).

**exoskeleton** The hard outer covering of an insect or a crayfish.

**far-field** Sound waves sensed at a distance by fish (see fig. 9.2B).

**front** The leading edge of a warm- or cold-weather system.

**fry** A newly hatched fish.

**gill rakers** The white projections coming off the inner curve of a fish's gill. They are designed to keep ingested food in the mouth while water escapes through the gills.

**global positioning system (GPS) unit** A satellite communication device that allows very accurate location of one's position on water or on land.

**harling** A technique of trolling a fly with a weighted fly line and a long leader.

**hertz (Hz)** Cycles per second as it relates to sound waves.

**hummock** A mound of vegetation, usually some kind of grass, protruding from the surface of shallow water.

**hypolimnion** The cold water below the thermocline in a lake (see fig. 2.1).

**imago** The sexually mature adult form of a mayfly and certain other insects (see fig. 3.1).

**in-line spinner** A fishing bait with a spinner on a straight wire just ahead of the hook (see fig. 7.5B).

**instar** A stage in the development of an insect larvae. As the larva grows, it molts and proceeds to the next instar stage (see fig. 3.1).

**jig** A fishing bait consisting of a hook attached to a lead head and usually dressed with hair, feathers, or rubber strips (see fig. 7.6).

**kit** The name given to a young beaver.

**lake survey** A field study of the fish, plants, and physical characteristics of a lake.

**lateral line** A faint line of scales along the side of a fish. Each scale in the lateral line has a pore leading to a vibration receptor, which is connected to a nerve (see fig. 5.3).

**limnology** The study of freshwater lakes and ponds.

**littoral zone** The ecological zone associated with the shoreline and shallower waters of a lake (see fig. 2.3).

**marl** A whitish crust of mainly calcium carbonate that covers the bottom and vegetation in certain regions of a lake, often near springs.

**mesotrophic** A moderately fertile lake in the middle of its life cycle (see fig. 1.3B).

**moraine** A hill of rocks and gravel that was dropped by a receding glacier. A terminal moraine represents the farthest extension of the glacier's advance.

**near-field** Reception of vibrations, mainly by the lateral line, in the vicinity of a fish (see fig. 9.2B).

**neuromast** A specialized cell of a fish that is sensitive to vibration (see fig. 9.2A).

**neutrally buoyant** A fishing bait of roughly the same density as water, which suspends at a given level when one stops reeling it in.

**nictitating membrane** A thin membrane that covers and protects the eye of an aquatic mammal when it swims underwater.

**nociception** The perception of a painful stimulus.

**nymph** The aquatic larval form of many insects (see fig. 3.1).

**oligotrophic** An infertile lake with clear water, usually in the early stages of its life cycle (see fig. 1.3A).

**operculum**  The gill cover of a fish (see fig. 5.3).

**otolith**  The ear bone of a fish. A mass, usually composed of calcium carbonate, that abuts upon a neuromast or sense receptor. Otoliths can be sectioned and used to age fish by counting rings, much like those in a tree trunk.

**pectoral fin**  The paired fins on the sides of a fish, just behind or under the gills (see fig. 5.3).

**pelagic zone**  The zone of open water in a lake (see fig. 2.3).

**pelvic fin**  A pair of fins on a fish located behind the pectoral fins (see fig. 5.3).

**pH**  A measure of acidity or alkalinity. A neutral pH is 7.0. Each pH unit above or below 7.0 is 10 times more acidic or basic than the previous one. For example, a pH of 5.0 is 100 times more acid than a pH of 7.0.

**pheromone**  A chemical released in minute amounts by animals that serves as a communication mechanism, often over long distances.

**photosynthesis**  The process by which a plant converts sunlight to energy.

**physoclistous**  A fish, like a walleye, whose swim bladder isn't directly connected to the gut.

**physostomatous**  A fish, like a whitefish, whose swim bladder is directly connected to its gut by a thin tube (see fig. 4.7).

**phytoplankton**  Tiny forms of plant life suspended in the water.

**plankton**  Tiny plants or animals suspended in the water. They are the food of some invertebrates and very small fish.

**poikilothermic**  A cold-blooded animal, whose body temperature corresponds to that of its environment.

**preoperculum**  The cheekbone of a fish, which in walleyes is razor sharp (see fig. 5.3).

**profundal zone**  The deepest region of a lake (see fig. 2.3).

**pupa**  The stage of a higher insect when it is undergoing metamorphosis (see fig. 3.4).

**Purkinje shift**  The greater sensitivity of eyes to colors in the blue/violet range in dim light.

**rafting**  The aggregation of loons in late summer and fall before they migrate.

**rods**  Cells in the retina of the eye that operate in very sensitive black-and-white vision in dim light (see fig. 9.1).

**Schreckstoff** A warning chemical secreted from the skin of some types of injured fish.

**Secchi disk** A metal disk that is lowered into the water on a string to determine the clarity of the water. The Secchi disk reading is the depth at which the disk disappears from view.

**seine** A long net that in lakes is usually pulled by two people to catch or sample fish from shallow water.

**shuck** The discarded exoskeleton of a mayfly (see fig. 3.1).

**slot limit** A set of fish lengths between which one is not allowed to keep a fish.

**solunar table** Tables devised by John Alden Knight that purport to forecast major and minor feeding periods of fish and other animals throughout the day.

**spawning** The act of reproduction by fish.

**spinner** (1) A spent mayfly that has fallen onto the water and is still flapping its wings; (2) A spoon-shaped piece of metal that revolves about a wire and is then dragged through the water.

**spinnerbait** An open-safety-pin-shaped fishing bait with a spinner on one limb and a hook covered with a rubber skirt on the other (see fig. 7.5).

**spoon** A metal fishing bait that wobbles in the water.

**structure** The term given by anglers to drop-offs, underwater islands, etc., where game fish are likely to congregate.

**subimago** See *dun*.

**sublittoral zone** A transitional ecological zone in a lake where the shallow bottom covered with vegetation gives way to deeper water, often in the region of the thermocline (see fig. 2.3).

**suction feeding** The means by which a fish commonly ingests food through flaring out its gills and drawing water and prey into its mouth.

**tannin** A brownish pigment in the water, derived from decaying leaves and other organic matter.

**tapetum lucidum** The reflective layer behind the retina of many nocturnal animals that increases their acuity of vision after dark (see fig. 9.1).

**test net** A gill net with various sizes of mesh used to sample fish populations in a lake.

**Texas rig** A plastic worm on a hook immediately behind a cone-shaped sinker (see fig. 7.8A).

**thermocline (mesolimnion)** The intermediate layer of a lake in which the water temperature drops very rapidly (see fig. 2.1).

**three-way rig** An arrangement of a sinker on a short stretch of leader that drops down ahead of another leader attached to the bait (see fig. 5.7B).

**treble hook** A fish hook with three pointed ends equally spaced apart.

**tube jig** A rubber or plastic body with a fringed tail into which is placed a hook with a lead mass attached to it (see fig. 7.6).

**turnover** A phenomenon occurring in the fall and spring when the surface water of a lake has a greater density than that of the deeper water. The denser water sinks and displaces the lighter deep water, which moves to the surface.

**two-story lake** A deep, usually oligotrophic, lake that is managed for cold-water species, like trout, below the thermocline and warm-water species above the thermocline.

**uropygial gland** A gland located by the tail of birds that produces an oily secretion which is rubbed on the feathers to waterproof them.

**vibrating bait** A thin, lipless bait that vibrates rapidly when retrieved through the water (see fig. 7.3).

**vulture posture** A threatening posture used by loons to scare loons or other animals that have invaded their territory (see fig. 10.1).

**wake-tracking** Following the trail of turbulent water that is left behind a swimming fish.

**water column** The designation of the vertical stretch of water from the top to the bottom of a lake.

**Weberian ossicles** A set of bones connecting the swim bladder to the inner ear of some types of fish. This greatly increases their auditory acuity.

**year class** A name, commonly used in fisheries management, given to all the fish of a species that were born in a given year.

**yolk** The nutritive material from a fish egg that nourishes a newly hatched fish for the first few days of its life before it is able to feed independently.

**young-of-the-year** Fish in their first summer of life.

**zooplankton** Tiny animals that are suspended in the water of a lake or stream and that provide food for small fish (see fig. 2.11).

## Aquatic Invertebrates

Hoffman, G. L. 1999. *Parasites of North American Fishes.* 2nd ed. Ithaca, NY: Comstock Publishing.

Knopp, M., and R. Cormier. 1997. *Mayflies.* New York: Lyons Press.

McCafferty, W. P. 1998. *Aquatic Entomology.* Sudbury, MA: Jones and Bartlett.

Pennak, R. W. 1978. *Fresh-water Invertebrates of the United States.* 2nd ed. New York: John Wiley & Sons.

Pobst, D., and C. Richards. 1998. *The Caddisfly Handbook.* New York: Lyons Press.

## Aquatic Plants

Blickenderfer, M. 2007. *A Field Guide for Identification of Minnesota Aquatic Plants.* Minneapolis: University of Minnesota Extension Division.

Fassett, N. C. 1957. *A Manual of Aquatic Plants.* 2nd ed. Madison: University of Wisconsin Press.

Riemer, D. N. 1993. *Introduction to Freshwater Vegetation.* Malabar, FL: Krieger Publishing.

## Beavers and Other Mammals

Gunderson, H. L., and J. R. Beer. 1953. *The Mammals of Minnesota.* Minneapolis: University of Minnesota Press.

Morgan, L. H. 1868. *The American Beaver and His Works.* Philadelphia, PA: J. B. Lippincott.

Müller-Schwarze, D., and L. Sun. 2003. *The Beaver.* Ithaca, NY: Cornell University Press.

Warren, E. R. 1927. *The Beaver.* Baltimore, MD: Williams & Wilkins.

Whitaker, J. O., and W. J. Hamilton. 1998. *Mammals of the Eastern United States.* Ithaca, NY: Comstock Publishing.

## Fish

Becker, G. C. 1983. *Fishes of Wisconsin*. Madison: University of Wisconsin Press.

Bone, Q., N. B. Marshall, and J. H. S. Blaxter. 2004. *Biology of Fishes*. 2nd ed. Abingdon, UK: BIOS Scientific Publishers.

Eddy, S., and T. Surber. 1947. *Northern Fishes*. Minneapolis: University of Minnesota Press.

Halpern, T. N. 1990. "A Comparative Study of the Seasonal Energy Dynamics of the Cisco, *Coregonus artedi*, in Three Minnesota Lakes." PhD diss., University of Minnesota.

Hubbs, C. L., and K. F. Lagler. 1964. *Fishes of the Great Lakes Region*. Ann Arbor: University of Michigan Press.

Kelber, A., and L. S. V. Roth. 2006. "Nocturnal Colour Vision: Not as Rare as We Might Think." *Journal of Experimental Biology* 209:781–88.

Scott, W. B., and E. J. Crossman. 1973. *Freshwater Fishes of Canada*. Ottawa: Fisheries Research Board of Canada.

Shields B. A., K. S. Guise, and J. C. Underhill. 1990. "Chromosomal and Mitochondrial DNA Characterization of a Population of Dwarf Cisco (*Coregonus artedi*) in Minnesota." *Canadian Journal of Fisheries and Aquatic Sciences* 47:1562–69.

## Glacial History

Melchior, R. C., and J. O. Annextad. 1996. *Glaciers and Glacial History of the Leech Lake Watershed*. NASA.

Tester, J. R. 1995. *Minnesota's Natural Heritage*. Minneapolis: University of Minnesota Press.

Upham, W. 1896. *The Glacial Lake Agassiz*. Vol. 25 of *Monographs U.S. Geological Survey*.

## Lake Management

Anonymous. 2004. *Guide to Lake Protection and Management.* Excelsior, MN: Freshwater Society.

Sorensen, J. A., G. E. Glass, K. W. Schmidt, J. K. Huber, and G. R. Rapp. 1990. "Airborne Mercury Deposition and Watershed Characteristics in Relation to Mercury Concentrations in Water, Sediments, Plankton, and Fish of Eighty Northern Minnesota Lakes." *Environmental Science and Technology* 24:1716–27.

Wendelaar Bonga, S. E., and L. H. T. Dederen. 1986. "Effects of Acidified Water on Fish." *Endeavour* 10:198–202.

## Limnology

Cole, G. A. 1994. *Textbook of Limnology.* 4th ed. Prospect Heights, IL: Waveland Press.

## Loons

Klein, T. 1989. *Loon Magic.* Minocqua, WI: NorthWord Press.

McIntyre, J. W. 1988. *The Common Loon: Spirit of Northern Lakes.* Minneapolis: University of Minnesota Press.

## Natural History

Bennet D., and T. Tiner. 2003. *The Wild Woods Guide.* New York: HarperCollins.

## Weather

Brenstrum, E. 1998. *The New Zealand Weather Book.* Nelson, New Zealand: Craig Potton Publishing.

Douglas, P. 2005. *Restless Skies: The Ultimate Weather Book.* New York: Sterling Publishing.

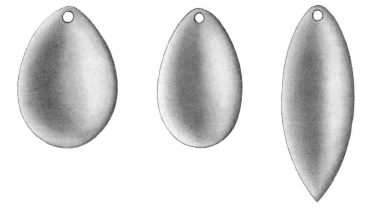

exotic species: alewives, 217, *218;*
  big-headed carp, 220–21;
  Eurasian milfoil, 219, *220;*
  gobies, *218,* 219; grass carp,
  220; lampreys, 217, *218;* ruffe,
  *218,* 219; salmon, 217; smelt,
  217, *218;* spiny water fleas, *218,*
  219; zebra mussels, *218,* 219
eyes, fish, 49, 142–45, *143*

**F**

far-field, 147
fish fly. *See* mayfly
fish kill: summer, 200, 213;
  winter, 207
fish senses: and baits and retrieves,
  52–53; electromagnetic, 153–54;
  hearing, 146–51, *149;* smell,
  152–53; taste, 152; vision,
  142–46
fishing: and docks, 117–18; in fall,
  86–87, 119–21, 203–5; ice,
  206–7; night, 52–53, 119–21
fishing baits, 107–14; buzzbaits,
  108; color of, 116; crankbaits,
  107, *color insert;* jig, 85, 108,
  *109, 110,* 113, 126; minnowbaits,
  63, *80,* 124; poppers, 107;
  spinnerbaits, 53, 108, *color
  insert;* spoons, 113; surface, 107,
  *color insert;* vibrating, 107,
  *color insert,* 121
fishing methods: bass, largemouth,
  114–21; bass, smallmouth,
  124–27; crappies, 138–40;
  perch, 89; pike, 96–101; sunfish,
  134; walleyes, 78–82, 84–87;
  whitefish, 63–67
frogs, migration of, 87
fronts: cold, 118, 199; warm, 196
fry, 26, 77

**G**

geese, 48, 213
gills, 34, *58*
grubs, 64, *110,* 113

**H**

harling, 82
hatch, 38
herons, 136, 191
*Hexagenia,* 38, 41
hook, circle, 114
hypolimnion, 18

**I**

imaginal disks, 45
inner ear, *150*
insects. *See under individual
  species*
instar, 39, *40*

**J**

jig 'n' pig, 109
jigging spoons, *64*
jigs. *See* fishing baits.
Jitterbugs, 53, 107

**K**

kingfishers, 136, 191
Knight, John Alden, 118
knot, Palomar, 112, *112*

**L**

Lake Agassiz, 6, *6*
Lake Superior, 20
lakes, acidification of, 170, 226–28;
  eutrophic, 7, *8;* glacial origins of,
  4–6; human impact on, 210–17;
  ice block, 4; life cycle of, 4–8, *8;*
  management of, 224–26;
  mesotrophic, 7, *8;* oligotrophic,
  7, *8;* surveys of, 224–25;
  turnover of, 202; two-story, 226
lampreys, 154, 217, *218*
larvae: caddis fly, *42;* damselfly, *27;*
  dragonfly, *27;* midge, 31, 44–*45;*
  mosquito, *46*

sound, 23–25; transmission of, in water, 23, 141. *See also* fish senses: hearing

spawning: bass, 105–6, 123; ciscoes, 61; crappies, 138–39; perch, 89–90, 192; pike, 94; rock bass, 131; sunfish, 133–34; walleyes, 75–77; whitefish, 67

spinnerbaits. *See* fishing baits

spoons. *See* fishing baits

stinkweed. See *Chara*

stocking, fish, 213

sturgeon, 154

suckers, 31, 99

suction feeding, 112

sunfish, 132–37

swamps, 7, *8*

swim bladder: physoclistous, 66; physostomatous, 65

swimmer's itch, 194–95

T

tannins, 19

Ten Mile Lake: aquatic plant species in, 232; Boy River, 9; background, 9–14; cabins, number of, 236; creel census data, 235; and fish age and growth, 234; fish species in, 233; Flowerpot Bay, *10,* 14; Kenfield Bay, *10,* 12; limnological data, 231; Long Bay, *11,* 14; Lundstrom's Bay, *10,* 12; map of, *10, 12*

thermocline, 18, *200*

thunderstorms, *196,* 196–98, *198*

*Triaenophorus, 68,* 68–69

trolling, 79–81, 86, 100

tubifex, 31

tullibee. *See* Cisco

U

ultraviolet sensitivity, 143

underwater cameras, 29, 82, 85, 99, 215

underwater noise, 23

V

vegetation, lake, 26, *26,* 28–29, *28, 29, 30*

W

wake-tracking, 151

walleye-cisco connection, *59,* 79

walleyes, 49, 50–51, *70, 74, 76,* 71–88

water, temperature and oxygen content of, 17, *18*

water lilies, 28

Weberian ossicles, 149

wetlands, 7

whitefish, 31, *56,* 61–69, *68,* 192

worms, plastic, 109–12, *111*

Y

yellow grubs. See *Clinostomum*

. . . . . . . . . . . . . . . . . . .

*Beneath the Surface* was designed and set in type at Cathy Spengler Design, Minneapolis. The typefaces are Miller and Franklin Gothic. Printed by Thomson-Shore, Incorporated, Dexter, Michigan.